Fifteen scintillating chapters in all – plus fourteen succinct appendices, from Magna Carta to General Summary, the influence of Christianity on Western Civilisation is minutely analysed and skilfully evaluated …

Mr Burrows' book is a must. No one who buys it, at such a bargain price, it has to be said, will be disappointed. All who read it will be thrilled. Those who study it properly, and act upon it, will be strengthened [illegible] ial. It is a mine of information, a tool for [illegible] aiting for. Hugely beneficial to wr [illegible]

Rt Rev.Dr Barry Shuck [illegible]

Mr Burrows draws on sou [illegible] hich we can follow up for ourselves. H [illegible] oroughly convincing. I cannot recor [illegible] . It is a splendid read, and powerfully illustrates the tr [illegible] Proverbs 14:34 "Righteousness exalteth a nation: but sin is a reproach to any people."

Rev. John Thackway, Holywell

"European history is a manifestation of the superhuman power and reality of the Christian faith." This book is the proving of that thesis. Quoting many authors throughout this text, Mr Burrows reveals his extensive study of both secular as well as Christian sources, as he surveys the whole period from the fall of Rome to the present day.

'Our Priceless Christian Heritage' is a much-needed antidote to the contemporary creeds of liberal secularism and multiculturalism, which demanded that no one culture or faith can be superior to any other. We are most grateful to Mr Burrows in helping us to understand the enormous blessing which Biblical Christianity has brought to the world, and, not least of all, to our own nation.

Pastor Peter Simpson, Penn Free Methodist Church

When Gospel light first burst onto the pagan world 2,000 years ago, it not only bestowed new understanding and eternal life on multitudes. But, in time, remarkably influenced whole societies and nations. This book traces the numerous ways Christianity has elevated life, even for the unbelieving masses in the West. Here is a sweep through history, which shows its effect on issues such as politics, slavery, home life, children, education, hospitals, literature, science, industry, commerce, social reform, conscience and economics. A fascinating review and a goldmine of quotes and information.

Christopher Laws, Metropolitan Tabernacle, London

Our Priceless Christian Heritage

by

Roland Burrows

ISBN 978–1–913133–07–8

Our Priceless Christian Heritage

Published by the Wakeman Trust

Distributed by Roland Burrows,
27, Beauty Bank, Cradley Heath B64 7HZ

* * *

* * *

* * *

Typeset using Minion Pro 11/12

“*By their fruits ye shall know them.*” Matthew 7:16.

“Christianity brought about the most audacious, the most original, the grandest spiritual revolution the world has ever seen. … The supreme object in life is the moral and religious perfection of the individual; … Man has only one real Master,—God; if he serves well that one and supreme Master, if he merits his love and praise, the rest does not count … It was this new conception of life by which Christianity revolutionised the intellectual and moral foundations of the ancient civilization from the top to the bottom and which triumphed finally over the awful disasters of the third century and produced a supreme reaction against disorder.”

Guglielmo Ferrero, *The Ruin of Ancient Civilisation and the Triumph of Christianity*, 1921, pp. 79–81

“In Christianity, and nowhere else, lie the roots of a higher valuation of history and of temporal life in general.”

Rudolph Eucken

“I say, choosing points of the most definitive character, that Christianity abolished gladiatorial fights, and other spectacles of horrid cruelty to men; human sacrifices; polygamy; exposure of children; slavery in its old form; cannibalism; drove into the shade all unnatural lusts, and indeed, all irregular passions.

Next, Christianity established, generally speaking, the moral and social equality of women, the duty of relieving the poor, the sick and the afflicted; peace, instead of war, as the ordinary, normal presumptive relation between nations.

Here is a goodly list. I speak not of what it taught. It taught the law of mutual love. It proscribed all manner of sin. But the preceding particulars refer to what, besides saying, it did, besides trying, it accomplished. In every one of these instances, except that of cannibalism, the exhibition of what it did is in glaring contrast, not with barbarous but with the most highly civilised life such as it was exhibited by the Greeks or Romans in the most famous ages of both. Now I think that is a fair statement, not easily shaken. I admit that many of these results are negative. And to those of them which are positive, there are other higher results in the excellence and perfection of the human soul individually; but I have taken such as are palpable, and I think undeniable.”

William E. Gladstone

"The coming of Christ was the creation of the sun in man's moral heaven, the opening of a fountain in man's moral desert; all that is wholesome in government, pure in morals, benevolent in institutions, also in the spirit and manners of the world, owes its existence to this fact. Insignificant as this planet is compared with other orbs, the fact that Christ has trod its soil has given it a lustre that pales the brightness of them all."

David Thomas

Gesta Christi … The achievements of Christ.

Contents

List of Illustrations

Author's Preface

The purpose of this book is to illustrate the vast and vital contribution Christianity has made towards the enriching, ennobling and well-being of individuals and societies through the centuries.

It freely acknowledges that it is not the primary concern of Christianity to create a Christian civilisation or culture. The main concern of Christianity is man's relationship with Jesus Christ. The chief responsibility of Christianity is to do as did John the Baptist and to cry, "*Behold the Lamb of God, which taketh away the sin of the world.*"

Neither do we argue that Christianity is to be solely taken up with this world. Indeed, one of its fundamental purposes, and one of its vital means of helping mankind is to remind him that his destiny is not in this world, but in the world to come. It is indeed by its otherworldliness that Christianity becomes the salt of the earth and the light of the world; our Lord Jesus Christ made it very plain when he said, "*My Kingdom is not of this world.*"

In order to make it clear that the object of this book is not to recommend the so-called Social Gospel, we might draw on some very useful remarks in Gresham Machen's, *An Introduction to The New Testament; Its Literature and History.* Machen makes it very clear that there is a world of difference between Christian service to society, as a fruit of the Gospel, and the view that social service is a fundamental part of the Gospel. Machen saw social reform as secondary to the Gospel, but also something that would develop normally under Christian influence. The *Social Gospel Movement* and its successors today come very close to making social service a kind of substitute for the Gospel of redeeming grace. "*Despite the importance of social reforms, the first purpose of true Christian evangelism is to bring the individual man or woman directly and consciously into the presence of God. Without that, all else is of but short temporary value.*"

We are seeking to look at and examine in these pages what we might call the by-products of Christianity. Though its main focus is on the soul of man, when widely embraced it inevitably has the effect of creating better societies and nobler civilisations.

Many people today are ignorant of the extent to which Christianity has enriched our Western nations. It is not widely known that it has formed the bedrock of Western society. Neither is it widely known that it has been the safeguard of our liberties, the inspiration of many of our social welfare provisions, as it has been the strengthening and stabilising influence that has held society together through many times of change, hardship and war.

Others have taken up the attitude of individuals like Voltaire who said, seemingly referring to Christianity: "*Religion is the chief cause of all the sorrows of humanity. Everywhere it has only served to drive men to evil, and plunge them into brutal miseries … It makes history an immense tableau of human follies.*"

It is the purpose of this book to challenge and correct such misapprehensions.

The first part of the book is an attempt to set out some of the underlying principles of Christianity which enable us to understand the nature of ourselves and the world we live in. Also at the same time to direct our thinking along the right channels and enable us to navigate the dangerous waters of false philosophies and theories that seek to dominate our society today. Such ideas tend to produce stagnation, of thought and action, ideas that act to the erosion of our liberties, and the corrosion of justice, integrity, humanity and kindness.

The main section of the book sets out on a journey through history, seeking to point out the numerous ways in which Christianity has spiritually, morally and socially lifted those societies in which it has taken hold. It has also formed the basis and rationale for the study of science, brought to reality the concept of universal education, and has been the inspiration for mankind's finest achievements in the realm of literature, music and the arts.

If Western societies are to survive they need to recover the strength of their Christian roots. Any continuance in the present secular course, is guaranteed to bring at last a dismal outcome. Certainly secularism has achieved an enormous erosion in popular commitment to the churches, and a widespread demoralisation in the ranks of the people of God. Some main-line churches have adapted their gospel and their moral teachings to secular trends. This is not the way, and we need to recover our confidence in the Gospel of redeeming grace. God has given to us his powerful and all sufficient Word; he has given to us the Words of everlasting life, and rather than adapt we must set these teachings against the destructive trends of modernism.

Finally, in regard to the book's contents I have included quotations and insights from a wide spectrum of authors pertaining to the subject before us. Not all hold to the same theological principles as myself, but I have included them inasmuch as they contribute to the issues before us here. Further let it be freely admitted, to slightly adapt Montaigne's line, I have gathered from many sources, and nothing but the thread that holds them together is mine own.

It is hoped that by God's grace these pages will inform and strengthen the hand of believers as they seek to witness and make known the greatness of Christ and his glorious achievements in this world.

I would like to express my grateful thanks to Dr Digby James for his much appreciated help and patience in the production of this book.

Chapter 1
Our Priceless Christian Heritage: The Foundation of Western Civilisation

Of all the speeches given by Sir Winston Churchill during the Second World War, perhaps the one delivered just prior to the Battle of Britain has the most abiding resonance and relevance for Christian people today. Churchill said:

> I expect that the battle of Britain is about to begin. Upon this battle depends the survival of Christian civilisation. Upon it depends our own British life, and the long continuity of our institutions and our Empire. The whole force and might of the enemy must very soon be turned on us. Hitler knows that he will have to break us in this island or lose the war. If we can stand up to him, all Europe may be free, and the life of the world may move forward into broad, sunlit uplands. But if we fail, then the whole world, including the United States, including all that we have known and cared for, will sink into the abyss of a new Dark Age made more sinister, and perhaps more protracted, by the lights of perverted science. Let us therefore brace ourselves to our duties, and so bear ourselves that, although if the British Empire and its Commonwealth last for a thousand years, men will still say, "This was their finest hour".

The speech refers to Christian civilisation, and sees that civilisation embattled and threatened by the most hostile and inhuman of foes. These two concepts give us an appropriate starting point for this work.

First of all, we may say that there is such a thing as a Christian civilisation or culture as we may call it. It is an incontrovertible fact that Western civilisation was built on a Christian foundation and in so far as these elements still exist, remains so to this day. It is also true that anyone with a knowledge of our history cannot deny the vast and extensive contribution that Christianity has made to the treasury of our Western culture and way of life.

Certainly, we need to avoid the illusion that there was ever a Christian Europe in the full evangelical sense of the word. Not everyone who professes and calls themselves a Christian is necessarily one in the fullest Gospel understanding of the word. However, when we are speaking of Christian civilization, we mean a situation in which there is an all-pervasive influence of Christian teaching within that culture. We are speaking of an outlook, a morality and an atmosphere, extending throughout, and moulding not only the lives of individuals, but governing and pervading the majority of the various institutions, standards and norms of that society.

We can say that in our own country, as well as others touched by the Reformation, Protestantism has been closely associated with the general culture of these societies.

We cannot emphasise too strongly the influence of Christianity on the culture of the Western world and this is well summed up by Emil Brunner in his Gifford Lecture "*Christianity and Civilisation*".

> European history is a manifestation of the superhuman power and reality of the Christian faith and of the New Testament message. This is so even where life has only been superficially touched by them, or where they are present in a very diluted and impure form.
>
> It is this which imposes itself as a manifest fact for everyone who studies the cultural history of the West: it is not only the Romanesque and Gothic cathedrals dominating the silhouette of many European cities, not only the frescoes of Fra Angelico in San Marco and of Michael Angelo in the Sistine Chapel, not only Milton's *Paradise Lost*, Rembrandt's engravings of Biblical stories, Bach's Passion according to St. Matthew, which are unthinkable without the Bible, and without the Church translating, conserving and promulgating this Bible. Our democratic state-forms, also public and private charitable institutions, colleges of English and American universities, a multitude of the most important concepts of our psychological, philosophical, juridical and cultural language are directly or indirectly products of Christian tradition and of Christian thinking, feeling and purposing. It was not for nothing that during many centuries the Christian Church had the monopoly of education and instruction, that the invention of the printing press primarily contributed to the spreading of the Bible, and for many centuries the most famous institutions of higher learning were foundations of Christian communities and churches and were primarily designed for the promotion of Christian knowledge. All that is easily understood if we consider that up to the nineteenth century every European individual was baptized and instructed by the Christian Church, and furthermore, at least in a superficial sense the contents

> of the Bible message were believed by almost everybody and shaped their judgement of what is true and false, good and evil, desirable and undesirable. Certainly, there were always some sceptics, doubters and heretics. But they could not manifest themselves as such. Certainly, there was probably in all ages a large majority of indifferent and lukewarm nominal Christians; but even they stood in an unbroken tradition of doctrine of faith, and even their conscience was formed by the Commandments of the Bible, whether they acted according to their conscience or not. Even towards the end of the eighteenth century, the typical thought of the Enlightenment, with its negative or doubting attitude, was confined to a decided minority within the higher ranks of society. The masses, even the large majority of educated men and women, always thought in the categories of Biblical Christian tradition, however diluted or misshaped and distorted the Gospel may have been in this tradition. It is therefore self-evident that in such a world of nations, civilisation was deeply imbued, determined and guided by Christian faith, its concepts, its norms, its concepts of value.
>
> The history of civilisation, as Christian, has not yet been written. What can be grasped of this history, however, by everyone who has any knowledge of it and who has any share in European culture, is sufficient to justify that catchword, "The Christian civilisation of the West". At least in the sense of an undeniable fact, however different may be the interpretations of this fact.
>
> Brunner, 1948, pp. 5–6

It has to be freely admitted at this point that Christianity is not the only root of Western culture. Recognition has to be given to the influence of classical antiquity, that is the influence of Greek and Roman culture, manifesting itself in forms of art, literature and philosophy, the influence of Greek concepts of democracy and Roman concepts of law etc. In recognising the contribution of these older civilisations, we must also note that there were, nevertheless, many aspects which were cruel and despotic. It is important therefore to remind ourselves that it was the Christian Church that salvaged, retained and indeed refined the best of these elements of classical and Roman culture for the use of further generations.

When the empire of Rome collapsed in the fifth century, the barbarian invaders came to burn, destroy, rape and plunder all that was left of the great Roman civilisation. It was the brave and intelligent actions of the Christian leaders of the time in negotiating with the invaders and thus subduing them that not only resulted in the preserving of the lives of thousands, but also in rescuing much of the Roman and pre-Roman heritage for posterity.

Some majestic scenes are recorded from this period, such as the occasion when Attila the Hun was overawed by the presence of Pope Leo III at Ponte Molino and listened obediently to the counsel he gave him.

> Even though the barbarians came as conquerors, at least they were not totally strange to the Romans, having lived on their borders for many years. But in the 450s, a tribe of Orientals from central Asia swept across Europe. These were the Huns, who had been driven out of China by the Chinese Emperor and were now pushing toward Rome. They were led by Attila, who wanted to establish an Asiatic Empire in Europe to replace the Roman Empire. In August 452, they swept through northern Italy, causing whole populations to scatter, a seemingly unstoppable advance. The people and the rulers panicked.
>
> Then, on the very day Attila was preparing to attack the city of Rome, he saw a strange procession marching slowly towards them, priests, monks and deacons bearing crosses and banners. From the entire column the rhythmical responses of hymns and Psalms were heard. In the midst of the procession rode an old man with a white beard, praying as he rode. The Hun galloped toward the river, urging his horse into it, and halted on a sandy islet, within hailing distance of the strangers. "What is your name?" Attila shouted to the old man. Came the answer: "I am Leo, the Pope". Attila hesitated, then urged his hosts to fall back. The Pope came forward to meet him.
>
> No one knows exactly what the two men said. A few hours later, Leo returned to Rome. All he would say to Emperor Valentinian III was, "Let us give thanks to God, for he has delivered us from grave danger". Attila ordered his Huns to retreat; Rome was safe. But not until Attila's sudden death the following year the Hunnish host was broken up.
>
> Carroll, 1994, p. 119

A similar occasion is on record when Genseric the Vandal in AD 455 was subdued by the Council of the Church leaders as he entered the gates of Rome. The Church and its leaders stood between the barbarians and the people. They won from the barbarians a promise that there would be no torture, no massacre, no burning, or sacking of the largest churches.

Dean Farrar comments:

> Already, they had heard the name of Christ; already, courageous missionaries had penetrated their savage forests and traversed their gloomy hills; and thus the fury of that onset was softened by the recognition of virtue more elevated than courage, and blessings more to be desired than strength. And thus, Christianity was not only saved, but became herself the bulwark of all that was valuable in the ancient civilisations. When the degenerate Romans had melted down the statue of Virtus to pay their ransom to Alaric, her bishops earned the title *Defensores Civitatis*. The Church saved the vanquished from extirpation, and the victors from decay. Barbarians who had seen such types of noble excellence as an Ulphilas or a Severinus, or in later times a Boniface or an Olaf, saw in the priesthood an institution for which they felt a genuine reverence; and this veneration was the means of fusing all that was valuable in two violently conflicting elements into one splendid, permanent, and progressive society. The churches of Christian Rome, built out of the marble of heathen temples, which had been levelled by barbarian hands, are at once a history and a symbol of the whole work which the Church did for the world.
>
> Farrar, 1875, pp. 112–113

Farrar also gives us three other quotations on this theme from writers, who, he notes, have no real sympathy for Christian truth, and yet cannot deny the facts of history.

> It was they (the Christian Church), who treated with the invaders in the name of the natives; it was their adhesion which guaranteed the general obedience; and after the conversion of the conquerors, it was to their sacred character that the conquered were indebted for whatever mitigation they experienced of the fury of the conquest.
>
> John Stuart Mill, *Dissertations II*, p. 243 quoted by Farrar, 1875, p. 112)

> In the face of the brute force of the corrupt and tottering Empire, whose frontiers echoed to the threatening footsteps of the barbarians, those bishops raised the banner of a moral idea, of a spiritual power, destined to win over the barbarians to its rule.
>
> Mazzini, *Fortnightly Review*, June 1870 quoted by Farrar, 1875, p. 112

> The progress of Christianity has been marked by two glorious and decisive victories over the learned and luxurious civilization of the Roman Empire, and over the warlike barbarians of Scythia and Germany, who subverted the Empire and embraced the religion of Rome.
>
> Gibbon *The Rise and Fall of the Roman Empire*, vol. 3, p. 38 quoted by Farrar, 1875, p. 112

Further by way of introduction to this subject we need to consider the question, how were the renowned civilisations which existed before the coming of Christianity brought about and developed?

We have already made reference to Roman and Greek civilisation but we could add to this number many others, such as the civilisation of ancient Egypt, (Moses studied at the University of Heliopolis such subjects as astronomy, law, medicine, chemistry, the philosophy of symbols, music, poetry and the religion of the Egyptians), to which other civilisations we could add Babylon, Assyria, India and China to name but a few. It is true that in them we find examples of magnificent art, architecture, literature, law and the institutions of state, highly developed systems of education, trade and manufacture. All these civilisations, we could say, grew up without any knowledge of God's revelation through Scripture.

We can speak of the magnificence of the Greek epic, its lyric or dramatic poetry, much of it unsurpassed even to this present day. We can speak of the Greek scientific mind, or the fact that the oldest democracy in the world was established there in Greece, not to mention the contribution of the great philosophers such as Parmenides, Plato, Aristotle, etc.

Some of the early Christian theologians put forward the hypothesis that the Greek philosophers had learned their best philosophy from Moses and the Hebrew prophets, but this theory might be contested.

Consideration of the existence of highly developed civilisations that grew up and existed outside the sphere of Divine revelation helps us in our consideration of and understanding of the unique nature of Christian civilisation.

Factors necessary in building cultures/civilisations

One necessary factor behind the development of culture and civilisation is the natural advantages of climate, fertility and the presence of a range of advantageous physical resources. Ancient Egypt prospered because of the fertility of the soil produced by the inundations of the Nile, the warm climate and the geographical location of the country, etc.

A second necessary factor is that of the human resources of a given area, namely the physical, mental and spiritual resources of the people who lived there. By this we mean the health, vitality, energy, talents and resourcefulness of the indigenous population.

Thirdly there is the all-important fact of the spiritual and moral beliefs which underlie any civilisation or culture. These elements will include the people's determination and motivation, the level of their freedom, the strength of their endurance, vision and character. The nature of that civilisation's religious beliefs, and philosophical outlook will undoubtedly play a massive part in determining the nature, strength and enduring character of that civilisation.

All these various elements must be present, but we cannot emphasise too strongly that the spiritual and moral beliefs of any people will ultimately be the decisive factors, determining the character, success or failure or period of survival of any civilisation.

Of course, the physical aspects will play a part, as also the resourcefulness and energy of the people, but it cannot be allowed, as naturalistic, positivistic philosophers are prone to do, to play down or ignore the spiritual factors. The nature of the moral and spiritual beliefs which undergird any civilisation are vital factors and cannot be ignored.

Every civilisation is undergirded by the system of beliefs it embraces

In regard to the Roman belief system, Gibbon in his *Rise and Fall of the Roman Empire* makes an interesting point when he observes that Roman civilisation was bound to reject Christianity, because of its (the Roman Empire's) concept of toleration.

Roman culture embraced a wide diversity of customs and religions. It gave respect to the many confused traditions and ceremonies of its constituent nations and peoples. All these however were ultimately required to give their supreme obedience to the Emperor/Caesar. Whatever religion was followed, homage to Caesar was paramount. Everyone was free to follow his own religion, but overall, that individual must bow to the supreme manifestation of divinity—Caesar, the embodiment of the state. All were united in giving their greatest honour and dedication to Caesar, and by doing so acknowledged their supreme obedience to the state.

Roman tolerance had its limits and the refusal of Christians to bow to Caesar was seen as a threat to the unity of the Empire, that is the unifying culture of the civilisation. This was in spite of the fact that in every other respect Christians were model citizens, and we can easily recall passages in the New Testament in which the apostle Paul calls upon Christians to give due honour, respect and obedience even to secular rulers (Romans 13:1).

We may also recall the words of our Saviour himself, "*Render unto Caesar the things that are Caesar's and unto God the things that are God's*" (Matthew 22:21).

Celsius accused believers of endangering the Empire by their withdrawal and refusal to give a whole-hearted commitment to it. The earliest Christians would not enter the ranks of the army because it involved acknowledgment of Caesar as god, and also held back from other elements in public life because of this kind of requirement.

In the same way, in modern times, Marxists have persecuted Christians because Christians will not engage in the wholehearted struggle to destroy the old order and build a new secular Marxist state.

The fundamental belief systems of any culture or civilisation are bound to have a great effect upon its nature and character.

Francis Schaeffer makes the following comments.

> In many ways Rome was great, but it had no real answers to the basic problems all humanity faces. Much of Roman thought and culture was shaped by Greek thinking, especially after Greece came under Roman rule in 146 BC. The Greeks tried first to build a society upon the city-state, that is, the *polis*. The city-state both in theory and fact, was comprised of all those who were accepted as citizens. All values had meaning in reference to the *polis*. Thus, when Socrates had to choose between death and exile from that which gave him meaning, he chose death. But the *polis* failed since it proved to be an insufficient basis upon which to build a society.
>
> The Greeks, and later the Romans, also tried to build society upon their gods. But these gods were not big enough because they were finite, limited. Even all their gods put together were not infinite. Actually, the gods in Greek and Roman thinking were like men and women larger-than-life, but not basically different from human men and women. As one example among thousands, we can think of the

statue of Hercules, standing inebriated and urinating. Hercules was the patron god of Herculaneum which was destroyed at the same time as Pompeii. The gods were amplified humanity, not divinity. Like the Greeks, the Romans had no infinite god. This being so, they had no sufficient reference point intellectually; that is, they did not have anything big enough or permanent enough to which to relate either their thinking or their living. Consequently, their value system was not strong enough to bear the strains of life, either individual or political. All their gods put together could not give them a sufficient basis for life, morals, values and final decisions. These gods depended on the society which made them, and when this society collapsed the gods, tumbled with it. Thus, the Greek and Roman experiments in social harmony (which rested on an elitist republic) ultimately failed.

In the days of Julius Caesar (100–44 BC), Rome turned to an authoritarian system centred in Caesar himself. Before the days of Caesar, the senate could not keep order. Armed gangs terrorized the city of Rome and the normal processes of government were disrupted as rivals fought for power. Self-interest became more significant than social-interest, however sophisticated the trappings. Thus, in desperation, the people accepted authoritarian government. As Plutarch (AD c.50–120) put it in *Lives of the Noble Greeks and Romans*, the Romans made Caesar dictator for life in the hope that the government of a single person would give them time to recover after so many civil wars and calamities. This was indeed a tyranny, since his power was now not only absolute but perpetual too.

After Caesar's death, Octavian (63 BC–AD 14), later called Caesar Augustus, grand-nephew of Caesar, came to power. He had become Caesar's son by adoption. The great Roman poet Virgil (70–19 BC) was a friend of Augustus and he wrote the *Aeneid* with the object of showing that Augustus was the divinely appointed leader and that Rome's mission was to bring peace and civilisation to the world. Because Augustus established peace externally and internally and because he kept the outward forms of constitutionality, Romans of every class were ready to allow him total power in order to restore and assure the functioning of the political system, business, and the affairs of daily life. After 12 BC, he became the head of the state religion, taking the title *Pontifex Maximus* and urging everyone to worship the "spirit of Rome and the genius of the Emperor". Later this became obligatory for all the people of the Empire, and later still,

> the emperors ruled as gods. Augustus tried to legislate morals and family life; subsequent emperors tried impressive legal reforms and welfare programs. But a human god is a poor foundation and Rome fell.
>
> Schaeffer, 2005, pp. 20–22

We say again that we can never put too much stress on the difference that an individual's or a people's fundamental beliefs, (or as we may put it world-view) makes to their whole outlook, strength and manner of life.

It was the inadequacy of the spiritual and moral foundations of even the most powerful nations and empires of the ancient world that was their undoing at the last.

> A culture or an individual with a weak base can stand only when the pressure on it is not too great. As an illustration, let us think of a Roman bridge. The Romans built little humpbacked bridges over many of the streams of Europe. People and wagons went over the structures safely for centuries, for two millennia. But if people today drove heavily loaded trucks over these bridges, they would break. It is this way with the lives and value systems of individuals and cultures when they have nothing stronger to build on but their own limitedness, their own finiteness. They can stand when pressure is not too great, but when pressures mount, if then they do not have a sufficient base, they crash—just as a Roman bridge would cave in under the weight of a modern six-wheeled truck. Culture and the freedoms of people are fragile. Without a sufficient base, when such pressures come only time is needed—and often not a great deal of time—before there is a collapse.
>
> Schaeffer, 2005, p. 22

In the year AD 410, Alaric and his Goths sacked the city of Rome. This event of course was of vast importance in the ancient world, not so much because of its direct effect on political or economic organisation, but because of its effect on the minds of men and women who shared in the Mediterranean civilisation. The sack was not the most terrible of visitations, but it was a profound shock, and it was likewise a revelation. For centuries men had thought of Rome as a stable feature of civilised existence, nothing could shake it. It had been intact from the invader for nearly 1,000 years. Provinces might revolt, provinces might be pacified, but Rome was the Eternal City.

She was the assurance of order, and men had come to believe, without argument or shadow of a doubt, in the dependability of that order. But the shock of invasion revealed to men throughout the Mediterranean and beyond the inadequacy of that on which they had depended with such implicit confidence. The consequence was that they were forced to question the entire civilisation on which they had relied. We see evidence of the enduring effect of the shock throughout the structure of St Augustine's great work, *The City of God*, which was not finished until sixteen years after the event that precipitated its writing. The whole book is a monumental attempt to speak to the condition of men and women suffering from a profound intellectual and spiritual shock. Augustine's arguments clearly show the questionings and probing's in men's minds. They recognised that the trouble was more than superficial and that the year AD 410 represented more than an isolated military defeat. The fall of Rome was not the cause of the decay of their culture, but rather a symptom of that decay. The decay, they realised, was in the foundations; their moral and spiritual foundations could not bear the weight of that which had been built upon it.

Our Western civilisation, and particularly, Great Britain and the United States, has been built on a Christian foundation. This foundation has now been under great attack for a considerable length of time. Our foundations are being destroyed. Albert Schweitzer, whose work amongst the lepers at Lambarene we may greatly admire, but whose theology we repudiate, nevertheless spoke the truth when in 1922 he observed:

> It is clear now to everyone that the suicide of Western civilisation is in progress. What remains of it is no longer safe. It is still standing, indeed, because it was not exposed to the destructive pressures which overwhelmed the rest, but, like the rest it is built upon rubble, and the next landslide will very likely carry it away.

The fact of the matter is that, though it was not clear to everybody else in 1922, it is much clearer now. Sometimes, we have to go outside the situation to see things clearly and it was clear to this lonely man, living, not in Europe, or America but on the edge of the African jungle. At that time, many of his contemporaries were wholly convinced that man had come into a new age, a time of general prosperity and happiness through the abundance of material benefits. It is much clearer now that these optimists were wrong.

We may at this point remember our Lord's parable of the house built upon the sand and the house built upon the rock in Matthew 7:24–27 and Luke 6:47–49:

> Therefore whosoever heareth these sayings of mine, and doeth them, I will liken him unto a wise man, which built his house upon a rock: And the rain descended, and the floods came, and the winds blew, and beat upon that house; and it fell not: for it was founded upon a rock. And everyone that heareth these sayings of mine, and doeth them not, shall be likened unto a foolish man, which built his house upon the sand: And the rain descended and the floods came, and the winds blew, and beat upon that house; and it fell: and great was the fall of it.

We turn now to look in some detail at the Christianity that has been the basis of our European civilisation since the collapse of the Roman Empire in the fifth century. We are beginning to look at its massive contribution and why it is imperative that this contribution is known, recognised, strengthened and restored.

Chapter 2
The Christian World-view: The Old Testament Foundation

FIRSTLY, WE NEED TO SAY THAT THE BASIS OF THE CHRISTIAN worldview is first built upon the revelation of God given to us in the Old Testament Scriptures.

The Old Testament tells us that "In the beginning God created the heaven and the earth" (Genesis 1:1).

These opening chapters of Genesis teach us to begin with God. As a foundational principle, the Bible teaches us to begin with God.

Calvin said:

> Nearly all the wisdom we possess, that is to say, true and sound wisdom, consists of two parts: the knowledge of God and of ourselves … Again, it is certain that man never achieves a clear knowledge of himself unless he has first looked upon God's face, and then descends from contemplating him to scrutinise himself. We always seem to ourselves righteous and upright and wise and holy—this pride is innate in all of us—unless by clear proofs we stand convinced of our own unrighteousness, foulness, folly and impurity. Moreover, we are not thus convinced if we look merely to ourselves and not also to the Lord, who is the sole standard by which this judgement must be measured.
>
> Calvin,, 1960, pp. 35, 37

We may also note the following observations made by Dr Martyn Lloyd-Jones on the same subject:

> If you consider the typical approach to theology and to biblical matters over the past hundred years or so, you will find that almost invariably the starting point is with man. Everything associated with what is sometimes called Modernism is always characterised by that; their theology is always subjective; it always starts with man himself. Because Modernism is interested in itself, and in so-called psychological ideas of origin, inevitably it starts either with man or with the world, and from that goes on to study the doctrine of God.
>
> But that is not what the Bible says. The Bible always starts with

> God; you remember the great opening statement which really tells us everything: "In the beginning—God".
>
> It is very important that we should emphasise this and grasp it clearly. The knowledge of God is ultimately the sum of all the doctrines; there is no sense, there is no meaning or purpose, in any other doctrine apart from this great central, all inclusive, doctrine of God himself. There is no point in considering the doctrine of salvation, nor the doctrine of sin, unless we have started with the doctrine of God. But quite apart from such more or less logical considerations, we start with the doctrine of God because God is God, and because if we put anything or anybody before him, we have thereby dishonoured him. We are failing to worship him as we should and failing to conduct ourselves in his presence as the Bible teaches us to do.
>
> Lloyd-Jones, 1978

The opening chapters of the Bible give a unique concept of history

This of course tells us that the created order of things—including human history—had a beginning. The Book of Revelation tells us that it will also have an end, a completion. This understanding of the world tells us that historic events follow a non-repetitive course from their beginning to their final goal and fulfilment. We sometimes forget that the whole of Western society is built upon and still holds to this linear view of history. Prior to this, and outside the sphere of Judeo-Christian influence, the understanding and concept of history is quite different, as for example in the classical thought of the ancient world. The ancient classical world thought in terms of a cyclical view of time. That is to say that historical events were believed to repeat themselves over and over through consecutive generations.

The directional view of history given by Christianity and Judaism was revolutionary in the eyes of many at that time. The importance of the biblical concept of history cannot be overstated; it alone gives us a purpose, and a goal-directed interpretation of history.

The Old Testament provides us with a profound passage illustrating the depressing nature of the cyclical view of history, especially when it is applied to the life of an individual. We have it in the well-known words of Ecclesiastes chapter 1:2–11.

> 2 *Vanity of vanities, saith the Preacher, vanity of vanities; all is vanity.* 3 *What*

profit hath a man of all his labour which he taketh under the sun? [4]*One generation passeth away, and another generation cometh; but the earth abideth for ever.* [5]*The sun also ariseth, and the sun goeth down, and hasteth to his place where he arose.* [6]*The wind goeth toward the south, and turneth about unto the north; it whirleth about continually, and the wind returneth again according to his circuits.* [7]*All the rivers run into the sea, yet the sea is not full; unto the place from whence the rivers come thither they return again.* [8]*All things are full of labour; man cannot utter it: the eye is not satisfied with seeing, nor the ear filled with hearing.* [9]*The thing that hath been, it is that which shall be; and that which is done is that which shall be done: and there is no new thing under the sun.* [10]*Is there anything whereof it may be said, See, this is new? it hath been already of old time, which was before us.* [11]*There is no remembrance of former things; neither shall there be any remembrance of things that are to come with those that shall come after*".

Solomon is lamenting in this phase of his reflection that in the understanding of the worldly man, we live in a world where there is constant activity, but where there is never any real progress. There is no actual getting anywhere. Everything goes on as it always has done, but there is no ultimate advance. The sun rises and sets, only to rise again and set. The wind blows and blows, only to come back to where it started. The rivers run into the sea, but never fill it, because the water evaporates and returns to its source. This is the way of the world; the activity never ends, but no destination is ever reached. Man is caught up in this endless and wearisome cycle. It is impossible to put into words or describe adequately the futility of it all. The eyes see, the ears hear, but neither knows what true satisfaction is. There is no ultimate understanding. History is as repetitive as nature; it is a tiresome round of activity which never ultimately produces anything new on this earth.

This is the sort of pessimistic, gloomy, depressing outlook that the cyclical view of life and history instils into men's minds and attitudes.

Another illustration and insight into the futility of the cyclical view of history is found in Psalm 12:8: "*The wicked walk on every side.*"

In Augustine's Latin version, the same verse reads: "*In circumitu impii ambulant*", which he translates as "The wicked walk in circles." He adds the comment:

> I think this fitting enough, not however because their life is really

> going to recur in the circles of which they speak, but because their false doctrine itself is of the circular kind.
>
> *The City of God*, XII, 13. quoted in Baillie, 1950, p. 76

Augustine rightly associated the cyclical doctrines of history with all the ideas of fate, fortune and destiny, astrological or otherwise, that were associated with it. Eloquently, and at great length, he insists on the hopelessness of such an outlook and the utter absence from it of any prospect of real blessedness.

> The pagan philosophers have introduced cycles of time in which the same things are in the order of nature constantly being restored and repeated, and have asserted that these whirlings of past and future ages will go on unceasingly.
>
> From this mockery they are unable to set free even the immortal soul, even after it has attained wisdom, and believe it to be proceeding unceasingly into false blessedness and returning unceasingly to true misery. For how can that be true blessedness which never has the assurance of being eternal, the soul being either most oblivious of the truth and ignorant of its coming misery, or else most unhappily fearing such misery while its so-called blessedness lasts? … It is only through the sound doctrine of a linear course of history that we can escape from I know not what false cycles discovered by false and deceitful sages.
>
> *De principiis*, II.iii. 4. quoted in Baillie, 1950, p. 75

Belief in these cyclical patterns of history have been widely held in various cultures from China, India, the Middle East and the ancient Greek and Roman empires. Their belief was that the life of any individual follows a pattern of growth to maturity, followed eventually by old age and death and another generation then rises and repeats the process. This way of thinking was projected onto the historical process. They came also to think that the yearly rhythm of the seasons was reproduced on a grander scale in the world of men. On the basis of these analogies, people concluded that history should be understood in a cyclical manner.

It is quite different with the Bible. The Old Testament is at the same time a theological statement and an interpretation of history. For Israel, its history is an encounter with Jehovah. The very idea that history is a process with a beginning, middle and end is original with Israel. It is the will and purpose of Jehovah which unifies the process of history.

The unfolding story of Israel is directed by the will of God and fulfils his designs. These designs are not revealed in their full clarity at any stage of the process. However, the serene confidence of these writings is that events, far from being the chance collisions of blind forces without meaning or purpose, or the ever-recurring cycles of nature, are rather the working out of the intelligent plan of God.

> The Old Testament view of history is that it is the execution of the designs of Jehovah. All through it runs the saving and judging will of Jehovah and this gives history both intelligibility and morality. It gives intelligibility, for it defines both the origin and the end of the human experience in history and the process by which the two are joined. It gives morality for it shows that history is governed by a supremely powerful and an entirely incorruptible moral will. The fulfilment of the process is conditioned neither by human success nor by human failure. Human achievement is not the agent that brings about the fulfilment of history and destiny, and human sin does not block the accomplishment of the purpose of history.
>
> The Israelites' consciousness of history is attested in such creeds or professions of faith as found in Deuteronomy 6:20–25; 26:5–10; Joshua 24:2–13. Similar examples are found in Psalms 77; 78; 105; 106. These statements of faith are liturgical. They are based on the historic memory of the deeds of Jehovah. When Israel wished to profess its belief in God, or its "knowledge" of him, it recited his deeds in history. From these deeds, Israel developed a consciousness of itself as an historical reality with an origin and a destiny. So deep was Israel's awareness of its place in history that, alone of the contemporary peoples in the ancient world, it exhibited a sense of its history as a career with a determined finality.
>
> This concept of Jehovah as the Lord of history was held in tension with the concept of human freedom and responsibility. It accepts the concept of Jehovah's will as being worked out through history, nothing able to ultimately thwart it, alongside the belief in man's responsibility.
>
> The Old Testament affirms both God's sovereignty and man's responsibility. Were people not responsible agents, they would not be objects of judgement. When the prophets charge Israel with sin, they do not fail to warn that Israel can escape the imminent judgement by conversion, until a point of cumulative malice is reached at which conversion can assure only survival, but not the reversal of the course

of history and judgement. The prophets show no awareness of any conflict between the sovereignty of God and human freedom; the theological concept of history demands that neither of these beliefs be maintained at the expense of another.

The Old Testament has a clear understanding that the function of Israel in history is to be that of mediating the knowledge of God to the nations.

Derived from J.L. McKenzie, *Aspects of Old Testament Thought*, 1974, pp. 1303–1304

The opening words of the Bible affirm both meaning and monotheism

Genesis 1:1 "*In the beginning God created the heaven and the earth.*"

The one-time Chief Rabbi, Jonathan Sacks, highly respected for his integrity and insights, commented:

> We cannot prove that life is meaningful and that God exists. But neither can we prove that love is better than hate, altruism and selfishness, forgiveness and the desire for revenge. We cannot prove that hope is truer to experience than the tragic sense of life. Almost none of the truths by which we live are provable, and the desire to prove them is based on a monumental confusion between explanation and interpretation. Explanations can be proved, interpretations cannot. Science deals in explanation. Meaning is always a matter of interpretation. It belongs to the same territory as ethics, aesthetics and metaphysics. In none of these three disciplines can anything of consequence be proved, but that does not make them insignificant. To the contrary, they represent three of the greatest repositories of human wisdom.
>
> Sacks, 2012, p. 32

Sacks goes on to comment that there is life-transforming truth in monotheism, the belief in one God.

> The discovery of a God beyond the universe has the power to redeem life from tragedy and meaninglessness … Only something or someone outside the universe can give meaning to the universe. Only belief in a transcendental God can render existence other than tragic. Individual lives, even within a tragically configured universe, may have meaning, but life as a whole does not. Bertrand Russell (the

pronounced atheist), who on this occasion we cannot but agree with, when he said: "Take God out of the equation, and we are left with unyielding despair". On this he was more honest than most of his successors.

It is said that it is possible to live without meaning. But it will be a strange, foreshortened, defensive kind of life. We know this because of the historical parallel. The world as conceived in the twenty-first century by the new atheists is recognisably the world of ancient Greece in the third pre-Christian century, the age of the Stoics, Sceptics, Cynics and, above all, the Epicureans. Epicurus, and his Roman disciple Lucretius believed that the material world is the only reality, that the world is made of atoms that simply reconfigure over time, and that the gods have no interest in the affairs of humankind. The Epicureans are the ancient counterparts of the new atheists in their reductive materialism and their hostility to religion. They held that there is no soul, no life after death, no meaning to history and no transcending purpose to life. The Epicurean formula for happiness is to maximise pleasure while minimising risk.

Here, roughly, is how an Epicurean would advise us to live. Do not make emotional commitments. Seize the day and harden yourself against the dark tomorrow. Do not pledge your life in marriage or suffer the burdens of bearing children. There is only one life, so there is no point in foreclosing your options or spending your time raising the next generation, for by the time your investment bears fruit you may no longer be here to see it. Do not get involved in public life: it is stressful and creates envy. Do not spend too much time on others: they seldom repay your efforts or even thank you for them. What matters is you. The others can look after themselves and if they cannot, that is their problem, not yours. Spend your time with friends. Live simply. Get used to solitude. Know that the highest form of freedom is the consciousness of necessity, and the highest form of knowledge is to know that we know nothing. Do not ask what life is for. Live it day by day. And when it becomes burdensome, end it at a time and place of your choosing.

This is a sane response to a universe without meaning. But it is also a symptom of a civilisation in advanced decline. Individuals can live without meaning. Societies in the long run cannot.

Sacks, 2012, pp. 29–30, 34

The opening chapters of the Bible reveal the far-reaching and highly consequential concept of God as Creator

Once again, the very first verse of the Old Testament lays down for us a fundamental truth for the understanding of life in this world.

> No man at the beginning ever thought of God as a Creator, not one. Wise people in these days say, the idea of a cause created the idea of God. But we must recognise this plain historical fact, that not a single primitive god of the race to which we belong, from India to Western America, had the idea of creation associated with him. Every god in the ancient world was a created being, and stood in the circle of nature, passionate, stormy, variable, manlike.
>
> Fairbairn, 1894, p. 111

This is a massive subject and we can only touch on it, but we might begin by asking: Did God have to create the world?

> Someone might say, Did not God then, if he is personal and if he loves, need an object for his love? Did he not *have* to create? And therefore, isn't the universe just as necessary to him as he is to the universe? But of course, the answer is, no. He did not have to create something face-to-face with himself in order to love, because there already was the Trinity. God could create by a free act of the will because before creation there was the Father who loved the Son. And there was also the Holy Spirit to love and be loved. In other words, God had someone face-to-face with himself in the three Persons of the Trinity. Our forefathers were certainly right when they formulated the Nicene and the Chalcedonian Creeds and insisted on the true Trinity in all its force. This wasn't just some passing Greek philosophic concept. When Greek thinkers raised these questions, the Christians saw that in what the Bible taught they had the answer.
>
> Schaeffer, 2005

The Bible teaches us that God created the universe to show his glory. Even in the inanimate creation, the stars and the Sun, the Moon and the sky, testified to God's greatness.

> Psalms 19:1 "*The heavens declare the glory of God; and the firmament sheweth his handywork.*"

Again:

> Revelation 4:11 "*Thou art worthy, O Lord, to receive glory and honour and power: for thou hast created all things, and for thy pleasure they are and were created.*"

When we affirm that God created the universe to show his glory, it is important that we realise that he did not need to create it. We should not think that God needed more glory than he had within the Trinity for all eternity, or that he was somehow incomplete without the glory that he would receive from the created universe. This would be to deny God's independence and imply that God needed the universe in order to be fully God. We must also affirm that the creation of the universe was a totally free act of God. It was not a necessary act but something that God chose to do.

Yet note:

> Revelation 4:11 "Thou art worthy, O Lord, to receive glory and honour and power: for thou hast created all things, and *for thy pleasure* they are and were created".

God desired to create the universe to demonstrate his excellence. The creation shows his great wisdom and power, and ultimately it shows all of his other attributes as well. It seems that God created the universe to take delight in his creation, and also to reveal his character.

This explains why we take spontaneous delight in all sorts of creative activities ourselves. People with artistic, musical or literary skills enjoy creating things and seeing, hearing, and reflecting upon and pondering on their creative work. God has made us to enjoy imitating, in a creaturely way, his creative activity.

If God created the universe to show his glory, then we would expect that the universe would fulfil the purpose for which he created it. This in fact is the case. Genesis 1:31 tells us that when God saw his creation,

> Genesis 1:31 "*behold,* [*it was*] *very good*".

Even though there is now sin in the world, the material creation is still good in God's sight and should be seen as good by us as well. This knowledge will free us from a false asceticism that sees the use and enjoyment of the material creation as wrong. Paul says that those who "*forbid marriage*" and "*insist on abstinence from food which God has created to be received with thanksgiving*" (1 Timothy 4:1–3) are giving heed to "*doctrines of demons*".

The apostle takes such a firm line because he understands that

> 1 Timothy 4:4 "*For every creature of God is good, and nothing to be refused, if it be received with thanksgiving.*"

By this fact Christians are encouraged to engage in proper industrial and technological development, and joyfully and thankfully to use the resources God has made and given—to ourselves and to those with whom we ought to share generously these good things.

The truth that God has created all things is full of comfort and encouragement

There is no peace for the mind apart from the knowledge that at the back of all that is around us, at the back of the stars and the sun, the earth and all that is in it, behind our own bodies, fearfully and wonderfully made as they are, there is the mind, the will and the purpose of God.

When we know that he created all these things, we can note that he has an eternal purpose. Even though the universe is marked by the eroding signs of judgement upon sin, we can be sure that our God who began his work will also finish it.

> 1 Samuel 3:12b: "*when I begin, I will also make an end.*"

God created the universe out of nothing

The Bible clearly requires us to believe that God created the universe out of nothing. (Sometimes the Latin phrase *ex nihilo* "out of nothing" is used). This means that before God began to create the universe nothing else existed except God himself. This is the implication of

> Genesis 1:1: "*In the beginning God created the heaven and the earth.*"

The phrase "*the heaven and the earth*" includes the entire universe. We can also read in the Psalms:

> Psalms 33:6, 9: "*By the word of the* Lord *were the heavens made; and all the host of them by the breath of his mouth. For he spake, and it was* [*done*]; *he commanded, and it stood fast.*"

At the beginning of John's Gospel, we read:

> John 1:3 "*All things were made by him; and without him was not any thing made that was made.*"

Many verses of Scripture could be brought out to prove that God is the Maker, Creator and Upholder of all things visible and invisible.

In Hebrews, coming to our point, we read that God made everything out of nothing.

> Hebrews 11:3: "*Through faith we understand that the worlds were framed by the word of God, so that things which are seen were not made of things which do appear.*"

In Paul's letter to the Romans, there is an interesting text, which states:

> Romans 4:17c: "*and calleth those things which be not as though they were.*"

Some of the modern translations render this text as:

> Romans 4:17c: "*and calls into existence the things that do not exist.*" (ESV)

Because God created the entire universe out of nothing there is no matter in the universe that is eternal. All that we see—the mountains, the oceans, the stars, the earth itself—came into existence when God created them. There was a time when they did not exist. This reminds us that God rules over the entire universe and that nothing in creation is more powerful than he, and nothing is to be worshipped instead of God or in addition to him.

If we were to deny creation out of nothing, we would have to say that some matter has always existed and that it is eternal like God.

The idea if true would challenge the independence of God, and also his sovereignty, and the fact that worship is due to him alone. If matter existed apart from God, then what inherent right would God have to rule over it and use it for his glory?

What confidence could we have that every aspect of the universe will ultimately fulfil God's purposes, if some parts of it were not created by him or under his control?

The positive side of the fact that God created the universe out of nothing is that it has meaning and purpose. God made everything for a purpose; therefore, everything has a purpose. God in his wisdom created it for something.

The practical application of this is that we should try to understand that purpose (these things contributed to the origins of modern science). We should use creation also in ways that befit God's purpose, namely, to bring glory to God himself. Moreover, whenever the creation brings us joy, we should give thanks to the God who made it all.

> 1 Timothy 6:17: "*Charge them that are rich in this world, that they be not high-minded, nor trust in uncertain riches, but in the living God, who giveth us richly all things to enjoy.*"

The Biblical doctrine of creation contradicts the man-made doctrine of materialism

Materialism tells us that the universe is eternal and self-existent. The materialist has to say the universe exists, because it exists. Materialism has no place for God. God is pronounced by the materialist to be a creature of the human imagination, the product of the human mind at a particular stage of its development. In its most elaborate modern form, materialism proposes the substitution of two self-existent factors in place of the God of heaven. In place of God, it substitutes two blind, all powerful agencies—matter and force. It pronounces the origin of the universe to be the result of innumerable combinations of self-existent force with self-existent matter; and it maintains that while the quantity of this eternally existing force is invariable, force can transform itself into light, heat, electricity and magnetism; it is, by turns, weight, affinity, cohesion, mechanism. It is inherent in matter; it is light and heat in the sun and in the fixed stars; it is mechanical impulse in planets which move around a central globe; it is cohesion or magnetism in the ponderable material of the heavenly bodies.

Its action is regulated by self-existent laws. These are sometimes called the laws of nature, and they have been described by some materialist as "barbarous inflexible forces; which know neither justice nor benevolence". The materialist says that beyond nature there is nothing—except in the "diseased" imagination of man.

One German materialist, Feuerbach, is supposed to have said:

> No hand holds the earth in its course; no prayer can arrest the sun or lull the fury of the storm; no voice can raise the dead from their eternal sleep; no angel can deliver the captive; no hand stretched forth from the clouds can feed the hungry; no sign from heaven can tell us that we know anything beyond Nature. Beyond Nature, there is nothing; and Nature, [cries Feuerbach with all the ferocious exultation of despair,]

> Nature has no answer that she can make to the griefs or the prayers of man; she drives him back inexorably upon himself.
>
> Derived from Liddon, 1904, p. 4

We could also add the statement of a modern materialistic atheist, Bertrand Russell who stated the case as follows and in this matter, we can agree with him.

> We could question whether the materialistic outlook of the universe is even rational. The Greeks of antiquity were a very rational people and they looked out upon the universe and gave it a name; that name was the Cosmos. They meant by the word that upon the face of the universe there is stamped beyond any question whatsoever, the imprint of a harmonious beauty. None could look upon it or study it without discovering its order and breath-taking magnificence.

Materialism believes force moulds matter in obedience to laws. But law implies a legislator, and the question is, who has created the laws? Atheistic materialism replies, chance; out of millions upon millions of chances that might have been otherwise, one chance has carried the day: and the result has been in the reign of order, the order of all nature. Out of mere chance all worlds exist.

The philosophic theory of materialism holds that the only thing that exists is matter. This philosophy would then reject any existence of God, control by God or sustaining of life by God. Much like the theory of evolution, materialism promotes that there is not even a thought of God's existing, and as such leaves a very dangerous proposition. If there is no God, then there is no moral standard by which to live. In other words, if there is no God, then there is no influence that guides man toward not committing murder, stealing, telling lies, or committing adultery, etc. If there is no God, then who is to say that anything is wrong or immoral? The only standard or code by which mankind could live would be his own code, determining for himself what is right or wrong for himself. Without any sense of good and evil, without any standard of right and wrong, all man is left with is a philosophy of cold materialism.

The doctrine of creation gives the lie to Pantheism

While the atheistic materialist says, "There is no God", the pantheist answers "Everything is God". The universe is not made by God according to the pantheist; it is God, God passing into various manifestations of being. Some pantheists say that God is the soul of the universe. They say God manifests himself in all his infinite variety of being in life. Pantheism lays emphasis on, and exaggerates, two great truths—the omnipresence of God, and the interdependence of created life. But pantheism denies that God is independent of the world; it maintains that he has no existence apart from the universe which manifests him as being himself.

The pantheist cannot say that God is a Person; it cannot say that God has consciousness, memory or will. He is only an impersonal quality or force; or he is only an idea, slowly realising itself in being.

Pantheism often uses a religious kind of language. But if pantheism speaks of God, in practical terms it denies him. Pantheism speaks of God as infinite; but then goes on to say that this infinite only exists in that which is finite.

We can remind ourselves that the first element of our belief in God is that God is a Moral Being, and that he is Essential Right, Essential Justice, Essential Sanctity, Essential Purity, Essential Truth, Essential Law. But if we say with the pantheist that God is universal life, and universal life is God, we thereby destroy God's morality. We effectively make God the agent and producer of evil, as well as the agent or producer of good; or else we deny that the distinction between absolute good and absolute evil really exists.

We make God, indeed, the energy which produces deeds of charity, courage, justice, integrity; but we also identify him with the energy which issues in adulteries, fornications, murders, thefts, and all that is untrue, cruel and impure.

Pantheism as a belief system undermines the very basis of morality.

The belief that God is the Creator gives the lie to Dualism

Alongside the doctrines of materialistic atheism and pantheism there is another false philosophy that the doctrine of creation challenges. This is the supposition that the universe and God are both eternal; that an eternal universe has existed side-by-side with an eternal God. This is a sort of half-way house for those who reject the idea of the Creator God with all its implications morally and spiritually; but hesitate to think of a universe without God as utterly meaningless, or even the theory of the universe itself being God as the pantheists believe.

However, this half-way house is somewhat unworkable because it inevitably resolves itself into one of these two. Unless it goes so far as to say that there are two gods, two self-existent, co-eternal beings, it must say that the universe is the reality, and God the imaginary counterpart, or it must say that the universe itself is God.

Another difficulty that arises from this view is that if there exist two equal powers, the universe and God, it is difficult to see how the harmonious and perfectly balanced laws of nature as we call them have come about and can continue.

Putting these three alternative views together we have to agree with one who said.

> Dualism denies God's solitary supremacy.
> Pantheism buries God in moral darkness.
> Atheistic materialism denies him out-right.
>
> Liddon, 1904

The destructive consequences of the denial of the doctrine of Creation

We have already noted some of these consequences.

We may take for instance the modern theory of evolution; we call it modern, but its origins are far more ancient.

It is important to understand the incredibly destructive influences that the development of this theory has had on modern thinking. If in fact life were not created by God, if human beings are merely the product of matter, time and chance, and in particular were not created by God, or responsible to him, and are simply the result of random occurrences in the universe; then of what significance is human life?

If we are merely the product of mindless, ever-existing matter, or chance and time, then it is impossible to think that we have any real or ultimate significance at all. It is no wonder that not a few who have honestly reflected on this teaching have sunk into the profundities of despair.

If again all life can be explained by evolutionary theory, without any reference to God, and if there is no God who has created us, then there is no supreme judge to hold us morally accountable. Neither is there any God of grace to redeem and help us.

This then inevitably leads to the conclusion that there are no moral absolutes in human life at all except subjective preferences, only temporal and changeable contingencies, governed by the mind or will of the majority, or a totalitarian regime. In fact, we get to the situation where the only thing which is forbidden is to say that one knows that certain things are right and certain things are wrong in the absolute sense—a situation we are beginning to experience in everyday life today.

Another frightening consequence of evolution is that if the inevitable process of natural selection continues to bring about improvement in life forms on earth, through the survival of the fittest, then why should we bother with those who are too weak and less able to defend themselves? We can easily reason ourselves into thinking that they are not worthy to be cared for; it is better for the race if the weak and sickly or mentally defective are left to die.

Out of this thinking of course has developed, such scandals as the massive increase in abortions, and the now growing demand for the practice of euthanasia. These certainly were the ideas of the grand atheists, Marx, Nietzsche and Adolf Hitler.

Moreover, if human beings are continually evolving for the better, then it follows that the wisdom of earlier generations (and often the Christian religion is put into this category) is not likely to be as valuable as modern thought. Some of this kind of thinking has undermined people's trust in the reliability of Scripture.

Contemporary sociological and psychological theories look on human beings as simply higher forms of animals. Man is no more than a sophisticated ape. The Bible teaches that we were made in the image and likeness of God and thereby a tremendous dignity and value are attached to a human being. To believe man is just an animal is to denigrate and lower the value of human life.

Some extremes of the modern 'animal rights' movement reflect this sort of belief.

> Lord Balfour in his Gifford lectures (1923), speaking of the three great virtues, all vital to the highest life of mankind, Love, Beauty, and Truth, said that we could not maintain those virtues permanently at the highest level, if we banished from the world the idea of design, of creation, of God who is himself the author and sustainer of these high virtues.
>
> Irwin, 1928, p. 10

We now turn our attention to what the opening verses of Genesis teach us of the sovereignty of God. "In the beginning God" demonstrates his sovereignty and primacy over all things. Nothing can stand beside him or thwart his purposes.

> The recognition of an ultimate unity in the created universe is an astonishing assertion. … The first chapter of Genesis not only assumes the One God, who stands outside nature, but, with masterly certainty, ignores and thus effectively destroys entire mythological systems. … The sun and moon, worshipped in many ways in other cultures, are reduced to light bulbs, convenient markers set in the sky to show the passage of the day and the changing seasons. The terrible sea monsters of legend are his creation and under his sway as they move in the vast ocean. The great struggle between the gods of the cosmic waters of ancient Near Eastern mythology simply disappear without trace. And to crown it all, with an almost nonchalant gesture, the whole of natural time, the solar and lunar cycles, are subordinated to the regular pattern of six days of labour and one for rest. God's time and God's sovereignty are stamped upon the world.
>
> Adapted from Magonet, 1997, p. 8

A. W. Pink in his classic *The Sovereignty of God* made this observation:

> The doctrine of God's sovereignty is no mere metaphysical dogma which is devoid of practical value but is one that is calculated to produce a powerful effect upon Christian character and the daily walk. The doctrine of God's sovereignty lies at the foundation of Christian theology, and in importance is perhaps second only to the Divine Inspiration of the Scriptures. It is the centre of gravity in the system of Christian truth; the sun around which all the lesser orbs are grouped; the cord upon which all other doctrines are strung like so many pearls, holding them in place and giving them unity. It is the plumb line by which every creed needs to be tested; the balance in which every human dogma must be weighed. It is designed as the sheet anchor for our souls amidst the storms of life. The doctrine of God's sovereignty is a Divine cordial to refresh our spirits. It is designed and adapted to mould the affections of the heart, and to give a right direction to conduct. It produces gratitude in prosperity and patience in adversity. It affords comfort for the present and a sense of security respecting the unknown future. It is, and it does, all and much more than we have just said, because it ascribes to God—

> the Father, the Son, and the Holy Spirit—the glory which is His due, and places the creature in his proper place before him—in the dust.
>
> Pink, 1993, pp. 138–152

Pink also expounds upon these practical headings derived from this doctrine. We only have space here to give the actual headings.

1. It deepens our veneration of the divine character.
2. It is a solid foundation of all true religion.
3. It repudiates the heresy of salvation by works.
4. It is deeply humbling to the creature.
5. It affords a sense of absolute security.
6. It supplies comfort in sorrow.
7. It begets a spirit of sweet resignation.
8. It evokes a song of praise.
9. It guarantees the final triumph of good over evil.
10. It provides a resting place for the heart.

Pink, 1993, pp. 29–30

This same fact of God's sovereignty and priority is reiterated in the First Commandment.

> Exodus 20:3: "*Thou shalt have no other gods before me.*"

This command is a warning and a threat, but it is also a principle which the God who condescends to reason with us sets before us. Can we not see that if we worship a lie then the result will be our own ruin? To love and serve any master, any course, as though it were a god is to make a false god of it—for even if it is a good thing in its place, it then becomes a lie and a destroyer. If we make a god of our country, our race, our ideology, our self, our pleasure, our family, or any other creature, we change the truth of God into a lie, and worship and serve the creature more than the Creator, who is blessed for ever, as Paul states in:

> Romans 1:25: "*Who changed the truth of God into a lie, and worshipped and served the creature more than the Creator, who is blessed for ever. Amen.*"

The penalty of this transgression is as Paul puts it in the following verse:

> Romans 1:26a: "*For this cause, God gave them up unto vile affections.*"

These affections are vile, each and every one of them, if made the object of our supreme devotion or worship. There is immense moral power in this principle and truth. Elton Trueblood gave the following illustration of this. He said:

> We must never forget that Hitler was able to crush the moralists, but he was not able to crush thousands of men who thought the First Commandment was really first. Since this is a clearly established fact of history, we may find light by looking into it. Pastor Martin Niemöller was one of those uncrushable German Christians who put the First Commandment first. Hitler summoned him to explain why he was surreptitiously preaching a higher law than Hitler, and the pastor replied, "Not you, Herr Hitler, but God is my Führer".
>
> If you want to know what it is in practice to put the First Commandment first, there it is. It happens that Pastor Niemöller is an ardent compatriot. He loves Germany. He loves God also. There is no contradiction as he sees it. He can love and serve Germany to his heart's content as long as this falls naturally into the proper course of his loving and serving the one true God. But the order may not be reversed: no loyalty that conflicts with one's loyalty to God can ever be legitimate. In practice, in life, the living of this commandment always consists of simple, unswerving, uncompromising adherence to this rule. We see the issue most easily in terms of our various loyalties. On one side is our loyalty to God; on the other side—and not necessarily opposed to our first loyalty—are our loyalties to family, to friends, to self, to country, to society, to our special groups in circles. All these other loyalties can be properly and faithfully served in God, so long as God's claims upon us are always given absolute priority. So long as we do not stop even to ask what share of ourselves we shall give to God and what we shall give to this or that other object of our loyalty—so long as we steadfastly give all of ourselves to God, we are in no danger of transgression. This done, our other concerns and responsibilities have a strange way of taking care of themselves. This is the Lord's doing.
>
> By refusing to give the Third Reich any share of his ultimate in life-determining loyalty-which is due to God alone, Martin Niemöller served his country as a Nazi never could.
>
> Trueblood, 1948, p. 2

In the nineteenth century, Thomas Huxley, known in those days as Darwin's Bulldog, attacked the doctrine of God's sovereignty and God's providence. He said that, unless mankind is released from such notions, it is doomed to stagnation. He argued that such beliefs cause men to sit back and do nothing, deluding themselves that in some way or another the Lord would provide. This of course is a caricature of the truth of God's sovereignty and providence. We may let the great Calvin Memorial in Geneva bear witness to the fact that faith in God's sovereignty and wise providence was the belief which produced all the free governments of the modern world. Right and left of the Reformer of Geneva (John Calvin) are William the Silent of Holland, Coligny of France, John Knox of Scotland, a Pilgrim Father of New England, and Oliver Cromwell—Calvinists all. When we think of such men, we do not think of high pietistic acquiescence, or of their faith as "an opiate of the people", we think of firm endurance on the very edge of despair against overwhelming odds, and of volcanic activity for the City of God. One said:

> So far is Calvinism from producing slackness of will and feebleness of character, Calvinists have been the most strenuous of men. The true Calvinist feels himself to be an instrument of the Divine Will and bends to whatever task he undertakes in the unshakeable conviction that he is on the side of God. What a spring of moral energy lies in this thought I need not tell you. … Calvinism was the form of faith in the strength of which the Dutch Republic was sustained and the American Republic founded, to propagate which Tyndale gave the English people the Bible in their own tongue and with it his life; which formed the royal intellect of Cromwell and inspired the majestic verse of Milton. Shall I say more or is this enough?
>
> The sixteenth and seventeenth centuries were the age of the absolute monarchies, Francis I in France, Charles V and Philip II in Spain; and, in a new phase of the struggle, of the Stuart tyranny in Britain. Everywhere these absolute monarchs set themselves to destroy the Reform and the Puritanism that followed it. Everywhere Calvinism said to these absolute monarchs: "You are all usurpers; only One is absolute, and in his name we defy you all!"
>
> Without that faith the battle would have been too hard. There would be no hope, and hopelessness means paralysis or else individualistic stoicism or devout quietism. The Ultimate and Absolute Power was on their side, and though they might fall the battle must go on to victory. Their business was to advance this

> battlefront and win ground for those behind them, and leave the issue to their Commander. The spirit which thus flamed up in them was one of most-stubborn and formidable activity which wrought itself out not only in the overthrow of the absolute monarchs, but in the creation of the free modern states in the old world, and the pioneering of new lands where the Kingdom of God might be realised.
>
> Cairns, 1937, pp. 169–171

The opening chapters the Bible give us a unique concept of the nature of man; that is:

Man made in the image and likeness of God

This second premise is, in many ways, no less wondrous than the first, namely that God is intimately related to one particular part of his creation—human beings. God speaks of the creation of man and his formation:

> Genesis 1:26a: "*And God said, Let us make man in our image, after our likeness.*"

There is the obvious allusion to the doctrine of the Trinity in this pregnant statement, but we continue with the thought of God making man in his own image and likeness. Some have detected here, as it were, a momentary pause before this statement is made, as if we are to reflect not only on the tremendous versatility of the creating power of God, but also on his unspeakable goodness and generosity towards mankind, a God who from the very beginning knows all the consequences and cost of such an action. We record here a truth which for ever stamps a dignity and value upon every individual soul.

The statement that God created man in his own image is repeated more than once here at the beginning of Genesis.

1. One thing that it means is that men and women possess the attributes of *personality*, as God himself does. Neither animals nor plants nor matter possess such a distinctive and precious gift. To have personality, one must also possess knowledge, feelings (note this includes religious feelings), and a will. All this is part of being made in the image and likeness of God. We can say that animals possess a certain kind of personality, but an animal cannot reason as man can reason; it only reacts to certain problems and stimuli. Animals do not

really create; they only conform to certain behavioural patterns, though some of these behavioural patterns might include the constructing of a nest, hive or den. Animals do not love as human's love; they merely reproduce. Animals do not worship in the commonly accepted meaning of that term, though at the same time we can say that there is a sense in which the whole creation brings praise to God.

2. A second element that is involved in man being created in the image and likeness of God is *morality*. This of course includes the two further elements of freedom and responsibility. We say that man's freedom is not absolute. Even in the beginning, the first man, Adam, and the first woman, Eve, were not autonomous.

> They were creatures and were responsible for acknowledging this by their obedience in the matter of the tree of the knowledge of good and evil. Since the Fall, that freedom has been further restricted so that, as Augustine said, the original *posse non peccare* (able not to sin), has become a *non-posse non peccare* (not able not to sin), still there is limited freedom for men and women even in their fallen state and with that there is also moral responsibility.
>
> Boice, 2006, p. 78

3. A third element involved in man's being made in God's image is *spirituality*. This means that man was made for spiritual communion with God.

> John 4:24: "*God* [*is*] *a Spirit: and they that worship him must worship* [*him*] *in spirit and in truth*."

Here we remember Augustine's words again, "Thou hast made us for thyself, and our hearts are restless until they find their rest in thee".

Although it is true that man shares a body with such forms of life as animals and fish etc., he alone possesses a spirit or soul. It is on the level of the spirit that he is aware of God and communes with God.

> Here lies our true worth. We are made in God's image and therefore valuable to God and others. God loves men and women; he does not and cannot love the animals, plants or inanimate matter in the same way. Moreover, he feels for them, identifies with them in Christ, grieves for them, and even intervenes in history to make individual men and women into all that he has determined they should be. We get some idea of the special nature of this relationship when we remember that, in a similar way, the woman, Eve, was made in the

> image of man. Therefore, though different, Adam saw himself in her and loved her as his companion and corresponding member in the universe. It is not wrong to say that men and women are to God somewhat as the woman is to the man. They are God's unique and valued companions. In support of this we need only think of the Bible's teaching concerning Christ as the Bridegroom and the Church as his bride.
>
> Boice, 2006, p. 78

These opening chapters, however, show us that man, by disobedience, has become a fallen creature: that although he is made in the image of God, this image has been greatly marred by sin. There are vestiges of the image remaining, but man today is not what God primarily intended. He is a fallen creature, and the effects of the Fall are seen on every level of his being: in his body and his soul or spirit.

> Man's soul is the seat of his intellect, feelings, and identity, and from the point of the Fall begins to die. So people begin to lose a sense of who they are, and give vent to bad feelings and suffer the decay of their intellect. This is the type of decay described by Paul in Romans 1 where we are told that, having rejected God, men inevitably "become futile in their thinking and their foolish hearts were darkened". Although they claimed to be wise, they became fools and exchanged the glory of the immortal God for images made to look like the mortal man and birds and animals and reptiles. Eventually even the body dies. So it is said of us, "Dust thou art, and unto dust thou shalt return". (Genesis 3:19)
>
> Boice, 2006, p. 79

The opening chapters of Genesis speak to us of the concept of the Sabbath rest

We can only here touch on this extensive and vastly important subject. We might ask, what does it mean that God rested on the seventh day?

> Genesis 2:1–3: "*Thus the heavens and the earth were finished, and all the host of them. And on the seventh day God ended his work which he had made; and he rested on the seventh day from all his work which he had made. And God blessed the seventh day and sanctified it: because that in it he had rested from all his work which God created and made.*"

It does not mean that God closed his eyes and went to sleep. It does not mean that God rested in the sense that he was weary or that he became indifferent to what men and women were doing. We know God was not indifferent because, when Adam and Eve sinned there in the garden, he immediately called them to account. He pronounced judgement and held out the promise of a Redeemer to come. Rest is not to be understood in either of these ways.

What it does mean is what Augustine had in mind when he contrasted the rest of God with our restlessness. We have already quoted Augustine's famous line; "Thou hast made us for thyself, and our hearts are restless until they find their rest in thee". Augustine was thinking of the turmoil of the human soul. He was saying that our true destiny is to find the rest that is found only in God. When Genesis reminds us that God rested on the seventh day, amongst the many truths involved in this event one of the most important is to say that the ultimate destiny of man is to find his rest in God. Without God, man is a hopeless and restless wanderer upon the earth. There is no ultimate rest in all the creation, seek it though we will, we will never find it unless we find our rest in God. These words anticipate the promise and gracious words of our Saviour

> Matthew 11:28: "*Come unto me, all [ye] that labour and are heavy laden, and I will give thee rest.*"

The opening chapters of Genesis teach us of the blessed hope enshrined for us in the first Gospel promise—Genesis 3:15

The wonderful foundations of truth and light, revealed to us in these opening pages of the Bible, would be incomplete if we did not find therein an anticipation of God's abounding grace, and the first dawning of that bright and blessed hope in which the Scriptures abound.

> Genesis 3:15: "*And I will put enmity between thee and the woman, and between thy seed and her seed; it shall bruise thy head, and thou shalt bruise his heel.*"

Matthew Henry points out three things concerning Christ in this verse.

- One is his incarnation, that he should be the seed of the woman, that is Eve, the wife of Adam. We see this traced out in the first chapter of Luke's Gospel.
- Secondly his sufferings and death are pointed to in the reference

here to Satan's bruising Christ's heel, that is, in his human nature. The serpent wounds the heel that crushes him; and so Satan would be permitted to afflict the human nature of Christ, and to bring suffering and persecution to his people, but he cannot ultimately triumph; he can by no means in the end succeed, because Christ by his death will conquer death and destroy all Satan's power (Hebrews 2:14).

- Thirdly by the references to destroying Satan's head, is meant the real seat of his power. The reference to the head means that Christ by his coming and by his atoning death shall destroy all Satan's policies and all his powers and bring about a total overthrow of his kingdom and influence.

How sweet the name of Jesus sounds;
In a believer's ear!
It soothes his sorrows, heals his wounds,
And drives away his fear. John Newton (1725–1807)

Summary

The Old Testament lays down the fundamental framework, principles and foundations for the most noble and enriching view of life and of reality that is possible. It prepares for the giving of the fullness of this revelation in the coming of Christ in the New Testament, but even as it stands, it is a book of priceless worth.

One nineteenth-century scholar said of it:

> If you want to prove the truth, the wisdom, the sober and honest history of the Bible (the Old Testament) and the purity of its religion, place it among the sacred books of the East. In these books, there are many grains of gold, but they are hidden in mountains of the most extraordinary rubbish; and the extraordinary thing is that it is the rubbish that calls forth the enthusiasm and admiration of the people that own them. The sobriety of the Bible, the purity of its spirit, the elevation and devotion of its tone make it occupy an entirely unique place. Placed among the sacred books of the East, the contrast would make its truth only the more stand out.
>
> Fairbairn, 1894, p. 102

We can say the Book is the noblest heirloom of humanity. It is true that there are individuals who criticise the Old Testament because they find in it what they call, things that sound not too refined for our modern ears. There are, they say persons in it guilty of acts that, measured by modern standards, cannot be called good, but must be pronounced evil. There are statements in it that seem to conflict with our modern tastes. Such people will tell us, in all seriousness, that these difficulties are fatal to our taking this book seriously. It is true that some of the actions of Jacob or the sins of David are to be condemned. But to condemn the sins of these and other individuals is not to condemn the Bible, for the Old Testament does not record these things for our approval, but for our disapproval, or for our own personal instruction to avoid such things. We must not forget that the Old Testament was given to a fallen and stubborn race; its purpose was to prepare them, and to lift them, and to speak through them, in such a way that would prepare for the revelation they were receiving to be received by the wider world of fallen men. It is a revelation recording God's lifting men by degrees, so that they may recognise and appreciate him who is the Light of the world in the day of his coming.

We may also think of what the Old Testament has been to the most devout and pious men and women of subsequent ages; that is to the most moral, the most humane, the gentlest, and the most obedient to God of mankind. Has it not been the inspiration that made them such, has it not been the power that lifted them from the lowest levels of sensuous and selfish lives to the highest and noblest heights of spiritual light and principle? Ought not this simple fact alone make our objectors pause and ask whether it is the Bible or their theory of the Bible that is at fault?

What we have seen in this glance at the Old Testament is that the religion of Israel depicted there was an altogether unique order of religion and this was by virtue of its conception or thought of God and his holy law. By the means of these things, it laid the basis for a noble understanding of the nature of God, and a true understanding of man, his origin, purpose, destiny, state by sin, and what he can be by God's redemptive grace in Christ. It has laid down the basis for an inspired view of what society may be and what ought to characterise man's relationship with his fellow man.

> So long as men believe in a multitude of gods, they will never believe in the unity of man; so long as they believe in a deity without moral character, they will never live under what they feel to be a common moral law. Might will be right. Their world will be the strong man's

world, where the weakest goes to the wall, and the poor, unpitied, live or die to please the rich.

No code of antiquity possessed, in anything like the same degree, so exalted a notion of man, of the rights of man, of the dignity of man's labour, of his duties, of his moral worth and relations, of his claim to reap and to possess the harvest of the profit, or plenty, his own hands had sowed. It was not the priest's, or the king's law, it was God's. In that lay the secret of its power, the source of the great dignity it gave to man. Make the law the king's or the priest's, make king or priest own the people, and you have as an inevitable result despotism, oppression, wrong, sacrifice of the weak to the strong. Make the law and the people God's, and you have as an inevitable result the equality of all men before God, and, once that is clearly and fully understood, the equal freedom and the equal rights of all men. The law which came through Moses was, to the people as a whole, the most generous, the most righteous law of antiquity, reposing as it did on the most humane of all the ancient conceptions of God.

Fairbairn, 1894, pp. 137–138

Chapter 3
The Christian World-view: The New Testament Foundation

When we come to look at the New Testament, we may say that what in the Old Testament was principally directed towards and for the benefit of Israel, God's particular, preparatory people, is now intended for the whole world. We may also say that what was provisional or preparatory in the Old now exists as that which is general and permanent in the New.

We can go on and say, that which was shadowy and typical in the Old is now clearly fulfilled in the New. That which was partial in the Old is now complete in the New. In Christ, we have the fullness of God's revelation to mankind in regard to his purposes and our life in this world.

It is impossible to estimate the value and impact of the New Testament upon the life of the world.

Men of literature have waxed eloquent upon its style, for example Arthur Quiller Couch pronounced it "the most majestic thing in our literature"; and McNeil Dixon, "the chief ornament of our language". Robert Bridges pronounced the parable of the Prodigal Son "a perfectly flawless piece of work". The same writer said to praise Paul's "Song of Songs" in 1 Corinthians 13 is to "varnish sunlight". Charles Dickens said, "The New Testament is the very best book there ever was or ever will be known in this world".

When E. V. Rieu completed his translation of the Gospels in 1952 he commented:

> The Gospels bear the seal of the Son of Man and God; they are the Magna Carta of the human spirit. Were we to devote to their comprehension a little of the selfless enthusiasm that is now expended on the riddle of our physical surroundings, we should cease to say that Christianity is coming to an end—we might even feel that it had only just begun.
>
> Rieu, 1952

But not only has the New Testament been admired for its literary excellence, others have admired it and given it high praise for its moral content and teaching. Some have described it as the matchless guidebook to the good life, or God's way of making bad men good. Others have described it as the world's supreme textbook on ethics, and that it ought to be studied and taken heed of by all who are interested in the problem of right living.

However, the outstanding glory of the New Testament does not lie in its literary or ethical glories, significant as these are, but it lies in the fact that it is the supreme and unique self-revelation of God to fallen and lost mankind. It is the book that gives the key to the inner meaning of all history. It is the record of the inconceivable condescension of God towards undeserving men, taking flesh and dwelling amongst us in the Person of Jesus Christ his only begotten Son. It is the record of the redeeming love of God through the sacrifice and blood of Christ. It is God drawing near to man for our sake and salvation. "It is the Word of life, the Word that tells of peace, of comfort in the strife, and joys that never cease" coming and dwelling amongst us.

We might say without fear of contradiction that Western civilisation was centred and founded on the firm conviction that Jesus Christ is the true centre of human life and existence. Western civilisation escaped from the dark world of multiple idols, all made in the image of man, to the light of the supreme revelation of monotheism. Further, Western civilisation was built on the fact that Jesus Christ is the complete and only answer to the dilemmas posed by questions such as: What is true and what is false? What is the meaning of the movements of history? What is the answer to man's troubled moral conscience? How can men and women find peace with God?

In relation to the last of these questions, we can emphasise the fact that Western civilisation was built on Jesus Christ's being:

> John 1:29b: "*the Lamb of God, which taketh away the sin of the world.*"

Jesus Christ stands alone as the Redeemer of mankind, the only Saviour of the lost. Christianity is uniquely the religion of redemption. It is the culmination of all that the Old Testament sacrifices and offerings pointed to. Through the sacrifice of Christ, God wills that man's estrangement from himself will be changed into a state of reconciliation with himself. This, Christ achieved when he took upon himself his people's sins, their consequences, and their condemnation on the cross, where he suffered, the just for the unjust, to reconcile us to God.

> 1 Corinthians 1:18: "*For the preaching of the cross is to them that perish foolishness; but unto us which are saved it is the power of God.*"

It was this message that Paul preached in the city of Corinth, that cesspit of vice and corruption, the very epitome of the collapsing culture of the ancient world. It would seem that such a message would be lost on a people who had given way to every form of self-indulgence and depravity. But, as we shall see in the rest of this study, the preaching of Christ and the cross, together with the testimony of his glorious resurrection and ascension, saved the world from what it would inevitably have done at that point, that is, destroy itself. It went on to lay the foundation of a new age, a Christian civilisation, that which is to be the chief theme and purpose of this study and which we will shortly begin to unfold.

Chapter 4
The Christian World View: Its Principal Doctrines

TURNING FROM SOME OF THE ESSENTIAL CHARACTERISTICS OF THE Old and New Testaments we now, before entering into our main theme, look briefly at some of the central doctrines and ethical teachings of the Christian faith.

Christianity sets before us thoughts and teachings on such subjects as God, man, sin and salvation. In regard to Christian teaching on the nature of God, we find that his attributes are high and exalted; we speak of his eternity, his immutability, his omnipresence, the completeness of his knowledge, his unsurpassed wisdom, his power, his holiness, his goodness, patience, etc. We see that the Christian view of God is far removed from that of Polytheism, Dualism and Pantheism. He is the Author of all things, the Creator as well as the Ruler of the world; his actions are not fettered or hindered by conditions which are independent of him. In the Christian conception of the moral character of God, justice is not sacrificed to love, nor love deprived of all moral significance by being divorced from righteousness. The God of Christianity is not a capricious deity. The God of Christian teaching is the God who so loved the world that he gave his only begotten Son for its sake and for its redemption.

James Orr comments on the Christian view of God as follows:

> God in the Christian view is a Being who enters into the history of the world in the most loving way. He is not only actively present in the material universe ordering, guiding, controlling it,—but he enters also in the most direct way into the course of human history, working in it in his general and special providence, and by gradual and progressive revelation, which is, at the same time, practical discipline and education, giving to man knowledge of himself by which he is enabled to attain the highest ends of his own existence, and to cooperate freely in the carrying out of Divine ends; above all, discovering himself as the God of redemption, who, full of long-suffering and mercy, executes in loving deeds, and at infinite sacrifice, his gracious purpose for the salvation of mankind. The Christian

> view of God is thus bound up with all the remaining elements of the Christian system—with the idea of revelation in Christ, with a Kingdom of God to be realised through Christ, with redemption from sin in Christ,—and it is inseparable from them. It is through these elements—not in its abstract character as Theism—that it takes the hold that it does on the living convictions of men, and is felt by them to be something real.
>
> Orr, 1908, p. 78

To this we may add the unsurpassed description of God in Article 2 of the Westminster Confession of Faith:

> I. There is but one only living and true God, who is infinite in being and perfection, most pure spirit, invisible, without body, parts, or passions, immutable, immense, eternal, incomprehensible, almighty, most wise, most holy, most free, most absolute, working all things according to the counsel of his own immutable and most righteous will, for his own glory; most loving, gracious, merciful, long-suffering, abundant in goodness and truth, forgiving iniquity, transgression and sin; the rewarder of them that diligently seek him; and withal most just and terrible in his judgements; hating all sin, and who will by no means clear the guilty.
>
> II. God hath all life, glory, goodness, blessedness, in and of himself; and is alone in and unto himself all sufficient, not standing in need of any creatures which he hath made, not deriving any glory from them, but only manifesting his own glory, in, by, unto, and upon them: he is the alone Fountain of all being, of whom, through whom, and to whom, are all things; and has most sovereign dominion over them, to do by them, for them, or upon them, whatsoever himself please. In his sight all things are open and manifest; his knowledge is infinite, infallible, and independent upon the creature, so as nothing is to him contingent or uncertain. He is most holy in all his counsels, in all his works, and in all his commands. To him is due from angels and men, and every other creature, whatsoever worship, service, or obedience, he is pleased to require of them.
>
> III. In the unity of the Godhead there be three persons, of one substance, power, and eternity; God the Father, God the Son, and God the Holy Ghost. The Father is of none, neither begotten nor

> proceeding; the Son is eternally begotten of the Father; the Holy Ghost eternally proceeding from the Father and the Son.
>
> Westminster Divines, 1646, pp. 24–27

It is impossible not to consider the Christian view of God and see it as standing head and shoulders above all other non-Christian conceptions of God in its elevation, purity and nobility.

The following summary has been given of the fundamental doctrines of Christianity as barriers against false and despairing philosophies of life.

> Faith in God's creation of the world is a barrier against pessimistic nihilism and rude naturalism.
>
> Faith in the Incarnation is a barrier against modern relativism and the mood of spectatorship.
>
> Faith in the resurrection of Christ is a challenge to the sceptical mentality of indifference and carelessness.
>
> Faith in the ultimate Judgement is a basis of creative earnestness and moral vigour—a continuous protest against any kind of monism obscuring and obliterating the definite line between good and evil, truth and falsehood, right and wrong, holiness and wickedness.
>
> Faith in Christ, the supreme Lord, is a barrier against any kind of totalitarianism.
>
> Smith, 1981, p. 271

We may also briefly consider Christianity's view of mankind

We can say that it neither unduly disparages nor unduly exalts human nature. It teaches us that man is made in the image and likeness of God and therefore of infinite value, and capable of knowing and entering into a relationship with God, and being responsible to him, man having a sense of right and wrong conscience and a will. The Christian doctrine of man gives due weight to all the elements of man's complicated being. Its doctrine of sin traces the evil to its root in a self-centred will alien from truth and God. In its teaching as to salvation, it explains why man cannot save himself, why all the systems of philosophy and religion outside of Christianity, and all the great thinkers of all time failed utterly to remedy man's predicament or answer the deepest longings of his soul for pardon, meaning and purpose. It shows how Jesus Christ, the only begotten of God, is come into the world to save his people from their sins, to heal the brokenhearted and to set free those bound in spiritual darkness. God and man should no longer be apart—and that the divine should enter into humanity, seeking his wandering and disobedient children, and willingly to buy them back to himself by the greatest of sacrifices. Besides all this it brings to redeemed men and women, through the merits of Christ, not only to be forgiven of their sins, but to be set free from their power and influence over them. It is come also to purify, elevate and stimulate man's thought and intellectual life, to a degree no other philosophy or religion has achieved.

By comparing Christianity in certain of its aspects with the moral teaching of other religions and philosophies, we are able to see how far it goes beyond these in purity and power. We will see that not only do the truths and principles of Christianity commend themselves to our minds and hearts by their elevation, purity, and universal applicability, but that this religion has achieved such a work in the world, has exerted such an influence upon mankind and upon history, as shows it to be no beautiful theory, no dream, but a practical power, proved to be so by unchallengeable testimony, and the witness of experience.

Chapter 5
The Witness of History to the Benefits of Christianity

(1) *Its power to overcome evil*

In 1870, Dean Farrar preached five sermons before the University of Cambridge, these sermons constituted the Hulsean Lectures for that year. These lectures were later published under the title, *The Witness of History to Christ*. Farrar begins his third lecture with the following texts, the first taken from Acts 5:39, the words of Gamaliel, "But if it be of God, you cannot overthrow it". The second was taken from Matthew's Gospel 15:13, the words of our Lord Jesus Christ, "Every plant, which my Heavenly Father hath not planted, shall be rooted up". The third was taken from 1 Corinthians 1:25, the words of St. Paul, "The foolishness of God is wiser than men, and the weakness of God is stronger than men".

All these texts argue that the virtue and value of Christianity are to be proved and seen by its effects in and upon history and time. If its doctrines after all are discovered to be fictitious and erroneous, it is certain that time will reveal them to be so, and their pernicious and detrimental influences will be felt and ultimately be seen to bring about its decline.

If, on the other hand, these things are of God, we will see clearly that their course will be victorious and beneficial. It is true, and we will need to bear this in mind, that though the progress of Christianity has rightly been compared to the sun rising with healing in its wings, we will nevertheless concede that just as the sun is sometimes obscured by clouds and storms, and its rays hidden by temporary darkness, so from time to time there will be dark periods in the unfolding history of the Church of Jesus Christ. Nevertheless, the history of the Church is such that we soon learn that its light is never for long quenched and it soon breaks forth again in the fullness of its strength.

We may note how apparently weak Christianity appeared to the pagan world in which it first began

When the last memorable words of the cross were uttered, "It is finished" (this comprised of but one word in the original, "*tetelestai*",

John 19:30)—and even when the apostles had seen the risen Christ—nothing could have appeared to show or give indication of the far-reaching power and unspeakable benefits Christianity was to manifest in the world through the ages. As Farrar put it, it numbered only a handful of timid followers, of whom the boldest had denied their Lord, and the most devoted had forsaken him and fled. They were poor, many were not well educated, and they were as a group of people seemingly helpless in a hostile world. They owned no synagogue or public meeting place. When they spoke their own language, Aramaic, they were regarded as speaking a mongrel dialect, and if they attempted to speak the current Greek it was despised as a miserable patter.

Their two central doctrines were the crucifixion and the resurrection; the one inspired indignant horror, the other unbounded scorn. Massive were the forces arrayed against them; the current Judaism in which they had been brought up held their fellow countrymen in its vice-like grip, and was set fast to crush them. No less hostile was the Gentile world of the Roman Empire, which from the first burst of hatred in the Neronian persecution and the persecutions which lasted until the end of the third century, ruthlessly attempted to suppress these people who

> turned away with aversion from pagan temples and statues and who refused to witness the games of the amphitheatre, who would die rather than fling into the altar-flame a pinch of incense to the genius of the Emperors; who would decline even to wear a garland of flowers at the banquet, or pour a libation at the sacrifice; whose austere morality was a terrible reflection on the favourite sins which had eaten like a spreading cancer into the very heart of the nation's life.
>
> Farrar, 1875, p. 99

The first wave of persecution by the Roman state authorities seems to have come about in the summer of AD 64 under the Emperor Nero. Nero began to inflict horrendous tortures upon the Christians in Rome. Among the first of his inhuman and barbarous outrages committed against Christian people was that he took to lighting his garden at night by setting fire to a few fully conscious believers who had been covered with wax and then impaled high upon poles forced up their rectums. Nero went on to kill Christians by wild animals in the arena, and also crucified a number of them. According to the Roman historian Tacitus, he committed these atrocities to escape blame for the great fire that destroyed parts of the city of Rome: "Nero fastened the guilt and inflicted the most exquisite tortures on a class hated for their abominations, called Christians by the populace". It is said that among the victims may well have been the apostle Peter and his wife, as well as the apostle Paul.

Nero's persecution of Christians lasted for several years and most likely extended to other parts of the Empire. It is estimated that at this time, he may have put nearly 1,000 believers to death. This however was but the first episode in a long series of intermittent attacks upon Christians taking place between AD 64 and AD 250.

Well might the early Christians have shuddered under such a confederacy of hatred and malice. The truth of the matter was however that they stood firm. It was no earthly calling that commissioned them for their work, neither was it earthly strength that enabled them to stand. These people had been baptised with the Holy Ghost and with fire; each faltering heart had been equipped with God-inspired courage; each lowly furrowed brow had been mitred with Pentecostal flame.

The remarkable fact and reality is, however, that though many powerful forces opposed them, and few helped them, Christianity triumphed.

> The philosopher who met a Christian bishop on his way to the Council of Nicaea, stammered into a confession of belief, and the last of the pagan Emperors died prematurely in the wreck of his broken powers, with the despairing words, Vicisti, Galilæe, Vicisti! (Thou hast conquered, O Galilean, thou hast conquered.)
>
> Farrar, 1875, p. 101

Christianity spent her first three centuries in a long, state-sponsored, almost unbroken persecution. Godly bishops, such as Ignatius, Polycarp, and Hippolytus; some of her greatest writers and preachers, Justin, Athanasius, Origen, likewise perished, as did countless others such as the poor female slaves, Blandina, Felicitas and Potamiaena, undaunted by the rack or the prison or threats of sword or flame, "yet they stood safe" as Cyprian put it, "stronger than their conquerors; the beaten and lacerated members conquered the beating and lacerating hooks". "The nearer I am to the sword", said Ignatius, "the nearer I am to God". "We were condemned to the wild beasts", wrote the youthful Perpetua, "and with hearts full of joy returned to our prison".

We might speak next on the fate of Perpetua in regard to the utter cruelty of her treatment, and of her amazing steadfastness and courage in the face of such diabolical cruelty. It was in AD 202 when Perpetua, a 22-year-old Carthaginian noble woman, who was a new convert and with a nursing infant, was brought before the authorities. At that time, the Emperor Septimus Severus (ruled AD 192–211) ordered that no new conversions to Christianity or Judaism would be tolerated, under pain of death. Along with four others, Perpetua was taken to the arena and, on her refusal to deny her faith, was scourged, and then set upon by wild animals, and, when in spite of this she still survived, she was put to the sword.

A more horrendous outrage was perpetrated against another brave young woman named Blandina, one of the martyrs of Lyons in France in AD 177. Initially, she was suspended from a stake, and exposed as food for wild beasts. When the beasts ignored her, she was taken down and subsequently subjected to "every torture, again and again". Then, "after the scourging … she was presented to a bull. … Then she too was sacrificed, and even the heathen themselves acknowledged that never in their experience had a woman endured so many terrible sufferings". (Eusebius, *Ecclesiastical History*, quoted by Stark, 1966, p. 140)

What came to be known as the Great Persecution broke out in AD 303 under the Emperor Diocletian (284–305). Such was the extent of the Roman Empire at this time that Diocletian shared his emperorship with three other sub-emperors, that is Maximianus Herculius, Galerius and Constantius, (the father of Constantine the Great), though historians have long blamed the Emperor Diocletian for initiating the great persecution. Some have questioned this, as both Diocletian's wife and daughter, it seems, were Christians. Earlier, Diocletian had allowed Christians to build a large new church directly facing his palace in Nicomedia. The evidence seems to point to the fact that Galerius, as he rose in power, originated the persecution, and Diocletian, because he feared him, succumbed under pressure.

It would seem that Diocletian, like other persecuting emperors, believed that the fate of Rome rested with the gods and that Rome could only be strong if all other religions, particularly the ever-growing, increasingly popular Christianity were put down. An edict was made requiring all adult persons to offer sacrifice to the gods; the Christians refused. So it was that on February 23rd AD 303 the imperial soldiers marched into the church across the road from the palace, looted all valuables from the place, burned all the Scriptures, and demolished the building. It seems at this time that Diocletian suffered a kind of nervous breakdown and power fell almost exclusively into the hands of Galerius. Immediately, an edict was passed forbidding Christian gatherings, ordering the seizure or destruction of all churches, requiring that all Christian Scriptures be burned, barring Christians from public office or appearing in court, and prohibiting anyone from freeing a Christian slave. Though Diocletian did not originate this edict, later he did preside over many trials and tortures of individual Christians. In the case of a member of the Imperial household named Peter, being discovered to be a Christian, Diocletian had him "stripped, raised high, and scourged all over". Then salt and vinegar were poured on his wounds and he was slowly roasted alive. (Stark, 1966, p. 146)

All told, approximately 3,000 leaders and prominent members were executed, and thousands of others were sentenced to slavery or sent to the mines. The number that perished in this persecution throughout the Empire is unknown; figures are not available but some claim that in one month in the province of Egypt no fewer than 17,000 martyrs suffered death. Others do not believe that it was so many; some maintain that in the city of Alexandria, between AD 303 and AD 311, the number of individuals who so perished came to 660.

What is known however is that when the great persecution began at least 10% of the whole population of the Empire had become Christian. At this time, Christians were probably the majority in major cities. It is also known that, in many cities, the edicts against Christians were ignored. It is also fact that in spite of the persecutions the number of Christians continued to increase rapidly.

On his deathbed in AD 311, Galerius revoked all the decrees he had caused to have been issued against the Christians. He acknowledged that the persecutions had been ineffective anyway, but remarkably, he also ordered the Christians to pray for his recovery. The persecutions were over.

Eusebius, in his *The Martyrs of Palestine*, gives an account of some who suffered during the Great Persecution in that region, remarking:

> Those Holy Martyrs of God, who loved our Saviour and Lord Jesus Christ, and God supreme and sovereign of all, more than themselves and their own lives, who were dragged forward to the conflict for

> the sake of religion, and rendered glorious by the martyrdom of confession, who preferred a horrible death to a [5] temporary life, and were crowned with all the victories of virtue, and offered to the Most High and supreme God the glory of their wonderful victory, because they had their conversation in heaven, and walked with him who gave victory to their testimony, also offered up glory, and honour, and majesty to the [10] Father, and to the Son, and to the Holy Ghost. Moreover, the souls of the martyrs being worthy of the kingdom of heaven are in honour together with the company of the prophets and apostles. [13]
>
> lines 1–13 in Eusebius, 1861, p. 1

Thus, we may say that the Roman authorities were overmatched and defeated. To this we may add some of the testimonies of Tertullian who lived through these times.

> "Call us", said fervent Tertullian, "call us *Sarmenticii* and *Semaxii*", (names derived from the wood with which they were burned, and the stakes to which they were tied;) "this is the garment of our victory, our embroidered robe, our triumphal chariot".
>
> [footnote 4 reads] Christianity was never stronger than when Diocletian and Galerius symbolised it on their medals as a strangled hydra with the haughty inscription *Deleta Christiana Religione*. Two such inscriptions have been found in Clunia, in Spain, on one of which are the words, "*nomine Christianorum delete qui rempublicam evertibant*".
>
> Farrar, 1875, p. 106

We may also note that theirs (the early Christians) was the first stand against the concept of an all dominant and oppressive state control. Thus was born the concept of a free conscience before God.

D. James Kennedy comments:

> Jesus Christ is the greatest emancipator in the history of the world. What freedom we have in this world we owe to Christ, and to his Word. "Where the Spirit of the Lord is, there is liberty". Wherever the Word has gone, tyrants have trembled, despots have been cast from the throne, and people have become free.
>
> Kennedy and Newcombe, 2001, p. 107

(2) *The Initial Social and Political benefits of Christianity*

Having observed the resilience of Christianity, with its supernatural strength and capacity to endure and to triumph over the most hostile opposition which is one of the great proofs and evidences that it is of God, we must now move on to observe that it also evidences its divine origin and enabling in the fact that it has brought and continues to bring a wide range of benefits and blessings to the world.

But first, some general and broad applications of this influence for good must be noted.

We can begin by reminding ourselves that in the midst of the squalor, misery, illness, and loneliness of ancient cities, Christianity provided an island of mercy and security. We need, for a while, to glance at the state of some of these burgeoning cities of the Roman Empire.

Firstly, we need to remind ourselves that these cities were phenomenally crowded. To squeeze everyone in, it was necessary to compact the buildings tightly together and build them higher than was safe. Most streets in these cities were so narrow that today, they would only be considered as footpaths. Roman law required that all streets be at least 9½ feet wide, but many were much narrower. The main street through the city of Antioch was celebrated throughout the ancient world for its spaciousness. It was however only fifteen to twenty feet wide. In most of these ancient cities, streets were so narrow that people leaning out of their windows could chat with someone living across the street without having to raise their voices. We also need to bear in mind that many of these buildings, except for the huge temples and public buildings, were constructed of wood, covered with stucco. With the large number of people crowded together, their cooking and keeping themselves warm over open braziers, the dread of fire was a constant worry and threat. Fire could and did have a devastating effect; it contributed to great loss of life and was not an infrequent event in the cities.

There was also the equal danger of the collapse of buildings. In Rome, it was illegal to construct a building higher than sixty-five feet. Nevertheless, buildings regularly fell down, and it was said that Rome was constantly filled with the noise of collapsing buildings or buildings being pulled down to prevent collapse. Many, if not most of these buildings did not have chimneys, which meant that the smoke had to escape wherever it could. Neither were there any windows, so that when a fire had taken hold, the draught running through the building would soon produce an inferno.

It is not always realised that soap had not been invented at this time, and all the water had to be brought in from wells or public fountains. In big cities, water was always in short supply, so that there was little left for washing of clothes or personal hygiene, never mind the washing of crockery and cutlery. Even the public water supply was often contaminated. Pliny wrote that he advised that "all water is the better for being boiled".

Sanitation was a major problem; there was a public drainage system in Rome from the major baths, which also served the public latrines. The outfall of this effluent found its way into the River Tiber, which very often could be smelt for miles around.

In the tenements, chamber pots were mainly used for the household's toilet arrangements. The majority of the contents of these were simply poured out into open ditches which ran through the streets. More often than not these pots were simply tipped out of the windows in the dark of night.

Adding to all this effluvia was the fact that the transport of goods and personnel was solely by means of a horse, donkey or ox, which constantly traversed the narrow streets, and left their dung behind; at the same time, flocks and herds passed through the streets on their way to the abattoir. In short, the smell of sweat, urine, faeces and decay hung over the whole city. Things were so bad and inhuman that very often corpses of adults as well as new-born or unwanted children, were sometimes abandoned in the streets. Mosquitoes and other dangerous insects were everywhere not to mention rats and other vermin.

Crime was a major problem in these large cities, Carcopino described Rome thus:

> In normal times night fell over the city like the shadow of a great danger, diffused, sinister, and menacing. Everyone fled to his home, shut himself in, and barricaded the entrance. The shops fell silent, safety chains were drawn across behind the leaves of the doors; the shutters of the flats were closed and the pots of flowers withdrawn from the windows they had adorned. If the rich had to sally forth, they were accompanied by slaves who carried torches to light and protect them on their way. Juvenal sighs that to go out to supper

> without having made your will was to expose yourself to the reproach of carelessness.
>
> Carcopino, 1943, pp. 47–48

In addition to crime, the constant influx of strangers into the Greco-Roman cities caused a great deal of disorder, including riots—some involving ethnic conflicts, some involving political disputes. Riots not only cost many lives and ruined immense amounts of property, in which major fires often resulted, but the political riots aroused such extreme anxiety among the ruling elite that the secret police proliferated everywhere, generating an intricate network of informants. Subsequently "no class, high or low, could escape their prying". These also were commissioned to carry out political assassinations. All this added to the tension, threat and misery of everyday life.

We need to add to this the inevitable threat of disease. With such conditions prevailing, the heat of summer constantly brought with it the threat of disease and death. Illness, caused by the almost total lack of hygiene, produced tapeworm, whipworm and other parasitical occupations of the body. While these debilitating discomforts were not fatal, they left the individuals wide open to other more-deadly diseases. Such conditions also gave rise to periodic outbreaks of plague.

In the year AD 165, during the reign of Marcus Aurelius, a most terrifying and devastating plague swept through the Roman Empire. Many medical historians suspect that this was the first appearance of smallpox in the Western world. No one can be certain exactly what this disease was, but it was highly contagious. During the first fifteen-year duration of the epidemic, a quarter to a third of the population most likely died of it. At the very height of the epidemic, mortality was so great in many cities that the Emperor Marcus Aurelius (himself later dying of the disease) wrote of caravans of carts and wagons hauling out the dead.

A century after this, another plague struck the population of the Empire which once again trembled as on all sides friends, family and neighbours died suddenly and horribly.

We need to remember that no one knew how to really treat these various plague victims. It is on record that, during one plague, Galen, the renowned physician of classical times, left Rome to escape to the safety of his country estate.

The fact was that no one attempted to treat the victims of these plagues for fear of catching them themselves. The typical response was to avoid any contact with the victim, and hence they were often simply abandoned in the streets, where the dead and dying lay in piles.

We also have to appreciate that no help was given by the pagan religious priests and leaders which abandoned the temples and fled. This was not considered unusual or even wrong by the populace, because there was no belief that the gods cared about human affairs. Pagan gods could be bribed to grant wishes, but the idea of a merciful or caring God was utterly alien to them.

Under such circumstances neither did, nor could, the classical philosophers provide any help; all they could do was blame it all on fate.

It is against this background however that we see a total and completely different attitude to disease, plague and death shown by the Christians. In the midst of these troubles, Christian leaders urged their flocks to act and to tend the sick and the dying.

Bishop Dionysius of Alexandria described the circumstances of one plague that struck his city as follows:

> At the first onset of the disease, they, the pagans, pushed the sufferers away and fled from their dearest, throwing them into the roads before they were dead and treated unburied corpses as dirt, hoping thereby to avert the spread and contagion of the fatal disease; but do what they liked, they found it difficult to escape.

He wrote the following pastoral letters to his flock at the end of the plague, commending them for the fact that they had nursed the sick, and that some had even given their lives in so doing.

> At all events most of the brethren through their love and brotherly affection for us spared not themselves nor abandoned one another, but without regard to their own peril visited those who fell sick, diligently looking after and ministering to them and cheerfully shared their fate with them, being infected with the disease from them and willingly involving themselves in their troubles. Not a few also, after nursing others back to recovery, died themselves, taking death over from them and thus fulfilling in very deed the common saying, which is taken always as a note of mere good feeling; for in their departure they became their expiatory substitutes. At all events, the very pick of our brethren lost their lives in this way, both priests and deacons and some highly praised ones from among the

> laity, so that this manner of dying does not seem far removed from martyrdom.
>
> Feltoe, 1918, pp. 71–72[1]

Because so many Christians responded and helped the plague stricken, even in the realm of elementary nursing, i.e. providing food, water and practical help, many lives were saved, leading some to conjecture that Christian nursing could have reduced the mortality rate by as much as two thirds. Significantly, the fact that most stricken Christians survived did not go unnoticed and gave immense credibility to the Christian testimony, which, in turn, contributed to an increase in Christian numbers.

What went on during the epidemics was only an intensification of what went on every day amongst Christians. Because of their communities of mercy and self-help, Christians lived longer and better lives. This was apparent and must have been extremely appealing and impressive to the non-Christians around them.

It is not that the pagans were completely uncharitable; rather, their charity had nothing to do with their service to their gods. In order to gain favour, pagan gods only had to be appeased or obeyed; beyond that the gods had no interest in human beings at all. Neither could pagan priests demand or require from their followers that kindness, generosity or sympathy should be shown towards others.

Moreover, in the pagan temples there was no congregation as such; likewise, there was no real bond of unity between those who attended any particular temple. Each person went to the temple as an individual, and usually only when there was an ulterior motive for going.

On the other hand, the Church was a congregation of individuals committed to one another in the name of Christ; the Church was a place of mercy in the midst of a largely inhumane and uncaring Roman society. Also, Christians believed in a life everlasting. Most pagans believed in a future unattractive existence in the underworld. Christians, whilst appreciating this world, recognised it was only a place of pilgrimage and preparation for the world that was to come. This enabled them to overcome their fears of death, to see that there was more than merely life preservation in this world. It was because of this that, in the face of the danger and risk of catching the plague, they were able to go forward and do what they did to relieve the sufferers.

1 Also referenced in Stark, 1966, p. 117.

It can certainly be said that it was by the imitation of Christ that the Christians themselves were able to live longer and experience more comfortable lives, and at the same time witness to others that the Christian faith was far superior in every respect to anything that had ever gone before.

All these facts are plain and even secular historians recognise them. We may quote the remarks of the secular historian, Anthony Alcock in his contemporary study *The History of Europe*. Alcock does not hesitate to describe Christianity as one of the vital influences and chief pillars of European civilisation, and then asks and answers the question "So why did Christianity succeed?"

> The gods of Rome were really the gods of Greece, transported and given Roman names. Up to the end of the first century AD Roman religion had an important role to play. It provided through its rituals a sense of order and cohesion, and was essential in the building of patriotism. The weakness of this religion was that it could do nothing to relieve concern about a world in which everything depended upon oppressive, whimsical chance or fate. It could not fill the vacuum in the soul, so while retaining the forms and attending the ceremonies of the official cults, many people turned elsewhere in the search for strength to endure life on earth and find a happy life in the hereafter. Some sought the answer in astrology, others turned to the many mystery cults coming to Rome from the Middle East.
>
> Among the more famous of these mystery cults was Manichaeism, which sought to get around the problem of how a good Creator could allow evil to exist by postulating the co-existence of good and evil powers.
>
> A much larger and more popular cult was that of the Egyptian goddess Isis, with its theme of death and resurrection. According to Egyptian legend the husband of Isis, Osiris, a mythical king and bringer of Egyptian civilisation, was murdered by his brother Seth. His dismembered body was reassembled by Isis who posthumously conceived their son Horus, who fought and overcame Seth. Osiris was then resurrected as king of the Underworld and a symbol of immortality.
>
> The cult of Isis thus promised immortality in an afterlife. The cult was open to all people—Roman citizens, free men and slaves. But Isis was above all, the woman's goddess, "Holy Mother", and her statues would usually be with the infant Horus in her arms.

> A third cult was Mithraism whose origin was Persian. Mithraism stressed the struggle in the world between the forces of good and evil. The hero of the good, and identified with light or the Sun, was Mithras. Mithras and its theme of struggle particularly appealed to the military in the Empire.
>
> Alcock, 2002, p. 38

The superiority of Christianity to this multiplicity of cults was obvious.

Though there appeared to be superficial similarities between these mystery cults and Christianity, there were in fact vast differences between them. The superior depth, quality and strength of Christianity caused it to outstrip all its rivals. Christianity, we might say, bore precious fruit while the others brought forth nothing but leaves.

The Christian Gospel of salvation in Christ, answers the deepest longings of the human heart for forgiveness and reconciliation with God. Christianity was (and is) a Gospel of grace, where, without money and without price, destitute souls could come and purchase the very water of life. It was indeed a message of faith, hope and charity. It extended to women, children, the destitute, those who were ill, those rejected by society, criminals and even one's enemies. It was the message of the Beatitudes and uniquely, it was a message which fostered concern for others before self.

Thus, the early Christians were aggressively evangelistic. Their desire was that others could find the new life they had found in Christ. They believed that they had found the "pearl of greatest price", and their desire was that all around would come to know the Saviour who had made himself known to them.

It is well known that the peace and good order produced by the Roman Empire (*Pax Romana*) together with the sophisticated road networks that it established made travel easy and safe, which enabled the rapid spread of Christianity in the early years. Also, in the earliest part of the Empire, in the educated sections of society, there was the common language—Greek—the language in which the New Testament was originally written.

The following reasons account for some of the success of Christianity

(A) Christianity is a universal not a national religion

As universal, it was something generically new, absolutely unlike all that had been before, or were around at that time. A universal religion is capable of living anywhere and everywhere, suited to people of all classes and in all stages of their development, capable of satisfying the largest, yet stooping to the meanest nature; yet able also to fill the nature as to make it dissatisfied with its attainments, ever craving after something nobler and higher. A.M. Fairbairn described a universal religion as follows:

> A universal is more than a missionary religion. It must be missionary, but all missionary are not universal religions. Buddhism is missionary, yet we can see this, that it so hates life, it so hates society, it so dislikes whatever tends to create an order that shall prolong and lift the life of humanity, as to act as a sort of paralysis of progress, as to produce a sort of general collapse in all the more progressive and ameliorative agencies of time. Islam is missionary, but then it spreads not simply by power, but so as to deprave the civilized, as to lower the higher and nobler races. A universal religion must be one that can help man ever forward, enlarge his nature, give him for ever the idea that far as he has come, he has yet an infinite path to travel to a higher and nobler perfection.
>
> Now, the universalism of Christianity rose out of its cardinal ideas. The one God made mankind one. One God and one humanity could be expressed only by one religion. Now, mark, that was at first an unintelligible idea. To the early world all religions were local. Zeus could not be understood out of Greece; Jupiter could not be understood out of Rome. The Roman might carry his faith with him, but it was bound up with the being of his state, with the idea of his city. No man can be a Brahman out of India. If he comes here, he loses so much of his Brahmanism that he has to be purged and purified at his return. There was not then, as there is not now, any religion, but the religion of Christ that possessed universalism, that could be anywhere by any man believed and obeyed, and that tended to embrace all men in a glorious unity. That made it a most insoluble problem, a strange anomaly, to men possessed of the older ideas, and many a great historian and thinker stood puzzled and helpless before the notion that a faith could be universal, that there could be a religion expressing faith in one God, one Humanity, and one great Mediator between them.
>
> Fairbairn, 1894, pp. 180–181

(B) Christianity is a spiritual religion

In its essence, Christianity is a spiritual religion independent in its essential form and belief of all outward and material forms. It can exist unlike any other religion without temples; it ordains no priests or priestly order, instead all true Christians are a royal priesthood unto God, each believer has free access to God through the one and only Priest-Mediator, Jesus Christ. Essentially, it established no organisational hierarchy; it offers no continual sacrifices; because the sacrifice has been once and for all offered on Calvary. The only sacrifice it speaks of is that its followers seek to have clean hands and a pure heart, and a holy life dedicated unto God and his service.

In the world of the early Church, the absence of these forms traditionally associated with religion, meant that many looking on believed that Christians were atheists. For many, in the early days, the absence in Christianity of any sacerdotal system or outward ritual inevitably forced upon the casual observer the condemnation that Christianity was a godless cult. It was for this reason together with others—one significantly being that they rejected the idea of a totalitarian state—which doomed many early believers to the stake or the amphitheatre.

(C) Christianity is a moral religion

Christianity, as it appeared in the first century, was a religion which created a new moral impetus to both individual and corporeal life.

It has been seen over and over again that the ancient religions did not pretend to give a moral law, or a directive of personal and social and civil life.

Again, Fairbairn comments:

> The moralist was never the priest; he was always the philosopher. No man did good because his religion bound him. No, it was only the maxims of the schools that could direct and teach. If you want to find the highest ideal of morality in pagan times, where do you go? Certainly not to the oracles, certainly not to the mysteries, certainly not to the priesthoods. Nay, but you must go to the Academy, to the porch, or to the grove, and say to Plato, or Zeno, or Aristotle, "Teach me how to regulate my life". And as there was no morality connected with the religion, so the gods did not concern themselves about morality. Pagan moralists could say, "The gods give me life and fortune, but a cheerful, contented spirit I secure for myself". Or he

could say, "The gods send war and pestilence, and we offer sacrifices to propitiate their wrath; but the virtuous man is sufficient for himself; he needs no help of the gods".

Now the result of this was inevitable: where religion had no concern with morality, morality could draw from it no inspiration. But when Christ appeared, these were bound together in indissoluble marriage, the highest moral principle and the highest religious faith were united in eternal alliance. And the result was seen at once. First in this: man was placed in the centre of new moral forces; new moral forces were placed within the man. Then happened a wonderful thing. Where the schools had been powerless, Christianity became powerful, and men who never felt the inspiration to a good and noble life felt it now.

And, as a second result, the virtues were universalised. If you had wished to scandalise an ancient philosopher, you could not have done it more effectually than by associating him with the unlettered, with the people. Celsus, the great assailant of the Christian faith, held up the Christians to scorn because they were unlettered men, slaves, cobblers, weavers, men who were not equal to stand in an Academy, or speak in elegant Greek. Therein lay its power; it took the poor, the outcast, the despised, and it made them more moral than the schools had made the philosophers. You will get many a beautiful proverb in Seneca, you will get many a fine ethical principle in Plato, you will find in Stoicism some of the most exalted precepts that human ethics have ever known. But mark you one thing, you will never discover that these elevated the common life of man, affected the course of the lost, or made the bad good, or the impure holy. Where they failed, Christ succeeded with splendid, glorious success; he made out of the very outcast of men and women saints unto God.

And then followed a third thing. Virtues new and beautiful were created. Now I don't mean to compare the Greek "Eros", the Latin "Amor", and the Christian "Love". The man who knows classical life knows that the distance between these is an infinite distance. Love, what did it signify to the ancient world but a form of lust, or what at best carried with it every connotation of passion and its pain? But Love, what does it become to a Christian man? Read that wonderful chapter which stands as the thirteenth of First Corinthians, the glorious description of Christian love, the power that can inspire, can

> regulate, can ennoble a man, making him love his fellows the wide world over.
>
> Fairbairn, 1894, pp. 183–186

To these reflections we may add similar remarks from F.W. Farrar's *Seekers after God*.

> The morality of paganism was, on its own admission, *insufficient*. It was tentative where Christianity is authoritative; it was dim and partial where Christianity is bright and complete; it was inadequate to rouse the sluggish carelessness of mankind, where Christianity came with an inspirational and awakening power; it gave only a *rule* where Christianity supplied a *principle*; and even where its teachings were absolutely identical with those of Scripture, it failed to ratify them with a sufficient sanction; it failed to announce them with the same powerful and contagious ardour; it failed to furnish an absolutely faultless and vivid example of their practice; it failed to inspire them with an irresistible motive; it failed to support with a powerful comfort under the difficulties which were sure to be encountered in the aim after a consistent and holy life.
>
> Farrar, 1881, pp. 319–320

As we have seen, some of the ancient Greek and Roman philosophers spoke some high-sounding and attractive words on various moral issues, but they were powerless amongst the general degradation of the times to awaken conscience or guide men's lives into a better way. They have been described as being like gathered blossoms stuck in a child's garden; they may have had an attractive appearance, but because they had no root they withered away.

In modern times, several high-minded souls have also attempted to create philosophical systems aimed at inspiring men and women to live unselfishly with the spirit that is mindful of the needs of others. Auguste Comte in the nineteenth century was typical; he developed the altruistic philosophy of positivism and took for its motto "Live for others". His scheme however soon failed and passed from common memory, as many others have done since the earliest of times. For, separated from belief in the God of Scripture, separated from faith in Christ, such precepts are inoperative and impossible.

We are seeking at this point to show the superiority of Christianity over every other philosophy of life, or system of belief. Christianity, we might say, shows its superiority in that it comes to us not as a mere collection of dogmas or a series of aphorisms, but as a living faith able to bridge over the wide gap between knowledge and actions. Christianity has at its root the very saving, regenerating revelation of God in Jesus Christ, the soul redeemed by faith in his all-atoning sacrifice, goes on to know the life-changing energy of the Holy Spirit working in their daily life and experience. We see in Christianity a new enlargement and deepening of moral perception, together with a new spiritual power breathed into the soul that enables men and women to lead good and godly lives.

(D) Christianity works by persuasion not coercion

Christianity stands as radically different from all previous religions. It works by persuasion, and its great instrument is speech. It did not seek to exist by the protection or health of the state, but it sought to penetrate, as truth and love, the mind and the heart of men and women. It did not even ask the laws to favour it; it only asked to be allowed to live and work in its own way. When it appears, it speaks to the mind, the reason and the heart, and it seeks also to persuade the spirit. When Paul went to Mars' Hill (Acts 17:22) in order to reason with the philosophers, his aim was, through the preaching of the Word, to convert and to change them. It was as power living by speech, living by persuasion, that Christianity was seen to be vastly different in the ancient world.

It pointed to Christ, not a system; it sought to persuade men to trust in him for salvation full and free. When it had persuaded, it required that a man or woman live a holy life unto God empowered and enabled by the Spirit of God.

Where the old religions placed the emphasis on outward sacerdotal acts and rituals, Christianity placed the emphasis on purity, peace, faith, hope, love, and willing service. With the coming of Christianity, all was changed, and every man and woman it reached became a great factor of change, a means of making a new humanity, and a whole new outlook on the world. These precepts further illustrated in the way that new meaning and significance were attached to the three vital concepts of love, humility and humanity.

> Take for example the tenderness it brought into the life of man to woman, of strong to weak. There is no grander ancient character than Socrates, beautiful character he is in many a way. He the citizen, thinker, teacher, plying that wondrous dialectic craft of his

in the streets of Athens, is a form attractive to all eyes. And he is so attractive because he stands out from among the crowd, the creator of a new moral ideal, at once stronger, higher, and more humane than the old epic and heroic ideal embodied in the Homeric Achilles. But now, look how over against him stands the image of Xanthippe, his wife. She has had hard measure dealt to her; his contemporaries and historians have made her seem one who led the poor philosopher a hardish life, and have made her the type of a woman who makes life not pleasant to the man that has wedded her. And many a dry-as-dust commentator has grown somewhat humorous over the sweet relief that death brought to Socrates when it saved him from Xanthippe.

But if you examine the simple truth as it stands in history, that woman has no right to be so rated; the man, on the other hand, has reason to be be rated most soundly. His love is all for the state and not for the home; marriage is for him only a convenient institution, carrying with it no duties of loving affection, of mutual helpfulness and cheerful intercourse, and his conduct was but too good an exponent of his opinions. He cultivated an admiring friendship for Aspasia, but he had only the coldest neglect for poor Xanthippe. His duties are all to Athens and Greece, and not at all to home. He puns, questions, teaches for the good of philosophy and the state, but she has to provide for their children. She goes to him in the hour of death, grieved, distressed in a woman's way, and he sits as in the Phaedo, sublimely discoursing with his friends. When she comes he never feels a bit the loss to her, they do not feel the pain to the woman and to the children; nay, it is going to trouble the serenity of the philosopher to see the woman who was his wife, and the children she had borne him. And they send her away with no word of comfort, with scorn rather than with cheer. There now stands out clear and distinct one of the great differences the religion of Christ brought in, it brought in the spirit of love, made the weak dependent on the strong, made the strong thoughtful of the weak, made the man in his might, in his manhood, with all the rights of manhood upon him, to be to the weak generous, and to the dependent noble. This is but one phase of its action in universalising and creating a higher virtue, and so purifying and perfecting the whole notion of society. The state

> of life built up in harmony with these principles, according to these great ideals could not but be a kindlier, nobler, humaner state.
>
> Fairbairn, 1894, pp. 186–187

More than one sceptical writer has observed, with something of a disparaging sneer, that the best utterances of Christian moralists may be found in the writings of pagan philosophers. This was a claim clearly recognised from the earliest days of Christian history.

> The relation between pagan philosophers and the Christian religion was a subject of much discussion and a profound difference of opinion in the early Church.
>
> Lecky, 1890, p. 343

Some of the early Christian writers readily admitted that there were similarities between the writings of Plato, Socrates, Seneca and so forth to some degree which resembled their own moral teachings.

Even before the Christian era, the Jewish writer Aristobulus had contended that the Jewish writings, having been translated into Greek, had become the source of much of the pagan wisdom.

Justin Martyr amongst the early Church Fathers contended that the wisdom of antiquity had been derived from two sources, namely, the alleged union of women and angelic beings as described in Genesis chapter six and secondly that it had been discerned from the teachings of the Old Testament. (abridged from Lecky, 1890, pp. 344–345)

While we may not altogether accept the opinions of Justin Martyr and others who thought that all knowledge had been derived from these two sources, we can say without a doubt that modern thinkers and historians are clearly not the first to have noticed the parallels.

It is also clear that the pagan philosophers of old would have been the first to admit that what light they had was dim, and the conclusions they drew tentative and uncertain. These were men who longed and craved for more light, and a greater understanding. So strongly did that necessity appear to some of the wisest of them, that Socrates went so far as to express in words, that at some future advent there would come a heaven-sent guide.

Thus, it can be seen that, in the words of Dean Farrar:

> Those who imagine that *without* a written revelation it would have been possible to learn all that is necessary for man's well-being, are speaking in direct contradiction of the greatest heathen teachers,

> in contradiction even of those very teachers to whose writings they point as the proof of their assertion. Augustine was expressing a very deep conviction when he said that in Plato and in Cicero he met with many utterances which were beautiful and wise, but among them all he never found, "Come unto me, all ye that labour and are heavy laden, and I will refresh you" (Matthew 11:28). Glorious as was the wisdom of ancient thought, its knowledge respecting the indwelling of the Spirit, the resurrection of the body, and the forgiveness of sins, was but fragmentary and vague. Bishop Butler (18 May 1692–16 June 1752) has justly remarked that "The great doctrines of a future state, the dangers of a course of wickedness, and the efficacy of repentance are not only confirmed in the Gospel, but are taught, especially the last is, with a degree of light to which that of nature is darkness".
>
> Farrar, 1881, p. 319

Farrar continues:

> Seneca, Epictetus, Aurelius, are among the truest and loftiest of Pagan moralists, yet Seneca ignored the Christians, Epictetus despised, and Aurelius persecuted them. All three, so far as they knew anything about the Christians at all, had unhappily been taught to look upon them as the most degraded and the most detestable sect of what they had long regarded as the most degraded and the most detestable of religions. (1881, p. 321)
>
> Though there is value and interest in the study of pagan philosophy and no wise man would despise it, we must all guard against the closed-mindedness illustrated by the unhistorical anecdote of Caliph Omar.
>
> When he conquered Alexandria, he was shown its magnificent library, in which were collected untold treasures of literature, gathered together by the zeal, the labour, and the liberality of a dynasty of kings. "What is the good of all those books?" he said. "They are either in accordance with the Koran, or contrary to it. If the former, they are superfluous; if the latter, they are pernicious. In either case let them be burnt". Burnt they were, as legend tells; but all the world has condemned the Caliph's reasoning as a piece of stupid Philistinism and barbarous bigotry.
>
> Farrar, 1881, p. 324

However, whilst we must be careful not to be guilty of the Caliph's folly, we can also say again that the philosophy of the ancients had little moral influence, and indeed, in a sense, was never intended to be a moral force; it was chiefly a philosophical outlook. The point is that it had no real influence over the heart and the character of the general population, or indeed over the philosophers themselves.

> (It) was sectarian, not universal; the religion of the few, not of the many. It exercised no creative power over political or social life; it stood in no such relation to the past as the New Testament to the Old. Its best thoughts were but views and aspects of the truth; there was no centre around which they moved, no divine life by which they were impelled; they seemed to vanish and flit in uncertain succession of light. But Christianity, on the other hand, glowed with a steady and unwavering brightness; it not only swayed the hearts of individuals by stirring them to their utmost depths, but it moulded the laws of nations, and regenerated the whole condition of society. It gave to mankind a fresh sanction in the word of Christ, a perfect example in His life, a powerful motive in His love, an all sufficient comfort in the life of immortality made sure and certain to us by His Resurrection and Ascension.
>
> Farrar, 1881, pp. 335–336

It is often said that "the darkest night comes before dawn". Yet never did a deeper darkness or a thicker gloom of moral pestilence and decay brood over the face of society than at the time when the Sun of righteousness arose with healing in his wings. There have been many periods in the world's history when a dense gloom of heartless immorality has settled down with unusual weight. In the days of Pharaoh, we read of a darkness that could be felt, but never probably was there any age or time where the worst forms of wickedness were practised with such audacity and effrontery than in the city of Rome under the government of the Caesars. A deeply-seated corruption seemed to have permeated to the very heart and core of national existence. It is a repeated lesson of history, having deep moral significance, that, at the same time when men became most polished in luxury, they became most-cruel and vile in their manner of life. Horace bewailed the fact that "the age of our fathers, worse than that of our grandsires, has produced us who are yet baser, and who are doomed to give birth to a still more degraded offspring". Fifty years after this Juvenal bewailed the fact that the final goal of iniquity had been attained, and cries, in a burst of despair, that "posterity will add nothing to our immorality; our descendants can but do and desire the same crimes as ourselves". (Derived from *Seekers After God* pp.56–57)

If we would seek to get from the Scriptures themselves a fair analysis of what the world had sunk to at that very period when Christianity began to take root, we can find no clearer, and penetrating description than that which we find drawn by the Apostle Paul in the first chapter of the Epistle to the Romans.

Romans 1:21–32:

> [21]*Because that, when they knew God, they glorified [him] not as God, neither were thankful; but became vain in their imaginations, and their foolish heart was darkened.* [22]*Professing themselves to be wise, they became fools,* [23]*And changed the glory of the uncorruptible God into an image made like to corruptible man, and to birds, and fourfooted beasts, and creeping things.* [24]*Wherefore God also gave them up to uncleanness through the lusts of their own hearts, to dishonour their own bodies between themselves:* [25]*Who changed the truth of God into a lie, and worshipped and served the creature more than the Creator, who is blessed for ever. Amen.* [26]*For this cause God gave them up unto vile affections: for even their women did change the natural use into that which is against nature:* [27]*And likewise also the men, leaving the natural use of the woman, burned in their lust one toward another; men with men working that which is unseemly, and receiving in themselves that recompence of their error which was meet.* [28]*And even as they did not like to retain God in [their] knowledge, God gave them over to a reprobate mind, to do those things which are not convenient;* [29]*Being filled with all unrighteousness, fornication, wickedness, covetousness, maliciousness; full of envy, murder, debate, deceit, malignity; whisperers,* [30]*Backbiters, haters of God, despiteful, proud, boasters, inventors of evil things, disobedient to parents,* [31]*Without understanding, covenant breakers, without natural affection, implacable, unmerciful:* [32]*Who knowing the judgment of God, that they which commit such things are worthy of death, not only do the same, but have pleasure in them that do them.*

Such was the world when Christianity came into it, yet though men sinned there was also a growing weariness of it, but no remedy for it, until the light of the Gospel dawned.

> On that hard Pagan world disgust
> And secret loathing fell.

> Deep weariness and sated lust
> Made human life a hell.
>
> In his cool hall, with haggard eyes,
> The Roman noble lay;
> He drove abroad in furious guise
> Along the Appian Way.
>
> He made a feast, drank fierce and fast
> And crown'd his hair with flowers—
> No easier nor no quicker pass'd
> The impracticable hours.
>
> Arnold, 1867, II. 93–104

(3) *Christianity and its humanising influence*

We are looking at the way Christianity touched this fallen world and brought about more changes for the good than any other movement or force in history before or since.

The concept of man, made in the image and likeness of God, we have already touched upon, but we repeat in more detail the point here, as we begin to look at the changes Christianity brought in the days of the Early Church.

> Genesis 1:27: "So God created man in his [own] image, in the image of God created he him; male and female created he them."

There is an old story of a French engineer who asked his students the question: "What is the most important thing to come out of a mine?" The pupils then proceeded to name various minerals, but he was then quick to correct them and say: "The most important thing to come out of a mine is the miner". We could say the engineer was emphasising the importance of human life, and the life of every single individual.

This is an important concept and, prior to the coming of Christ into the world, human life on this planet was exceedingly cheap. In a world that was full of slaves who were regarded as no more than goods and chattels and could be put to death at a mere whim of their owner, the concept of the value of every single life was indeed revolutionary. The coming of Christ gave mankind in general a new perspective on the value of human life. Christianity bridged the gap between the Jews—who first received the divine revelation that man was made in God's image—and the pagans, who attributed little value to human life. It is a sad fact, as has been remarked by many, as in the post-Christian West we abandon our Judaeo-Christian heritage, life is once again becoming cheap.

The origin of the sense of humanity must be sought in the influence of Christianity. If Christianity did not create the sense, it contributed in the highest degree to the growth of the feeling of humanity, for which we look in vain in pagan civilisations. Even with the Hebrews humanity is the result of a slow growth. However, the Hebrew writings reveal a gradually advancing tendency toward the sentiment of humanity.

The next step was of the highest importance.

> The advent of the Founder of Christianity was the foundation of a new era of sentiment. To Him the immediate victims of wrong, the outcast, the destitute, the slave, owed the relaxation, if not the absolute removal, of their miseries. To Him who recognised the treasure lodged in every human form, and taught the sanctity of the body, the issues which depend upon life, and the brotherhood of mankind, were directly due the merciful spirit, the tender care for human suffering, and the reverent respect for man as man, which characterizes civilized nations at this day.
>
> Jones, 1903, p. 156

We may take the following example: in AD 251 the then Bishop of Rome wrote a letter to the Bishop of Antioch in which he mentioned that the Roman congregation was supporting over fifteen hundred widows and persons in distress. (Eusebius, *The History of the Church*, 6:43 in Stark, 1966, p. 113)

This was not unusual. In around the year AD 98, Ignatius, the Bishop of Antioch advised Polycarp, the Bishop of Smyrna, to be sure to provide special support for widows. (Stark, 1966, p. 113)

Paul Johnson in his *History of Christianity*, comments:

> It was the Christian spirit of mutual love and communal charity which most impressed pagans. Tertullian quotes them, saying: "How these Christians love one another!" And he adds that the funds which financed their charities were essentially voluntary: "Every man once a month brings some modest coin, or whatever he wishes and only if he does wish, and if he can—for nobody is compelled". And the funds were spent "not on banquets and drinking parties", but "to feed the poor and bury them, for boys and girls who lacked property and parents, and then for slaves grown old and shipwrecked mariners;

> and any who may be in the mines or on the penal islands, in prison … they become the pensioners of their confession.
>
> The Christians had enormously expanded the old charitable trusts of the Jewish diaspora. They ran a miniature welfare state in an empire which for the most part lacked social services. The Emperor Julian, seeking to revive paganism in the fourth century, tried to introduce similar charitable funds for the poor. In a letter ordering imperial clergy to set these up, he noted: "Why do we not observe that it is in their benevolence to strangers, their care for the graves of the dead, and the apparent holiness of their lives that they have done most to increase atheism?" (i.e. Christianity). He thought it "disgraceful that, when no Jew ever has to beg, and the impious Galileans support not only their own poor, but ours as well, everyone can see that our people lack aid from us".
>
> Johnson, 1979, p. 62

Tertullian (AD 155–222) explained how this welfare system functioned.

> There is no buying or selling of any sort of the things of God. Though we have our treasure chest, it is not made up of purchase money, as of the religion that has its price. On the monthly day, if he likes, each puts in a small donation; but only if it be his pleasure, and only if he is able; but there is no compulsion; all is voluntary. These gifts are, as it were, piety's deposit fund.
>
> Tertullian, n.d., p. 88

These charitable activities were possible only because Christianity formed congregations, congregations of truly committed believers who built their lives around their faith. It was because they were part of this community that Christians were insulated from many of the deprivations of ancient life. When trouble struck, there were people around them who cared enough to help them; indeed, there were people who had the distinct responsibility to do just that. All congregations had deacons whose primary job was to support the sick, the infirm, the poor, and the disabled. This is outlined in the Apostolic Constitutions:

> (Deacons) are to be doers of good works, exercising a general supervision day or night, neither scorning the poor nor respecting the persons of the rich; they must ascertain who are in distress and

> not exclude them from a share in church funds; compelling also the well-to-do to put money aside for good works.
>
> As quoted by Adolf von Harnack in Stark, 1966, p. 114

(4) *Christianity and Slavery*

It is well known that, at first, Christianity did not abolish slavery. It could not and it did not; yet it declared itself in its ideal the fall of slavery. In Christ, there is neither Jew nor Greek, bond nor free. In the Church, there was no slave and no master; they were all the servants of Christ, the children of God, and members one of another. Slowly, as Christianity prevailed, the idea of man's equality entered into the heart of society. When we come to the period of Justinian and his laws, slavery is still allowed, but to kill a slave is made a crime. Over the slave, the Christian law now extends its protection. When we move further down the years, the slave again gained new rights. He can become a free man, he can enter into a religious order, he can there become the leader and peer of another.

Of the state of the slaves in Greek civilisation much has been written. Largely, they were of the same blood as their masters. They were often prisoners taken captive in the wars between the various city states. Some of them were poor persons who had sold themselves because they were unable to support themselves. Those who could not pay public taxes were liable to be sold into slavery. The children of the poor were sold to buy food, or if they were simply unwanted. Children who had been exposed for death, and rescued, became the slaves of those who had found them; this is said to have been the case with Epictetus.[2] Captives taken by pirates were sold; and because it furnished such multitudes of slaves to the cities of Greece, piracy was held to be an honourable profession, which contributed much to the public welfare. The number of slaves was enormous. In Attica,[3] it was estimated that around 309 BC, there were 84,000 citizens, 40,000 aliens, and 400,000 slaves. In many cases, the condition of the slaves was unspeakably bad. Cato the Censor, who had himself sprung from the poorer class, used to flog his slaves severely when they failed to wait on him correctly; he

---

2 Epictetus was a Greek Stoic philosopher. He was born a slave at Hierapolis, Phrygia and lived in Rome until his banishment, when he went to Nicopolis in northwestern Greece for the rest of his life. His teachings were written down and published by his pupil Arrian in his *Discourses* and *Enchiridion*. Wikipedia

3 An historical region that encompasses the city of Athens

forbade them to practise any kind of religion, and when they were too old to work he exposed them to inclement weather, leaving them to the ravages of storms and starvation.

Slaves in ancient Greece were marked by their clothing and hairstyles and when they were sold in the public slave markets, they were required to stand naked. They often walked with their feet fettered to prevent their escape. They were not infrequently branded on the forehead, in punishment for slight offences.

> But, if conditions were bad in Greece, they were far worse and more severe in ancient Rome.
>
> Many of their lives were worn out and expended in the building of vast and magnificent works, porticos, temples, aqueducts, mausoleums whose ruins can still be seen today. Thousands were used as porters, often kept in a state of nudity and chained like dogs to the doorposts of the homes of their owners. Others were subjected to hard labour on farms, again often working in chains, and at night slept in the cells of an *ergastulum*,[4] underground, wet, filthy, and full of disease.
>
> No injury done to a slave was counted by law an injury to him, but to the master. If done by the master, no one had suffered. If the master were murdered in his house, all the slaves connected with that house were liable to be killed, and even the freed men with them. It was not until the time of the Emperor Hadrian—emperor from 117 to 138—that attempts were made to limit the master's absolute power over his slaves.
>
> The name of Vedius Pollio is remembered as a man of violent character, who kept slaves that he might feed them to the lampreys, which he kept in a pool for his table. On one occasion in the presence of the Emperor Augustus, he sentenced a young slave boy to this fate because he had slipped on a polished floor while carrying in his hand a crystal vase. The boy was only saved by the intervention of the Emperor who at the same time ordered that the pool be filled in.
>
> For slaves the punishment of the cross was reserved and one form of crucifixion, as we learn from Seneca, was by impaling. There were torturers by profession, whose business it was to exercise upon them (the slaves) their detestable craft. So cruelly complete was the power over slaves, and so benumbed the general sensibility, that when

4 The *ergastulum* was usually subsurface, built as a deep, roofed pit—large enough to allow the slaves to work within it and containing narrow spaces in which they slept. Wikipedia

the praetor Domitius had a slave crucified for killing a wild boar with a weapon appropriate to freemen, even Cicero only spoke of it afterwards as "perhaps appearing a harsh thing".

And so common was it, according to Suetonius, to expose decrepit and invalid slaves on an island in the Tiber, that there they might die without expense to the master, that Claudius himself, certainly one of the least exacting of imperial reformers, had by law to discourage the practice.

This was slavery in the European countries, civilised and cultured, into which came the new religion; where forum and palace faced each other; where the stateliest temples united with Porch, Lyceum, and Academy, to give to their sites perpetual renown; where orators like Cicero, moralists like Seneca, combined to instruct and to elevate the peoples; while among the barbarian tribes of the North, from whom we have sprung, it was common, and no less cruel.

Christianity entered on no superficial and obvious contest with this ancient, consolidated, and haughty iniquity, so general in the world, and so intricately involved with the customs of the rude, the laws of the advanced, with barbarian ferocities, Grecian philosophies and Roman power. It sent no formal challenge to the system, to which it was still as fatally hostile as it was to idolatry. But it smote it with blows more destroying than arms, and caused it to vanish as summer skies and melting currents consume the glacier, which we call an iceberg, which has drifted down from the Arctic coasts. The Sermon on the Mount, God's affectionate and watchful Fatherhood of all, the brotherhood of disciples, the mutual duty and the common immortality of poor and rich—these were the forces before which slavery inevitably fell. Where philosophies had utterly failed, and eloquence had been wanting, and the progress of arts, cities, or states, had only clenched tighter the manacles of the bondman, he who taught on the narrow Galilean beach overwhelmed by the mystic energy of his words the consummate oppression.

Christianity sought to reform society from within, outward; by working a true regeneration of spirit, and thus of laws and social customs. It planted the acorn, and was surer of the oak than if it had been built it in any manufactory. It sent the Spring on the earth; and left the old icefields, untouched of pick, or drill, or dynamite, to take care of themselves. But as fast as its power widened in the world, slavery grew milder, weaker, less crushing, narrower in its range and

> more merciful in its rule, until it ceased. This brief synopsis sums up in one sentence the crowded records of centuries of struggle.
>
> Adapted from Storrs, 1884, pp. 158–161

> From the first, slaves were welcome in the Christian congregations, on a level of equality with others. By the Church in the third century, the liberation of slaves was put on the same level of privilege with the rescue of martyrs. The emancipation of slaves was set forth as a principal duty of Christian righteousness. Prayers for slaves were early inserted among the solemn petitions of the Litanies. The financial offerings of harsh masters were refused, as bearing upon them the odour of a temper and not acceptable to God. Bond and free were on the same footing in the houses and in the offices of worship. Gladiatorial fights, as a matter of course, were forbidden to Church members; and the royal worth of the soul redeemed unto God by Christ was joyfully recognised, by prelates like Chrysostom, in the poorest disciple.
>
> Adapted from Storrs, 1884, pp. 161–162

Other details can be added such as in Rome slaves were not allowed to wear a distinguishing dress, lest it should acquaint them with the fact of their numerical superiority.

It is also true that laws were made to restrain cruelty to slaves, and to ensure to them adequate sustenance; but as the slave had no right of appeal to the law, of what use could the law be to him? Some of these laws showed the abject condition to which slaves were reduced: one law obliged masters to give each slave one pound of corn daily; another restrained mutilation of their persons, their limbs, and tongues; another law prohibited the compulsion of slaves to combat with wild beasts at the shows, and required for that purpose the licence of the judicial authorities; another law forbade the forcible subjection of female slaves to prostitution. In Rome, one named Scaurus had 80,000 slaves; and a Roman senator in the reign of Augustus left in his will, along with other properties, 4,116 slaves. In the reign of Julius Caesar, the slaves were more numerous than free men. They could be punished at the pleasure of their master and put to death by him at his own will. It is said that one Roman of wealth, when a guest at his table commented that he had never seen a man die, had the nearest slave put to death so that his guest might have his curiosity satisfied.

> The first incipient movements towards reform appeared at the time

of the rule of Hadrian and the Antonines, a century to a century and a half after the time of our Lord's crucifixion, when the atmosphere of society, however severe, was beginning to be imperceptibly modified by the new Faith. The master was then forbidden to kill his slave at his pleasure, or to sell him for a gladiator without permission of magistrates, or for combats with wild beasts. If the slave were subjected to excessive cruelty, the magistrate, on appeal, could constrain his master to part with him for a price. A right of sanctuary was granted to him beside the statue of the Emperor; and the formalities of enfranchisement were made perceptibly simpler. So far as this it was principally, no doubt, the direct or indirect influence of the Stoical philosophy which contributed to mitigate the condition of the slave; though neither jurist nor philosopher attempted to give him his full measure of rights, and a ruler as thoughtful, philosophical, and conscientious as Marcus Aurelius, left the ancient legal position of the bondsman substantially unchanged. But when that renowned Emperor died, AD 180, there was a force rapidly extending throughout the Empire, which he had recognised only with contempt, and had blindly combated with persecution, which was to do in this direction what he had not conceived to be possible; which was to accelerate, widen, and multiply, all the forces that had been slowly and partially working forward towards a future of liberty and hope for the slave, and was to add to them others, more powerful, to make that secure. This force was Christianity.

Storrs, 1884, p. 161

The laws of Constantine though scarcely consistent among themselves, helped on the powerful movement toward freedom; manumission under him was largely facilitated, and the practice of branding was finally forbidden. Under Theodosius the separation of families was prohibited. The laws of Justinian moved more strongly and steadily in the interest of humanity. By them emancipation was still further encouraged. Slaves were admitted as witnesses in court and recognised as having certain rights to be guarded. They were required to work five days in the week and had the privilege of the church-festivals (as holidays). They were under a higher law than the will of the master, obedience to which law brought perfect freedom, which was eloquently taught from the Metropolitan pulpits. Influential teachers early and emphatically condemned all slavery and declared the liberation of those in bondage the duty of Christians.

> The Council of Orange, AD 441, forbade the reducing of Christians to bondage. The Council of Reims, AD 625, prohibited bishops from breaking up sacred vessels *except* for the redemption of slaves. Gregory the Great only expressed the growing, at least the governing feeling of the Christendom which he ruled, when he based his own manumission of slaves on the fact that the Lord had come from heaven to redeem all men, without distinction, from the bondage of sin.
>
> Slavery disappeared in Italy by the 15th century; and in parts of Germany before the end of the 13th century; though it lingered longer—to our shame!—in our own country. In Britain it was argued and justified on the grounds of its alleged tendency to civilise and in the end to Christianise the individuals concerned.
>
> Storrs, 1884, pp. 162–163

Dean Farrar adds these words:

> Christianity did not at once abolish slavery—which would have been revolutionary and impossible—but by sapping its very foundations, rendered certain its final abolition.
>
> The most prejudiced historians do not deny that to Christianity mainly the abolition of slavery was due. It preached emancipation as a duty, and rewarded it as a privilege; it elevated the slave into a serf, ennobled by the sense of mutual obligations between his seigneur and himself, and then, flinging over him a shield of adamant, it told the proudest baron who dared to do him wrong that he did so at the peril of his own soul. And thus it removed from labour, both manual and agricultural, the unworthy brand of shame. Greeks and Romans spoke of artisans and barbarians with contemptuous disgust; but Christians never forgot that their Lord and Master had chosen the earthly position of the barbarian and an artisan.
>
> The proudest bishops were not ashamed to dig; a Benedict worked six hours a day with hoe and spade; and it is said that Thomas à Becket helped regularly to reap the fields. The monks at once practised labour, and ennobled and protected it.[5]

---

5 "They knew", says Mr Mill, of the Benedictines, "and taught that temporal work may be a spiritual exercise; and, protected by their sacred character from depredation, they set the first example to Europe of industry conducted on a large scale by free labour". Mill, *Dissertations*, II. 154. See too Lecky, *Hist, of Rational.* II. 261 seqq; Farrar, 1875, pp. 176–178.

(5) *Christianity improving the life of children*

We are all familiar with the descriptions in the Old Testament of the records of children being offered as sacrifices in pagan temples. The Old Testament clearly condemned the practice amongst the Canaanites and other ancient peoples for offering child sacrifices to Baal and Ashtoreth. Early in the twentieth century, excavations in Samaria revealed the ruins of one of the ancient temples of Ashtoreth. Just a few yards away from the temple was a cemetery, where many jars were found containing remains of infants who had been sacrificed in that temple. Such was the perversity of human nature that those ancient priests of Baal and Ashtoreth were the official murderers of countless little children.

The lives of children even in classical Greek and Roman times was little better. In these cultures, abortion was rampant. Abandonment was commonplace. It was quite normal for infirm babies and unwanted little ones to be taken out into the forests or mountainsides, where they would be eaten by wild animals, or simply starve to death, or be picked up by unscrupulous people who would bring them up to slavery, beggary or worse.

Virtually all deformed babies were so abandoned; some would abandon their small children if they had not the money to raise them. Others abandoned female children because women were considered inferior. Infanticide was not only legal; it was normal, and even applauded. In the city of Rome, there were special high places or walls where new-born children could be taken, usually by night to be exposed to die.

By the sixth century, so much had the feeling grown against such practices that the Christian Emperor Justinian was able to have the practice explicitly declared illegal.

> Those who expose children, possibly hoping they would die, and those who use the potions of the abortionist, are subject to the full penalty of the law—both civil and ecclesiastical—for murder. Should exposure occur, the finder of the child is to see that he is baptised and that he is treated with Christian care and compassion. They may be then adopted as *ad scriptorum*—even as we ourselves have been adopted into the kingdom of grace.
>
> Kennedy and Newcombe, 2001, p. 28

St Luke's Gospel particularly reveals to us the sacredness of

Pages 95–103 are an article from The Expositor, *Third Series, Vol. V. ed. W. Robertson Nicoll (Hodder & Stoughton, 1887) showing that Paul, in Philemon, did not condone slavery as is often claimed.*

THE EPISTLE TO PHILEMON.

THE OLDEST PETITION FOR THE ABOLITION OF SLAVERY.

M. Renan has called the Epistle to Philemon a *note*. It is indeed a letter in few words, but this very brevity only enhances the greatness of its contents.

There are other writings in the New Testament which might be described in the same way, as, for example, the second and third Epistles of John.

This group of short letters seems to have been regarded by the primitive Church as scarcely worthy of a place in the canon of sacred writings. Many Churches did not receive the second and third Epistles of John, and Jerome tells us that the Epistle to Philemon was rejected by many writers. From the absence of any approach to doctrinal teaching in this Epistle, they concluded that it was not by St. Paul, or that, if it was his, it did not belong to the canon, since it contained nothing by which the Church might be edified. This decision arose out of a narrow view of the canon, and the primitive Church, as a whole, did not ratify the verdict. Preserved at first as a precious relic in the family of Philemon, this apostolic document was subsequently placed among the archives of the Church at Colosse, in the house of one of its elders. We find the first mention of it, as forming part of the Pauline collection, in the writings of Marcion, son of the Bishop of Sinope in Pontus, who about the year 140 went to Rome from Asia Minor. Soon after this it finds a definite place in the Canon of Muratori, in the fragment found at Milan in the middle of the last century, which dates from about the year 170, and contains a list of the writings received and publicly read at that time in one of the Western Churches, either that of Italy, or more probably that of Africa.

We observe, moreover, that the Epistle to Philemon formed part of the Western canon, included in the old Latin translation, usually called *Itala*, and that in the Church most remote from this, the Church of Syria, it also found a place in the authorised translation of the Scriptures, the *Peshito*, in the latter part of the second century.

It is obvious then that the Church very early learned to appreciate the importance of this brief letter. It differs undoubtedly from the other writings of the Apostle, inasmuch as it refers to a purely personal and private matter. But this private matter came within the scope of the work which Christianity was to accomplish among men. And even if it had not been so, how full of interest for us must be the one opportunity supplied by this letter of studying the character of the Apostle Paul in this private relation which brings him into such close contact with our daily life.

We read in Col. iv. 7 that when the Apostle sent to Colosse the letter intended for the Church of that city, he entrusted it to one of his fellow-helpers named Tychicus, and that Tychicus was accompanied by another brother—Onesimus—whom Paul describes by the honourable terms, "faithful and beloved," and speaks of him as "one of us." It is impossible to doubt that this Onesimus is the subject of the Epistle to Philemon, and that it also was therefore sent to Colosse. If any doubt at all existed on this point, it would be set aside by the statement of Theodoret, a Syrian bishop of the fifth century, who says positively that "the house of Philemon at Colosse was still standing in his time."

In the city of Colosse, in the beautiful basin of the Lycus in Phrygia, there lived then at this time a rich citizen named Philemon. This man, as we gather from the Epistle, had been brought by Paul himself to the knowledge of Christ; and as Paul had never visited the Churches of the district in which Colosse was (Col. ii. 1), we must conclude that the rich Phrygian burgher had been converted by the Apostle at Ephesus during a visit which he paid to that capital. The wife of Philemon, we find from the second verse of the Epistle, was named Apphia, and as Paul mentions immediately afterwards in the same

verse the name of Archippus, it is highly probable that this third personage was no other than their son.

Chrysostom indeed speaks of Archippus as a friend of the house, and Theodoret supposes him to have been a Christian teacher receiving the hospitality of Philemon; but these suppositions are not so natural. To us it seems more probable that Archippus, as a young Christian and the son of Philemon, should have been entrusted (in the absence of Epaphras, who had gone to Rome to see Paul) with the care of the Church at Colosse, and that it was in order to make him feel the responsibility resting upon him, that in the Epistle to the Colossians Paul wrote these words: "Say to Archippus, Take heed to the ministry thou hast received in the Lord, that thou fulfil it."

The Greek and Roman names of this household show what a hold the authority of Rome and the culture of Greece had taken of the once barbarous nations of Asia Minor.

After saluting the three principal members of the family, Paul goes on to greet the Church gathered in the house. This does not mean simply the household of Philemon; the name *Church* does not allow of such a restricted signification. On the other hand, the distributive preposition *κατά* equally excludes the whole body of Christians at Colosse. It refers rather to that portion of the Church which was accustomed to meet in the house of Philemon.

But it may be asked, if Paul was writing to Philemon on a private matter, why should he have addressed his letter to the section of the Church of which Philemon's house was the centre? And out of this question arises another. Why should he have associated the name of Timothy with his own in such a letter?

It must be admitted that the case of Onesimus interested in some degree the whole of the little community that was wont to meet in the house of Philemon. They had all heard of the wrongdoing and of the flight of his slave; and now that Onesimus had come back as a Christian, Paul wished to secure for him from them all the same brotherly welcome which he desired Philemon and his family to give him. Hence he wrote commending Onesimus to the confidence and love of them all. It was doubtless with the same end in view that he introduced the name of Timothy. Perhaps Timothy had himself visited Colosse. At any rate his recommendation would take away any semblance of favouritism or personal weakness on the part of Paul. That which Paul asked as the "prisoner of Jesus Christ," Timothy asked in the name of the Christian brotherhood (" Timothy our brother ") which united him to the Church at Colosse and formed a plea for the kindly reception of the new brother. We hear nothing further, however, of Timothy in the letter, and Paul speaks throughout in the first person singular, because it was really his affection for and personal interest in Onesimus which made him write.

What was the wrongdoing which had caused Onesimus to run away? The Apostle refers to it in *v.* 18. The expressions used do not necessarily imply that the fugitive slave had committed a theft. They may be explained on the supposition that he had been guilty of culpable negligence which had brought serious loss on his master. However this may be, it was the fear of well-merited punishment which had caused Onesimus to run away. Where had he escaped to? and where had he met Paul? Many commentators think that it was at Cæsarea, in Palestine, where Paul was kept a prisoner from the summer of 59 to the autumn of 61. It is urged in favour of this opinion that Cæsarea was less distant from Colosse than Rome. But a fugitive slave does not seek to hide as near as possible to his master, and it was far easier to get from Ephesus to Rome than to Cæsarea. The runaway would obviously be much less likely to be found by

his master in the great capital of the world than in the little residence of Cæsarea. The other reasons urged in favour of Cæsarea are still more feeble and bordering on the absurd, as the reader may judge by reading those alleged by Meyer. We have already observed, in our paper on the Epistle to the Colossians, how much more natural it seems to date that Epistle from Rome than from Cæsarea, and this would suffice to decide the question with regard to Philemon. We find moreover in *v.* 22 what seems to me an irrefutable argument to show that that letter was written during the captivity in Rome, that is, between the spring of the years 62 and 64.

Let us now turn to the Epistle itself.

A modern commentator has shrewdly observed that the Epistle to Philemon was a practical commentary on the injunction of the Apostle in the Epistle to the Colossians (iv. 6): "Let your speech be always with grace seasoned with salt." As we study the letter in detail, we shall be struck with the truth of this remark.

In the opening words *v.* 1–3, the Apostle speaks of himself as the prisoner of Jesus Christ, delicately substituting this description for the usual one, "servant of Jesus Christ." He is indeed at this time fulfilling his apostolic calling, not by active missionary labours, but by bonds and imprisonment.[1] This thought is well adapted to open the heart of Philemon to grant the request Paul has to make. He calls Philemon his "beloved and fellow worker," because when he became a Christian, he had placed his strength, his property, and his life at the service of the same work in which Paul himself was engaged—the salvation of men (*v.* 6). In *v.* 2 he gives Archippus a somewhat different title. He calls him his "fellow soldier," because, as Epaphras' deputy, he had to contend at Colosse for the truth, and specially to combat the false doctrine which threatened to invade the Church.

[1] The expression is equivalent to "captive servant of Jesus Christ."

These opening words are followed, as usual in Paul's epistles, by thanksgiving for that which God has already wrought in the readers, followed by a prayer for the continuance and increase of the work (*v.* 4–7). In *v.* 5 the Apostle says: "hearing of thy love," and not as in the corresponding passage of the Epistle to the Ephesians (i. 15) "hearing of the faith in the Lord Jesus which is among you." The conversion of the readers of the Epistle to the Ephesians was an *accomplished fact*, of which the Apostle had been assured once for all, while the love of Philemon was a present and constant disposition of mind, the ever new manifestations of which gladdened the heart of Paul. The Apostle adds, "and of the faith which thou hast toward the Lord Jesus, and toward all the saints." It is not without advertence that Paul brings out in this instance alone, the faith which a Christian should have, not only towards the Lord, but also toward those who belong to Him. He had spoken of faith in an analogous sense in 1 Cor. xiii. 7. "Love covereth all things, believeth all things." In speaking of the faith which Philemon has not only in the Lord, but also in the work of grace which the Lord can perform in the heart of the vilest of men, Paul is certainly thinking of the welcome he is about to ask for him who was formerly the unfaithful slave; which welcome must depend entirely on the confidence felt by Philemon in the work of grace wrought in Onesimus. A succession of disappointing experiences often produces among Christians, particularly among those who are older, a religious scepticism which paralyses love and kills enthusiasm. The good there is in the saints must be always with their fellow Christians, a matter of faith. It was this faith toward all the saints which was about to be tested in the case of Philemon.

In thanking God for this gift bestowed on him, there is an implied exhortation that he should be faithful to it in

the case in question. In *v.* 6 Paul gives the substance of his prayers for his friend Philemon.

"*The fellowship of thy faith*," must refer to the beneficent communications of which his faith is the source.[1] These become more and more abundant and effectual by the knowledge of the beauty and holiness of the work which God performs in Christians,[2] *to the glory of Jesus Christ*, through whom it is done. In desiring for Philemon a growing knowledge of the work of God in his brethren, Paul certainly wishes to prepare him to recognise with gladness and confidence the, to him, almost incredible change wrought in Onesimus. We see how free Paul's style is from anything that is stereotyped. Every word has its peculiar fitness. The language of the Apostle is the ever fresh garb of a truth ever new.

After this preamble the Apostle passes to the subject of his letter, the commendation of Onesimus to his master. But before making his request, as he does in *v.* 17, he carefully prepares the way (*v.* 9–16).

In *v.* 8, 9, he reminds Philemon who it is who makes this claim on him; it is he who, as the apostle of Jesus Christ, might have all boldness to declare to Philemon the will of the Lord, and to enjoin him what was fitting to do under the circumstances. But he prefers to appeal to his heart, asking that of him as a proof of his love which he might have enjoined as a duty. His claims to the affection of Philemon are all comprised in that name *Paul*, which recalls to him so many memories, and in those two epistles which renders its appeal still more forcible, "the aged," and "a prisoner." Paul's age at this time would be about fifty-five. His conversion took place in the year 36 or 37, and he could not have been then less than thirty years old. Had he been younger than this he would not have been

[1] The active sense of the word κοινωνία is proved by Rom. xv. 26.
[2] The reading "*in us*" is certainly to be preferred to "*in you*."

competent to receive from the Sanhedrim the important commission entrusted to him. But the labours, the sufferings, the persecutions he had endured, had prematurely aged him, and he knew well how these two words, "aged" and "a prisoner," would touch the heart of Philemon.

After thus reminding Philemon who it is that asks, he goes on to speak of the one for whom he intercedes. He is careful not to name him at first, knowing what painful associations the name would call up. He begins by describing the close bond which his conversion had formed between himself as the spiritual father and this child whom he had begotten in his bonds. And only after this does he mention him by his name Onesimus, which means "helpful," and which would be merely ironical if applied to the part played by him in the house of Philemon, but which has become now a true description, because of the kindly offices he has already done for Paul, and is anxious now to do for Philemon also if he will consent to forgive and receive him back. Paul is evidently playing here upon the name of the slave, but not as a mere *jeu de mots* to display his wit; rather as a delicate way of recommending the faithful slave to his master, by substituting for the remembrance of his past failures the hope of the services he might now render. It is in this capacity of a servant who will prove himself in the future worthy of his name (helpful) that Paul sends him back.

The same idea—"profitable to thee and to me" (*v.* 11) —is worked out in the succeeding verses. Only we must rectify the unfortunate modification introduced by the copyists in *v.* 12—"thou therefore receive him that is mine own bowels," which is an anticipation of the request in *v.* 17. According to the best manuscripts, *v.* 12 ought to read simply, "whom I have sent back to thee in his own person, that is, my very heart (or mine own bowels)." This expression is very common in Latin (*mea viscera, cor*

meum), meaning that which fills my heart. The sense is: "He is one with me in such a way that whatever you do to gladden him, my bowels will feel it as if done to myself."

Ver. 13, 14 enlarge on this idea of the value of Onesimus to Paul himself. He would fain have kept him in Rome, as an evangelist, all the more that his captivity rendered such help very needful to him. But he had refrained, not wishing to anticipate that which Philemon might feel prompted to do of his own accord, in granting the Apostle this welcome help. Paul does not wish to take Onesimus away from Philemon. If he is privileged to have his help, it shall be as a living proof of Philemon's affection for himself.

In *v.* 13 the Apostle says "that in thy behalf (ὑπὲρ σοῦ) he might minister unto me." This explains *v.* 15, 16, in which Paul enlarges on what Onesimus is to become to Philemon himself. Providence had perhaps permitted all that had happened in order that the temporary relation of master and slave, in which Philemon and Onesimus had stood to each other, might be exchanged for the eternal relationship of brothers in the Lord. Not that Philemon must on that account necessarily keep Onesimus with him; on the contrary, Paul has just hinted (*v.* 13, 14) at his hope that Philemon might perhaps spare Onesimus to him. But in this way the master would really benefit by the service of his slave; for the services which Onesimus would render to Paul in his Roman prison would be the very same kind offices which Philemon himself would gladly do him if he could. This is the explanation of the words, "on thy behalf," in *v.* 13. In *v.* 16, Paul says, "a brother beloved specially to me, but how much more to thee, both in the flesh and in the Lord." These words show how little even slavery excluded the gentler domestic affections. Onesimus is henceforward beloved by Paul as by no one else ("specially to me") unless it be by Philemon, in whom the old affection of the master will now be reinforced by the new affection of the brother in Christ ("both in the flesh and in the Lord"). Before leaving this passage, which is one of inimitable grace and delicacy, we may call attention to the word "*perhaps*" at the beginning of *v.* 15. The Apostle is going to try and show the good results of the parting "for a season" of Onesimus from his master. But it is always very difficult to interpret the ways of Providence, especially when man's own misdoing has to be taken into the category of causes working for good. Therefore, feeling that it might be rather startling to Philemon to represent Onesimus' offence in this light, Paul discreetly adds "*perhaps.*" God might no doubt have brought about the conversion of Onesimus by some other means; but as a matter of fact He had condescended thus to overrule evil for good.

After these preliminaries, each one of which has its due weight in the balance, the Apostle at length comes (*v.* 17–21) to the request he wants to make. He has reminded Philemon who it is that asks—Paul the aged and a prisoner; he has said who it is for whom he pleads—his own son in the faith, and henceforth a brother to Philemon, one capable of doing immense service to the Apostle in the great work laid upon him and which is dearer than aught else to the heart of Philemon also. He thus comes in *v.* 17 to the request which is the keynote of this short epistle. "If then thou countest me a partner, receive him as myself." Let us imagine Paul arriving at Colosse and knocking at Philemon's door. What rejoicings there would be through the whole household, alike in master and slaves! What delight in all hearts, on all faces! Just such a welcome he now asks for the wandering sheep that has come back to the fold. His request is not only for pardon and complete restoration, but also for the welcome of a brother in the household of faith.

There remains however one dark spot on the picture. Onesimus had caused considerable loss to Philemon, either by his own dishonesty or by the results of his negligence. In any case the loss had not been made good. Here then Paul offers himself as security for the reparation which is still due. "If he hath wronged thee at all, or oweth thee aught, put that to mine account." This offer might scarcely appear serious. In order that his reader may see that it is so, Paul repeats emphatically, "I, Paul, have written it with mine own hand, I will repay it."

Some interpreters have supposed that Paul wrote only this passage of the letter with his own hand. This seems to me a strained and childish explanation. He meant to call attention to the fact that, the whole letter being written by himself, the offer contained in these last words was well guaranteed: "I will repay it: *I* (ἐγώ), Paul, have written it with mine own hand." The past tense, "*I have written,*" is a common form in Greek, by which the writer places himself by the side of the reader when the communication is received.

Bonâ fide as the offer is, it is clear that the Apostle thinks it impossible that Philemon will accept it; therefore he adds: "that I say not unto thee how that thou owest to me even thine own self besides"; which evidently implies that beyond the remission of this debt, Philemon owes himself, all that he is and all that he has, to St. Paul, inasmuch as he owes to him his eternal salvation.

In contrast to such unworthy conduct on the part of Philemon as demanding the payment of this debt by Paul, (who has, even in that case, taken the burden upon his own shoulders and released Onesimus), the Apostle goes on to describe in loving words what he really expects from his old convert: "Yea, brother, let me have joy of thee in the Lord; refresh my heart in Christ." It is in Christ that he pleads; in Christ that he hopes to gain a hearing;

and this granting of his request will remove any uneasiness he might have felt for his dear son Onesimus. He hopes for even more than the obedience to which he feels he has a just claim. He is confident that Philemon will do beyond what he asks. Are not these words sufficiently clear? How can they have been misconstrued by so many commentators? De Wette, who sees the idea of the enfranchisement of Onesimus already expressed in *v.* 16 (ὑπὲρ δοῦλον), thinks that here something more is asked, some further benefit to be granted to Onesimus with his liberty. Meyer and Wiesinger, who refuse to see even here a request for the emancipation of Onesimus, also regard these words as indicating some special benefaction to be added to the pardon granted him.

We can but hope that Philemon read the thought of Paul more truly than these interpreters. Paul had clearly asked him to give up Onesimus to him for the work of an evangelist. Now it is perfectly plain that such a gift must imply the liberation of Onesimus, and that this is what Paul means by the words, "knowing that thou wilt do even beyond what I say." The Apostle has been accused of sanctioning the institution of slavery by restoring to his master a slave who had escaped from the yoke. On the contrary, the way in which Paul sends him back, reminding his master that it is not a slave, but one better than a slave, a brother beloved who returns to him, contains the moral premisses from which must follow, not only the immediate emancipation of that one slave, but the ultimate abrogation of slavery itself.

We have seen that the Epistles of Paul usually conclude with some personal references, greetings and commissions to the various brethren. It is so in this Epistle. There is something very touching in the request to Philemon in *v.* 22. Paul has just been asking him to receive Onesimus as himself; now he adds, as though with a smile,

"Withal prepare me also a lodging; for I hope that through your prayers I shall be granted unto you." If there remained any doubt about this letter being written from Rome, these words would be conclusive. When Paul was imprisoned at Cæsarea, he had just taken leave, and as he believed for ever, of the Churches in Asia Minor (Acts xx. 22), and all his thoughts were turned towards Rome. How could he at that time have been cherishing the hope of again visiting Colosse? In order to do so, he would have had to cross by sea from Cæsarea to Ephesus, and travel thence inland to Colosse; or to traverse the whole of Asia Minor, passing through Phrygia. We know that nothing was farther from the Apostle's thoughts than such a journey. But the case was altogether different when, after his captivity in Cæsarea, he had already passed one or two years in Rome. Circumstances had materially changed in the East, and particularly in Asia Minor. Colosse itself was in danger through the introduction of false doctrine. The evil had come of which he had forewarned the Ephesian elders (Acts xx. 29). "I know that after my departing grievous wolves shall enter in among you, not sparing the flock." Before starting for Spain, the extreme limit of the then known world, and so cutting himself off finally from his old field of labour, the Apostle had a longing to go once more to the East to consolidate his work there. He expresses the same desire in writing from Rome to the Church at Philippi (Phil. ii. 24). "I trust in the Lord that I myself also shall come shortly." It may be said that the Apostle thus himself contradicts his farewell words to the elders of Ephesus (Acts xx. 25). "Now behold I know that ye all among whom I went about preaching the kingdom, shall see my face no more." But in any case the contradiction remains between these words and the passage in Philippians which we have just quoted, a passage which, as all critics agree, must have been written from Rome. At the time when the Apostle took leave of the elders of Asia, he was leaving for the West, to fulfil a mission which, as far as he could judge, would absorb all the rest of his life, and it was very natural that he should look upon his farewell as final. And even if this presentiment had not proved true, there would have been nothing contrary to apostolic inspiration, rightly understood; for that inspiration only extended to the great facts of salvation. (See the Pastoral Epistles.)

The salutations contained in *v.* 23, 24 are the same as those in the Epistle to the Colossians, with the exception of those addressed to the Church at Colosse generally and to neighbouring Churches. These would have been inappropriate in a private letter.

After this detailed study of this short Epistle, which is at once so simple and so *naïf*, so full of heart and fine of wit; so appropriate to the particular circumstances, and, with all its playfulness so earnest, we find it difficult to understand how any critic could ever have been found to call in question its genuineness. This has been done, however, by Ferdinand Baur, who, to use his own expression, discerns in this Epistle "the embryo of a Christian novel, in which the author proposed to illustrate by a short narrative this great idea: that that which is lost in this world and for time, is found again in Christianity for all eternity. It was in order to work out the idea that the Gospel united for ever those who have been severed for a time by outward circumstances, that the unknown author conceived this fiction of the relation between Onesimus, Paul, and Philemon." Only a theologian very much preoccupied with erudite ideas, could have come to regard the simple fact which forms the basis of the Epistle to Philemon as only the fictitious illustration of a theory; or rather the author must have been very much driven into a corner by the consequences of his own system before he could

have invented such a way of escape. Baur was forced by his own theory of primitive Christianity to deny the authenticity of the Epistle to the Colossians, because the Christology of that Epistle was inconsistent with the limitations which he had laid down for the Apostle Paul, and approached too nearly the theology of the Apostle John. Now the Epistles to the Colossians and to Philemon are so closely linked together that it would be impossible to accept the one and reject the other. Hence Baur was compelled to sacrifice this innocent little Epistle, and to perpetrate a sort of critical murder.

We are now in a position to estimate the full importance of this short Scripture, and to pay our tribute to the wisdom of those who were not afraid to give it a place in the canon of the New Testament. It brings out two points of inestimable value and interest. First: It shows us what St. Paul was in little things. We know what he was in the treatment of great principles, and in carrying out the main work of his life, his mission to the Gentiles. But there are many great philanthropists who have undertaken to reform the world, and yet in their private life have shown themselves the proudest, most hard and self-seeking of men. In theory they have been full of the love of humanity; in fact, full of self-love. The Divine charity which the love of God had enkindled in the heart of Paul showed itself in little unnoticed things no less than in the great overt acts of his public life. We see him in this letter concerned (and with what tender solicitude!) for the reception which a poor guilty slave would meet with from his master. He writes in his behalf a letter as carefully considered, both in form and substance, as those which he addressed to the Churches of Rome and of Corinth. He throws as much heart into it as if the gravest interests of his apostleship were involved. And in order to show the importance he attached to it, instead of dictating it, as was his custom, he writes it with his own hand. Such is the difference between true Christian love and that of mere humanitarian reformers.

This Epistle brings out secondly the marked difference between the Gospel method of action and the way in which men set to work to accomplish social revolutions. It was not by calling on the unhappy slaves to rise in armed rebellion against their masters that the Gospel struck off their fetters. It rather melted them by the fervour of Christian love, and so penetrated society with the principles of the Gospel that emancipation became a necessity.

The Epistle to Philemon was the first indication of the tendency in this direction, and may therefore be fairly called the first petition in favour of the abolition of slavery. In this respect Wilberforce was but a follower of St. Paul.

F. Godet.

infancy. Luke tells us of the birth and infancy of John the Baptist; the Annunciation; the meeting of Mary and Elizabeth; the songs of the Herald Angels; of our Lord's circumcision and presentation in the Temple; of our Saviour's growth in wisdom and knowledge, and favour with God and man. He alone preserves the one anecdote of our Lord's confirmation at twelve years old. Luke records the life of our Saviour before birth, (1:42); as a boy (2:40); and as a man (3:22).

The early Church Fathers were relentless in their opposition to cruelty to children.

> "The wicked alone can expose his children; for us, this impiety only inspires horror: first, because the most of these unfortunate little ones are destined for debauch; then, because we would fear the accusation of murder if they should die". Clement says, "Man is more cruel to his offspring than animals".
>
> Brace, 1897, p. 77

The great obstacle to reform, however, was the prolific and terrible pauperism of the Roman Empire. When, under Constantine, the spirit of Christianity began to affect Roman legislation on this subject, there came up always the practical difficulty—what shall be done with the exposed child? He will only be preserved from death by those who would make a slave of him. To forbid such slavery may only increase the evils of exposure. These difficulties constantly modified legislation on this evil. Constantine, in the year AD 315, was obliged to issue the following proclamation:

> Let a law be at once promulgated in all the towns of Italy, to turn parents from using a parricidal hand on their new-born children, and to dispose their hearts to the best sentiments. Watch with care over this, that, if a father brings his child, saying that he cannot support it, one should supply him without delay with food and clothing; for the cares of the new-born suffer no delay, and we order that our revenue, as well as our treasure, aid this expense.
>
> Brace, 1897, p. 78

Further Constantine announced in AD 321:

> We have learned that the inhabitants of provinces suffering from scarcity of food, sell and put in pledge their children. We command then that those found in this situation, without any personal resource, and only being able with great trouble to support their

> children, be succoured by our treasury before they fall under the blows of poverty; for it is repugnant to our morals that any one under our empire should be punished by hunger to commit a crime.
>
> Brace, 1897, p. 78

Constantine was further obliged in AD 331 to enact the following law:

> In view of the increasing calamities of the Empire, anyone "taking up" an exposed infant had the power to adopt him as a child, or to keep him as a slave, and the natural father had no right to reclaim him. He was however permitted to obtain his child again, if he pays the full price, or replaced him by another slave.
>
> Brace, 1897, p. 78

> In 553, Justinian invited the Archbishop and Prefect of Thessalonica to give to exposed infants all the assistance possible, while threatening a severe fine on all who disobeyed. [80]
>
> Houses of mercy for children were founded also by Justinian. The churches and Church charities became refuges for this unfortunate class. Christian charity attempted to alleviate the great evil which law could not correct or the usual spirit of humanity prevent. A marble vessel was provided for exposed infants at the door of each church. In a later age, this simple provision of humanity was imitated in a manner which produced great evils, in the well-known 'turning-slide' (*tour*) of French asylums for foundlings.
>
> Brace, 1897, pp. 80–81

However, Christian charity early began efforts to relieve these evils and we find systems for their protection gradually developing and becoming more sophisticated and effective. In the year AD 787, Archbishop Datheus of Milan reported:

> I desire that as soon as an infant shall be exposed in church, he be received by the superintendent of the hospital, and entrusted to the care of nurses employed for this purpose. These children are to learn a trade, and when they have arrived at the age of eight years, I desire that they be freed from all servitude, and be at liberty to go and dwell where they please".
>
> Brace, 1897, p. 83

It was certainly the case that Christianity sounded the death knell of the maltreatment of children, and with every successive generation, society increasingly recognised that their helpless condition constituted a claim on the compassion of adults.

> The eighteenth century furnishes us with an instance to show how little value is set on child-life when the sanctions of religion lose their power. It is stated on unimpeachable authority (his own) that Rousseau sent his five children to the Foundling Hospital. Even in the Nineteenth Century there were ominous indications of a similar callousness arising from a similar indifference to religion. Some years ago, a French writer, J. K.-Huysmans advocated the legalization of infanticide, and denounced St. Vincent de Paul for his "odious precautions in deferring for years the death of creatures without intelligence".
>
> Footnote 2 in Jones, 1903, p. 167

The situation as we have it today demonstrates this principle even more tragically and starkly.

Perhaps we could say of all the practical changes which Christianity encouraged and commenced in the history of the world, the respect for and value of children is one of the most important, as it affects the foundation of all society and government, and influences the far distant future.

(6) *Christianity raising the status of women*

Under the Hebrew system found in the Old Testament, the position of women was relatively high, in comparison with that afforded her in the surrounding nations. She certainly was granted more liberty, and a greater variety of opportunities and employments than found amongst many other people of that time. The Hebrews honoured Miriam who led other women in triumphant song at the overthrow of her people's enemies. Deborah was a leader of armies and was also a prophetess and a judge. Hannah's song of thanksgiving is given a high place amongst their literature, and women like Huldah were consulted alike by High Priest and king. The tribute to womanhood in the 31st chapter of the Book of Proverbs is a perfect description of this high regard.

In the New Testament, much honour is given to women such as of course the Virgin Mary, Elizabeth mother of John the Baptist and many others who played important and honoured roles in the life of the early Church. The Gospel of Luke particularly emphasises the honour given to women. Luke records the graciousness and tenderness of Christ towards many women in the course of his ministry. He tells us how our Lord raised from the dead the widow of Nain's son, being touched with compassion because "he was the only son of his mother, and she was a widow" (Luke 7:12). Luke alone tells us of the remarkable fact that our Lord, in his earlier mission journeys, was accompanied not by warriors like David, or by elders like Moses, nor by nobles and kings like the Herods, but by a humble band of ministering women (Luke 8:1–3). His narrative in the first two chapters must have been derived from the testimony of the Virgin Mary and has been thought to show in every line the pure and tender colouring of a woman's thoughts. He alone mentions the widow Anna (Luke 2:36), and tells us about eager Martha cumbered with serving, and Mary choosing the better part (Luke 10:38–42). He alone showed how our Lord once addressed a poor, crushed, trembling, and humiliated woman with the tender name of "daughter" (Luke 8:48). Further, Jesus spoke of another as the daughter of Abraham (Luke 13:16); he alone tells how our Lord had once consoled and warned the "daughters of Jerusalem", who followed him weeping to Calvary (Luke 23:28). The scribes and Pharisees gathered up their robes in the streets and synagogues in case they should touch a woman and held it a crime to look on a veiled woman in public; our Lord suffered a woman to minister to him out of whom he had cast seven devils (Luke 8:2–3).

However, in the surrounding nations, the role of women was not in any way so highly respected. The greatest of the Greek philosophers represented the State as radically disorganised in which wives should claim to be equal to their husbands. Aristotle regarded women as beings of a certain intermediate order between free men and slaves. Plato suggested a community of wives, on the ground that children so brought into life would be more wholly devoted to the State. It was only the women recognised as unchaste who were permitted to frequent public lectures, and to be on terms of equal association with artists and scholars. An Athenian daughter legally inherited nothing from her father. In that society, a woman was always regarded as a minor, and never free. "A woman's glory was", as Pericles said, "that no one should speak of her". It was declared that a woman is never fit for independence.

A similar attitude to women was also held in Roman civilisation as well as in many of the other civilisations of the ancient world. We have already noted the high level of exposure of female babies at birth. Even philosophers like Seneca stigmatised women as "foolish, wild creatures, unable to control their lusts". Divorce, both by men and women, was however extensive. Juvenal spoke of a woman who had eight husbands within five years. Tertullian said that divorce was the very purpose and end of Roman marriage.

Though in Roman society there were significant numbers of instances where women, while retaining their virtue, and in spite of their sex, rose to distinguished positions, there was still a negative image of females.

> It was said by Metellus, the Roman Censor, that if nature had allowed man to exist without women, he would have been spared a troublesome companion, and that marriage could only be recommended as a sacrifice of pleasure to public duty.
>
> Storrs, 1884, p. 149

> Habitual and contemptuous distrust of women was in the very life of the governing classes of Rome. It ruled custom, shaped statutes, and entered with depriving and dominating force the highest minds. Seneca wrote with passionate outbreaks against the women of his time, though he is almost singular among philosophers of the more refined class for speaking with affection and honour of his mother (Helvia). One would not know from any allusion in the manifold and elaborate writings of Cicero that he ever had one. Pliny speaks in his letters, with urbane complacency, of the excellency of his wife; but it seems to have been largely because she gratified his vanity by admiring both his writings and himself, and singing his verses to the cithern [ED. a stringed instrument]; and he applauds the example of a friend who celebrated the funeral of his wife with a fight of gladiators, only regretting that the African panthers intended for the occasion had been delayed by stormy weather.
>
> Storrs, 1884, p. 150

> In revolt against the system so harshly oppressive towards Roman women, because founded on a conception of their nature so false and debased, there came into use a form of free marriage, in which the wife retained relationship to her kindred and control of her property, and under which either she or the husband could perfect a divorce by giving to the other a written declaration of a wish to that effect. Concubinage, too, became customary, familiar, and was legalised by Augustus. The tendency to moral laxity, starting in such a natural

> reaction against the offensive and tyrannical radical strictness of previous rules, went swiftly forward, till at last the wrongs which had for ages been inflicted on women in civilised Europe were terribly avenged in the downfall of the Empire before those fierce Germanic hosts who had associated their women most closely with themselves, both in toil and in battle, and the stern chastity of those daughters and wives to whom even Tacitus, sad and cynical as he was, pays honourable tribute.
>
> Storrs, 1884, pp. 150–151

The influence of Christianity however brought an almost instantaneous improvement in the way that women were regarded. We have already noted that the Lord himself included women amongst his devoted disciples.

> Women had been the first converts in Europe: Lydia at Philippi, the honourable women at Thessalonica, the woman named Damaris—another Athenian Magdalen she may have been—upon Mars' Hill, the Priscilla whose name is more than once placed before her husband's, as if to indicate a certain conceded and beautiful leadership in her genius and spirit.
>
> Storrs, 1884, p. 151

We find salutations addressed to them in the Epistles. Second John is addressed to, "The elect lady and her children"—though many regard this to be a reference to the Church. The grandmother Lois, the mother of Eunice, is remembered by Paul in his prison in Rome. Women were later to show their faith and courage in the arena and at the stake.

Well might Libanius, a pagan orator, exclaim with envy, "What women these Christians have!"

It is no exaggeration to say that the standard of character, and of moral aspiration, was rapidly and permanently raised amongst women as a result of the influence of Christianity. Monogamy was made to be universal in the Church and marriage became a free and solemn covenant for life, taking even a near sacramental character.

> The tendency of Christianity always has been—to give to women larger opportunities, more effective control of all instruments for work: to put her side-by-side with man in front of all the great achievements, in letters, arts, humanities, missions, as illustrated by the majestic south portal of Strasbourg Cathedral where the figure of

> Sabina, maiden and architect, faces the figure of Erwin of Steinbach; and though the old traditions of law are hard to change, the entire movement of modern society is toward the perfect enfranchisement of the sex to which the religion brought by Jesus Christ gave at the outset pre-eminent honour.
>
> Storrs, 1884, p. 153

Outside Christianity pagan girls were usually married off at a very young age, usually to much older men, and rarely had they any choice in the matter. The Cambridge historian Keith Hopkins argues that it was possible to calculate that many famous Roman women had been child brides: Octavia (daughter of the Emperor Claudius) married at eleven years old. Nero's mother Agrippina married at twelve years old; Quintilian, the famous rhetorician must have married a twelve-year-old, since we know she bore him a son when she was thirteen; the historian Tacitus married a thirteen-year-old, and so on. However, in none of these instances was this fact seen as sufficiently interesting to be mentioned in the women's biographies. Plutarch (46–120) reported that Romans, "gave their girls in marriage when they were twelve years old, or even younger". Another Roman historian Dio Cassius (AD 155–229) stated: "Girls are considered to have reached marriageable age on completion of their twelfth year".

Very few Christian girls suffered similar fates. Most married when they were physically and emotionally mature; most had a say in whom they married and enjoyed a far more secure marriage. (Stark, 1966, p. 128)

(7) *Christianity elevating the concept of home*

It would not be an exaggeration to say that the reality of a happy family life is the direct creation of Christianity. Farrar said:

> '*Familia*' to the ear of a Roman meant a multitude of idle, corrupt, and corrupting slaves, kept in subjection by the cross and the *ergastulum*, ready for any treachery, and reeking with every vice. It meant a despot who could kill his slaves when they were aged, and expose his children when they were born; it meant that matrons among whom virtue was rare, divorce was frequent, remarriage easy, and who, for no stronger motive than that of vanity, sacrificed the lives of their infants yet unborn; it meant, children spectators from their infancy of insolence and cruelty, incivility and sin. But the

new faith, while it sanctioned the authority of parents, checked their despotism; it made marriage sacred and indissoluble; it encircled the position of womanhood with all that was pure and divine, and tender, in the names of mother and wife.

For families in which, like sheltered flowers, spring up all that is purest and sweetest in human lives; for marriage exalted to an almost sacramental dignity; for all that circle of heavenly blessings which result from common self-sacrifice; for that beautiful unison of noble manhood, stainless womanhood, joyous infancy, and uncontaminated youth; in one word, for all that there is of divinity and sweetness in one word *Home*; for this, to an extent which we can hardly realise, we are indebted to Christianity alone.

Farrar, 1875, pp. 182–183

The Christian view was that the child was of the kingdom of heaven. The fact that Christ was born of a woman lifted the concept of womanhood from the depths to a high pedestal. Christianity certainly taught reverence and respect for women, as it at the same time expected a high degree of purity and devotion from women, and in doing so created a noble ideal of home.

The man who is capable of despising his mother, of disowning or neglecting a wife, or being cruel to a child, is no man; he wants the soul of chivalry. The faith that brought out that great latent passion in man for gentleness to woman and child, has achieved a right noble work, has done a grand thing.

Fairbairn, 1894, p. 204

(8) *Christianity and charities for the alleviation of the hardships of the poor and needy*

[We do not know] how destitute of true and generous action the ancient world was! It was a new thing that Lucian laughed at—the sight of Christians visiting the prisons and ministering to the captives. He thought them simpletons, weak people who offered themselves as easy prey to the designing and crafty. He did not know that their act expressed a new passion, the enthusiasm of humanity, and had in it the promise of redemption for the world. It was a new thing, despised of many a man, to see poverty relieved, to see disease nursed, to see pestilence faced … (yet) when the barbarian hordes swept over Italy or across Africa or into Spain, rich Pagans

> fled far into their retreats, and left pestilence and famine and death to rage as they listed. But brave men like Ambrose and Augustine, faced the desolation and death. The matrons and the maids of the new faith went out to nurse in hospitals, in churches, by many a bedside, creating, where only misery had been, a sweet and gentle peace. The religion of Christ created charity; at its very birth it stood forth to organize the beneficence of man into the instrument of the providence of God.
>
> Fairbairn, 1894, pp. 204–205

Previous to its coming, amongst the pagan world there had been no suggestion of right behaviour between man and man, set out in the prevailing religions. The general attitude was that the individual existed for the interest of the state; and classes thus inevitably arose, with rights varying according to their position in society. One class held no responsibility for the other and it is said that Plautus remarked that "a man is a wolf to another man whom he does not know". Pericles is also reputed to have said that "poor and hungry, being condemned by their appeals for assistance, should be expelled from marketplace and city and the country be cleared of that sort of animal". (Adapted from Storrs, 1884, p. 164)

John Stuart Mill in an essay *On Liberty* given in 1863 criticises the Christian scheme as dwelling too little on public duties and public virtues. He was answered by Richard S. Storrs as follows.

> It is characteristic of the school of thought represented by him, which expects some time to regenerate man by improving his conditions, rather than to improve his conditions by regenerating the man. But I read in face of his critical words the words of St Paul—the manliest, most intrepid and high-minded person whom the age of Seneca presents to our view—"I am debtor both to the Greeks and to the Barbarians; both to the wise and to the unwise" (Romans 1:14) and there I see not merely the temper which made that trained and converted Cilician a master-builder in civilisation, but the temper which afterwards shot forth its missions on every side, and which enabled the early Fathers, in the midst of the fearful oppressions of the Empire, to see slavery, with its pagan theory of two races, falling at last before the holy words of Jesus that all men are brothers, as the children of God.
>
> We sharply object to the vast Church-establishment which ruled

> Europe for centuries; but it is, at least, to be remembered to its honour, that obscurity of birth, poverty of resources, weakness of the frame, were not barriers to eminence in it, and that some of its chief prelates and princes came from the classes from which in Athens slaves were supplied, which in Rome were content with bread and the games. The one English Pope, Adrian IV, who held himself lord of Barbarossa and who fought him with relentless severity, while he claimed to bestow the sovereignty of Ireland on the English monarch, was so ignorant at the outset that the monks of St Albans would not receive him, and he became a servant in a monastery at Avignon. Alexander III, who followed him in the Papacy, from an origin hardly less humble, who conquered Barbarossa, and nearly laid England under an interdict, subduing the stubborn Henry II and forcing him to an ignominious penance, was the same who asserted the general principle that nature has made no man to be a slave, and who has been credited with that scheme of universal liberation which Voltaire declared should make his name dear to the world.
>
> Storrs, 1884, pp. 166, 167

It is the same power from which came the creation of hospitals for the sick, homes for the aged, refuges for the homeless and the orphan, which was the impetus behind the efforts to help the blind, the deaf and the dumb to lead fuller and happier lives. The pages of history, carefully studied, bring more of this spirit of humanity and selfless caring for the well-being of others to light; again we may quote the example of the monks of the German forests and of the Pyrenees who seem to have been the pioneers of work to assist the insane and the mentally handicapped. (Adapted from Storrs, 1884, p. 167)

(9) *Christianity's early impact on legal reforms*

As early as AD 125 the Athenian philosopher Aristides brought before the Emperor Hadrian a defence of the Christian faith, in which he described his fellow believers as follows:

> (T)hey do not commit adultery nor fornication, they do not bear false witness, they do not deny a deposit nor covet what is not theirs: they honour father and mother; they do good to those who are their neighbours, and when they are judges they judge uprightly; and they do not worship idols in the form of man; and whatever they do not wish that others should do to them, they do not practise towards any

> one, and they do not eat of the meats of idol sacrifices, for they are undefiled: and those who grieve them they comfort, and make them their friends; and they do good to their enemies: and their wives, O king, are pure as virgins, and their daughters modest: and their men abstain from all unlawful wedlock and from all impurity, in the hope of the recompense that is to come in another world: but as for their servants or handmaids, or their children, if any of them have any, they persuade them to become Christians for the love that they have towards them; and when they have become so, they call them without distinction brethren: they do not worship strange gods: and they walk in all humility and kindness, and falsehood is not found among them, and they love one another: and from the widows they do not turn away their countenance: and they rescue the orphan from him who does him violence: and he who has, gives to him who has not, without grudging; and when they see the stranger they bring him to their dwellings, and rejoice over him as over a true brother; for they do not call brothers those who are after the flesh, but those who are in the spirit and in God: but when one of their poor passes away from the world, and any of them sees him, then he provides for his burial according to his ability; and if they hear that any of their number is imprisoned or oppressed for the name of their Messiah, all of them provide for his needs, and if it is possible that he may be delivered, they deliver him.
>
> And if there is among them a man that is poor or needy, and they have not an abundance of necessaries, they fast two or three days that they may supply the needy with their necessary food. And they observe scrupulously the commandments of their Messiah: they live honestly and soberly, as the Lord their God commanded them: every morning and at all hours on account of the goodnesses of God toward them they praise and laud Him; and over their food and over their drink they render Him thanks.
>
> Harris, 1891, pp. 105–108

As the early centuries unfolded, permanent legal reforms were set in motion by the Emperors Constantine (272–337), and Justinian (483–565) that can be only attributed to the influence of Christianity. Licentious and cruel sports were prohibited; new legislation was ordered to protect slaves, prisoners, mutilated men, and outcast women. Children were granted important legal status. Infant exposure was abolished. Women were raised from the status of degradation to that of legal protection. A large number of new hospitals and orphanages were created to take care of foundlings. Legislation was issued to curb personal feuds and private wars. In some cities, freedom of conscience was established by law. Branding of slaves was forbidden. Property reforms were instituted. A new spirit pervaded society and it began to be considered the right thing to do to be involved in almsgiving, charity, kindness to others, and the performance of good works.

We might at this point also make reference to the Council of Vaison (fifteen miles north east of Orange, France), which was held on 13 November 442, which emphasised the need to care for the unwanted and to give relief to the distressed. The Council specifically opposed the desertion of children and encouraged the faithful to take them into adoption.

It is almost impossible to emphasise the importance of the role of the Emperor Justinian in enshrining these principles in common law. Justinian had his chief jurists compile what they believed to be the best of previous codes of law and judicial opinions into one summary, which along with a few of Justinian's own edicts is now known as the "Justinian code" (also known as—*Codex Justinianus*, or *Corpus Juris Civilis* (Body of Civil Law)). The Justinian Code was explicit in declaring infanticide and abortion illegal.

> Those who expose children, possibly hoping they would die, and those who use the potions of the abortionists, are subject to the full penalty of the law—both civil and ecclesiastical—for murder. Should exposure occur, the finder of the child is to see that he is baptised and that he is treated with Christian care and compassion. They may be then adopted ... even as we ourselves have been adopted into the kingdom of grace.
>
> Kennedy and Newcombe, 2001, p. 28

The Code of Justinian, it is said, has had an influence on nearly every legal system of the present day.

Traditional English Civil Law has clearly been influenced by it, and the classic English treatise writers, Bracton, Coke, Hale, etc., clearly reveal its influence on their thinking.

Referring to the Justinian Code, Samuel G. Green comments:

> The influence of Christianity on social political life first apparent in the laws of Constantine is now distinctly evident.

> No doubt it was in many respects far below the Christian ideal of life. But there were already sown the seeds of justice, freedom and philanthropy. Slavery was not abolished, but its severities were greatly mitigated. Human life was respected; gladiatorial shows were absolutely proscribed. Family relations were placed upon a noble footing, the right of parents over the children was restricted, and infanticide was rendered a crime; the position of women was raised. Laws against seduction and other forms of immorality were made more severe. Divorce was severely limited, the prohibition of marriage between near relations was extended and it is a singular proof of the ascendency of Christian ideas that sponsorship in baptism was ranked with the parental relationship as a bar to conjugal union.
>
> Green, 1904, p. 346

Later, we have the Doom Book, or Legal Code of Alfred the Great.

> The Doom Book, Code of Alfred or Legal Code of Ælfred the Great was the code of laws ("dooms" being laws or judgments) compiled by Alfred the Great (c. 893). Alfred codified three prior Saxon codes—those of Æthelberht of Kent (c. 602), Ine of Wessex (c. 694) and Offa of Mercia (c. 786)—to which he prefixed the Ten Commandments of Moses and incorporated rules of life from the Mosaic Code and the Christian code of ethics.
>
> Alfred's admonishment (was) "Doom very evenly! Do not doom one doom to the rich; another to the poor! Nor doom one doom to your friend; another to your foe!" This reflects Mosaic Law, which says "You shall do no injustice in judgment! You shall not be partial to the poor; nor defer to the great! But you are to judge your neighbour fairly!" (Leviticus 19:15).
>
> The Christian theologian F.N. Lee extensively documented Alfred the Great's work of collecting the law codes from the three Christian Saxon kingdoms and compiling them into his Doom Book (*Alfred the Great and our Common Law*). Lee details how Alfred incorporated the principles of the Mosaic law into his Code, and how this Code of Alfred became the foundation for the Common Law. In the book's extensive prologue, Alfred summarises the Mosaic and Christian codes. Dr Michael Treschow, UBC Faculty of Creative and Critical Studies, reviewed how Alfred laid the foundation for the Spirit of Mercy in his code, (*The Prologue to Alfred's Law Code:*

> *Instruction in the Spirit of Mercy*, Florilegium 13, 1994 pp. 79–110) stating that the last section of the Prologue not only describes "a tradition of Christian law from which the law code draws but also it grounds secular law upon Scripture, especially upon the principle of mercy".
>
> Anon, 2018

Later, in the thirteenth century, Henry de Bracton produced his *De Legibus et Consuetudinibus Angliae* (On the Laws and Customs of England). In this work he argued that the king ought to be under the law as everyone else.

> … and that he (the king) ought to be under the law appears clearly in the analogy of Jesus Christ, whose vicegerent on earth he is, for though many ways were open to him for his ineffable redemption of the human race, the true mercy of God chose this most powerful way to destroy the devil's work; he would use not the power of force but the reason of justice. Thus he willed himself to be under the law that he might redeem those who live under it. For he did not wish to use force but judgment.
>
> [T]here ought to be no one in his kingdom who surpasses him in the doing of justice, but he ought to be the last, or almost so, to receive it, when he is plaintiff.
>
> Volume 2, p. 33 of Bracton, n.d., II. 11–17, 21–23

In other words, God by sheer feat could have crushed Satan in his revolt by the use of his all sufficient power, but because of God's character being what it is, justice came before the use of power alone. Therefore, Christ died that justice, rooted in what God is, would be the solution. Bracton codified this by arguing that Christ's example, because of who he is, is our standard, our rule, our measure. Therefore, power is not first, but justice is first in society and law. The prince may have the power to control and to rule but he does not have the right to do so without justice. This was the basis of English Common Law.

Magna Carta Libertatum, commonly called Magna Carta, is a charter of rights agreed to by King John of England at Runnymede, near Windsor, on 15 June 1215 and was written within thirty-five years of Bracton's great work and in the midst of the same universal thinking in England at that time.

Examples of individuals who lived according to these new influences. It is not difficult to look into the lives of eminent Christians at this time to find examples of Christian concern for the poor, the needy and the downtrodden for example:

> *Benignus of Dijon* was a missionary from Lyons who was martyred in Epagny in the late second century. He was renowned for his generosity and charity especially to the sick and suffering. A mob of superstitious citizens in that pre-Christian Gallic region slew him because he nursed, supported, and protected a number of deformed and crippled children that had been saved from death after failed abortions or exposures.
>
> *Callistus of Rome* was a Christian slave who was imprisoned and sentenced to hard labour in the Sardinian quarries late in the second century after becoming involved in a scandalous financial scheme. After his release he was emancipated and put in charge of the church's shelter and cemetery on the Appian Way which still bears his name. He faithfully occupied himself with his duties—caring for the poor, comforting the bereaved, and giving refuge to the dispossessed. His compassion for abandoned children was especially noteworthy—it was Callistus that helped to organize the famed "Life Watches" that placed hundreds of exposed children into Christian homes. Eventually, he was chosen to serve as Bishop of Rome.
>
> *Alban of Verlamium* is widely venerated as the first Christian martyr on the island of Britain. During the last few decades of the second century, he offered refuge to those fleeing the persecution against the church. He succoured the sick, cared for the poor, and saved abandoned children from certain death. Bede the historian records his brutal martyrdom on Holmhurst Hill after he tried to intercede on behalf of a pitiful family of refugees.
>
> *Afra of Augsburg* developed a ministry to the abandoned children of prisoners, thieves, smugglers, pirates, runaway slaves, and brigands. Herself a former prostitute, she cared for the despised and the rejected with a special fervour, taking them into her home, creating an adoption network, and sacrificing all she had—that out of her lack they might be satisfied. Ultimately, her work came under the scrutiny of the authorities, and she was martyred during the great persecution of Diocletian.
>
> Grant, 1991, pp. 27–28

(10) *Christianity at the time of Constantine: advantages and disadvantages*

We will now consider the influence of Constantine, the first professedly Christian Emperor.

It is not our business here to set out a life of Constantine (*c.* 274–337). Some authorities say that he was born in Naissus, Moesia (now Nis, Serbia). All are agreed that his mother, Helena, was a Christian and there is strong evidence for assuming that Constantine was born in Britain. His father, Constantius, a sub-emperor under Diocletian, was responsible for Gaul and Britain and married Helena the Christian daughter of the British tribal leader King Cole.

Constantine's father Constantius, also known as Constantine Chlorus, though a heathen, favoured the Christians, and when the last edicts of persecution were issued by Diocletian he refused to put them into force.

Many believe that Constantine was crowned Emperor at York. The old London Wall dates back to his time and he has given his name to lakes, rivers, and countless women. Strange to say, he was for some time brought up like Moses, in the court of the enemy, Diocletian, and was compelled to spend a considerable time as a hostage in the hands of one of the other sub-emperors, Galerius, at the time one totally hostile to Christianity. Galerius is often called Christianity's last and most-cruel persecutor.

Constantine escaped from the hands of Galerius and returned to England where his father Constantius lay dying. When his father saw him, he is said to have leapt from his bed, saying "I will now die in peace".

Constantine's mother, Helena, is generally regarded as exerting a great deal of influence on his life.

When he was 32 years old in AD 306, he was crowned Emperor in York. At this time, the Roman world was governed by six administrators, but within twenty years Constantine became the sole Emperor.

It was while marching against one of his rivals, Maxentius, Governor of Italy, that Constantine met with his life-changing experience. In the campaign near Verona, on his way to Rome, he saw in the sky a burning cross, with the inscription in Greek written upon it, "By this symbol, conquer".

The night before the battle, the famous Battle of the Milvian Bridge, one of the main entrances over the Tiber into the city of Rome, he dreamt that he was commanded by an angel to inscribe the sacred monogram of Christ upon his soldier's shields. This was the origin of the famous Labarum, which was a vexillum (military standard) that displayed the 'Chi-Rho' symbol, a christogram formed from the first two Greek letters of the word 'Christ' (Greek: ΧΡΙΣΤΟΣ, or Χριστός)—Chi (χ) and Rho (ρ). This standard was borne before the army.

Chi-Rho

A stylised vexilium

The vision of the fiery cross produced a profound impression upon Constantine, who resolved, as he alleged, to embrace the cause of Christianity. Also in the previous year, an edict of toleration had been issued by the cruel Galerius, who was conscious of his fast approaching death and seems to have suffered from a deep pang of remorse.

However, when Constantine became sole Emperor, he issued edicts not only tolerating but legalising Christianity within the Empire and later acknowledged it as the religion of the realm. It will be debated to the end of time how far Constantine was actuated by political motives and how far he was a genuine convert to Christianity. Whichever view we take of this he was certainly conscious of the fact and able to see how indispensable it was to protect Christianity in order to promote the unity and bring about a consolidation of his Empire.

What becomes quite clear in all this is that the Empire, both morally and spiritually was in a deplorable state and Constantine grasped the fact that Christianity was the only resource with the power, cohesion and strength to remedy the situation.

The French nineteenth century historian Gosselin comments:

> Long before the conversion of Constantine, the Roman Empire carried within itself those seeds of dissolution, which were gradually weakening, and at last completely destroyed it. The number of different nations which it contained, the infinite variety of their customs and characters, the relaxation of military discipline, the universal depravity of morals, all conspired to shake the constitution of the Empire; while the ceaseless eruptions of the barbarian hordes aggravated the dangers resulting from the combination of so many different causes.
>
> In this wretched state of affairs, the Christian faith presented to the government one of the surest means of strengthening its authority and of securing the obedience of the people. A strong constitution of the Church, the beauty of its moral doctrine, the sublime virtues which it taught its children, the reformation which it everywhere produced in public morals, naturally pointed it out as the agent for the regeneration of the social system; it alone could breathe new life into that exhausted frame, by restoring morality, order and all the other bonds of harmony between the different members of the state. The Christians were at once the most fervent servants of the Deity, and the most loyal subjects of the Emperors. Submission to the powers of the earth was one of their principal maxims and their most sacred duties. They had never been implicated in any of those seditions and revolts which so often deluged the Roman provinces with blood and overturned the imperial throne. Constant and daily experience proved to the Emperors that they could nowhere find more faithful subjects, more devoted soldiers, more upright magistrates, than in the bosom of Christianity … "The most virtuous of our seniors", observes Tertullian, "preside in our assemblies; an honour which they attain, not by money, but by the suffrages of the Church, for holy things cannot be purchased".
>
> Gosselin, 1853, 2 vols. i.29–30

Later, Gosselin states:

> The pagans themselves could not refrain from respecting the character and the virtue of the ministers of the Christian religion. Their example was cited by the Emperor Alexander Severus, as a model of the care to be taken in the election of public offices. Origen in his works against Celsus, composed in the third century, supposes as a certain fact, acknowledged by the pagans themselves, that the conduct even of very imperfect Christians, was far superior to that of the pagans, and that the virtue of the least perfect bishops far surpassed that of the civil magistrates. "The assemblies of the Christians", he says, "compared with the popular assemblies of the cities which they inhabit, resemble those stars which illumine the world. For, can anyone deny that the most imperfect portion of our assemblies is better than the popular assemblies? Compare the Senate of the Christian Church with that of each city, and it will be seen that among the senators of the Church, there are men fit to govern a city of divine beings, if such could be found on this earth, whilst the others are entirely devoid of the morals required in the high dignity which they occupy. If you compare, moreover, the bishop of each church with the first magistrate of the city, you shall find that amongst the chiefs and governors of the Church of God, those least evident for their virtues, are nevertheless better than the chiefs and governors of the cities". It must be remembered, that Origen expresses himself thus, in a work directed against pagans, who could manifestly overwhelm him with the ridicule, if the facts which he states were not notorious and undeniable.
>
> Gosselin, 1853, 2 vols. i. 34–35

The admiration and respect with which the greatest enemies of Christianity were compelled to admire it was clear proof to the governments of that time of what a powerful influence such a faith and its ministers could exercise in the regeneration of society, and in the maintenance of public order.

However, there was also another factor which must be borne in mind and that was the influence that Christians had upon the barbarian invaders from time to time, who with ever-increasing regularity, now harassed the Empire.

> In the year 350, the city of Nisiba, which was the principal barrier against the Persians, was saved from their assaults by the prudence

> and sanctity of its bishop James. A few years later in 383, the Empress Justinia, when compelled to negotiate the interests of her son Valentinian II with the tyrant Maximus, thought she could not entrust the matter to safer hands than St Ambrose; and so successfully did that holy bishop conduct his negotiation, that he arrested the usurper in his march, and concluded a treaty with him far more favourable than could be expected in circumstances so unfortunate.
>
> Rome itself was twice saved from the most frightful calamities by the mediation of Pope Leo with the barbarian kings Genseric and Attila.
>
> The city of Troyes in particular owed its preservation to the mediation of its bishop Lupus with the haughty Attila, who yielded in the same manner to the prayers of Aignan in favour of the city of Orleans.
>
> Germain of Auxerre, and Lupus of Troyes, while on a mission in Great Britain to oppose the Pelagian heresy, had saved that province from the invasion of Saxons and of Picts.
>
> Gosselin, 1853, 2 vols. i. 38–39

History is replete with similar situations in which the example and doctrine of Christians on public morals benefitted the State.

Returning to the advantages of this closer union between Church and State, we may name some of the following:

> It became the accepted rule that ministers and office bearers of the Church at times of war were not called or conscripted into the army but were allowed to continue their Church obligations. These people were exempt from military service by law.
>
> Monies for the building of churches were made available from the Imperial funds. At the same time churches that were confiscated in times of persecution were now returned to their owners. Many heathen temples were converted into churches.
>
> At the time when the Church herself forgot her own persecutions, monies from condemned heathens or heretics were given to the Church.
>
> Up to this point no one could legally leave their wealth to the Church; private wills were not valid where the Christian Church was the beneficiary. But now a law was passed legalising such wills, a law,

> the result of which very soon filled the treasuries of the churches and extended the landed property of the Church.
>
> Jerome tells us that the Church soon came to own a tenth part of all landed property.
>
> Cameron, 2016, p. 63

The voluntary system of supporting the clergy as it existed before the union of the Church and state gave place to State aid for their support.

Ministers and teachers received a fixed income from the Church funds, and from the Imperial and municipal treasuries. While this improved the external condition of many of them by raising them above the oppressive and distracting cares of making ends meet, it also enabled them to devote their whole strength to the duties of their office. Nevertheless, at the same time, it had a detrimental effect of fostering ease and luxury, as well as attracting a host of unworthy people into the service of the Church. It also discouraged the exercise of free giving amongst the people.

It is worth noting that both Chrysostom and Augustine spoke of their preference in principle to the voluntary system in support of the Church and the ministry. Augustine said that believers should support the clergy and the poor by free gifts.

The State brought about many changes to the old ways:

(a) The Lord's day became a recognised day of rest. The sitting of law courts and all secular labour on that day, together with all military exercises, was officially prohibited.

(b) The status of women was raised, and they were given power over their own property and houses. Marriage also became respectable with certain prohibitions taken from the Old Testament teachings on degrees of consanguinity.

(c) The Church was given the power to afford refuge to the oppressed within the various churches until the situation of the oppressed was properly examined. Ministers could also intercede for those who had so fled to ensure that proper justice was carried out. However, this privilege was not much appreciated by the clergy of those times.

Freely adapted from Spence-Jones, 1906, pp. 224–225

We must not forget that the greatest advantage of these changes however was the simple fact that Christians were now no longer persecuted and could live their lives without fear of being exiled or put to violent deaths simply because they professed Christ as King and Lord.

We cannot but be aware that although there were many *advantages* to the uniting of the Church and State under Constantine and subsequent Emperors of Rome, there were also many *disadvantages* and dangers.

We will now consider some of these disadvantages.

> With the Church at this point occupying a position of power and privilege it inevitably drew into it many new adherents. As it is said, "make anything popular, the new will soon draw a crowd". The popularity of Christianity drew the crowd from among the heathen. They joined it, and they became professed Christians. They did not know why they joined, but their coming in such a spirit brought a downgrade into the Church.
>
> The Court of Constantine became recognised as a professed Christian court. Sadly, the Court of Constantine was proverbial for its extravagance in servants, "employing no less than 1000 barbers, 1000 cup bearers, 1000 cooks, and so many eunuchs that they could be compared only with the insects on a summers day". When the Emperor was seen in public, he was surrounded by a vast multitude of attendants of the higher ranks, "their horses glittering with golden ornaments, and their riders with golden shields and golden lances". When Julian the Apostate, the last of the house of Constantine, became Emperor, he discouraged this extravagance, his desire and aim being to show to disadvantage, as indeed he might well do, the Christian faith of his predecessor.
>
> Into the Church, so closely connected with the court, much extravagance of a similar kind was gradually introduced. The dignitaries of the ecclesiastical world vied with those of the sovereign. The people followed suit. The heathen multitudes adopted Christianity just because it was the religion of the State and being accustomed to a grand and gorgeous ritual liturgy, they wished to hold by the same in some form in their new condition. They found the door of the Church wide enough to admit them with all, or at least, with a very considerable amount of their heathen rites and superstitions.
>
> The second evil that the Church suffered through this union was State oppression. At first, Constantine disowned having any power to interfere with the bishop's decisions. The bishop's decision was by him regarded as final, but gradually, he moved away from that

> position and claimed the right of being supreme. According to the custom of ancient Rome, the Emperor was *Pontifex Maximus*, or the real high priest of the State religion. When however, he became a Christian, there was a temptation to maintain the same power, to which temptation he and his successors unhappily yielded, and so we find the imperial power having a very prominent influence in all the decisions of the Church.
>
> When heresies broke out, as they frequently and violently did, and the Church was divided into sections, the support of the State authority was eagerly sought after by each section. Thus, the section which failed to secure the royal favour was suppressed, and often banished from the land. At one time the Arians were outlawed, and another time the Nicaeans, just as the Emperor's whim turned, or as one Emperor agreed with or differed from his predecessor. This appeal to imperial power was constantly fanning the flame of divisions and even multiplying them.
>
> Based upon Cameron, 2016, pp. 66–70

Before we leave Constantine let us not forget his great contribution; he deserves to be acknowledged as a great deliverer and protector of the Church whatever verdict we may pass on his own Christian life or Christian faith. His passing of the Edict of Milan in AD 313 gave complete toleration to Christianity, which in turn was the gateway to a new era in the history of the Church. We must not forget that the first decade of the fourth century saw the Church in the fiercest fire of persecution, which threatened its total extinction. The last decade of that century saw it dominant, established and secure.

Though we are tracing out the beneficial aspect of Christianity in this work, it is only fair and fitting to note those times when the Church has been overmuch influenced by the world, and its beneficial power has become compromised.

Constantine had gone a long way to making Christianity the state religion of the Roman Empire. However, his sons, who divided the empire amongst themselves at his death, and above all Constantius (who was master of the East), pursued a fanatical and intolerant policy against pagans and introduced the threat of the death penalty for the practice of superstition and the offering of pagan sacrifices. He also closed all pagan temples calling upon the Christian mob to storm them.

It was the Emperor Theodosius the Great (AD 379–395) who formally made Christianity the state religion of the Empire, and at the same time made heresy a state crime.

It took less than a century for the persecuted Church to become a persecuting Church. An enemy of the Church was now regarded as an enemy of the Empire and was punished accordingly. In AD 385, a Spanish aesthetic and enthusiastic lay preacher, Priscillian, together with six companions, was executed in Trier for heresy, a bad sign for the Christian centuries to come. This was the first time Christians killed other Christians over a difference in faith. Despite objections from different sides, people soon got used to this. Leo the Great already had expressed his satisfaction with this procedure.

When compulsory state measures were introduced against pagans and heretics, they were welcomed even by prominent Christians even such highly respected believers as John Chrysostom.

Not surprisingly paganism increasingly disappeared from public life in the cities, and the Roman Senate solemnly abjured the old faith, removing the altar of *Victoria adveniens* from the hall in which it met, and abolishing all privileges for pagan priests and vestal virgins.

At the same time Christian anti-Judaism began to develop from the anti-Judaism which had already existed in the pagan state.

Under Theodosius II (AD 401–450), the Jews were effectively excluded from public life. They were not to be exterminated but segregated from public life and isolated from the main channels of society.

At the same time, theologians and Church leaders like Augustine still felt that there was a missionary task and responsibility to bring the Gospel to the Jews. Augustine's views ran contrary to the popular idea that Jews were God's murderers. Augustine believed that, despite their guilt, the Jews had a hope of conversion, while other earnest men like Ambrose prevented the rebuilding of synagogues, and bishops, as we mentioned above, like Chrysostom preached fiery sermons against them: "the synagogue—a place of hostility to the Law, a quarter of the evil done, a bulwark of the devil; the Jews—gluttons who delight in feasting and greedy rich people who, unfit to work, are suitable only for slaughter".

However, in spite of this hostility Judaism remained present as a living religion throughout the Empire. Indeed, at the time of Chrysostom, there were still Christians (Judaizing Christians) who went to the synagogue on Sabbaths and feast days and took part in Jewish ceremonies.

However, there was also a healthy reaction against Church and State integration, which can be seen in the rise of sects such as the Donatists.

The Donatists were so called after their leader Donatus, Bishop of Carthage. They believed that those Church leaders who had succumbed in the time of persecution to a denial of Christ, but afterwards repented of what they had done, were no longer worthy to administer the sacraments of the Church. This was also coupled with the belief that the sacraments were only valid if those who administered them were in a right relationship with God. This position was advocated by many and threatened to split the Church.

> The Donatists were a large body who seceded from the Church in the beginning of the fourth century, on the ground of the Church's impurity, as they maintained. They gradually increased till in Africa they numbered four hundred bishops. Their dioceses must have been very small; they should rather be called ministers. Those Donatists were the first to ask the question, What has the Emperor to do with the Church? This question they were taught to put by the Oppression they suffered. They denied the right of the State to meddle with ecclesiastical affairs. In some of the views of this sect, one can discover the germ of the Protestant faith, and of the noble and patriotic spirit that for centuries strove for and finally secured liberty of conscience in this and other lands.
>
> Cameron, 2016, p. 67

Chapter 6
The Benefits of Christianity in the Second Part of the First Millennium

The impact of Monasticism

Influential paganism by the end of the fourth century was finally defeated. From this time pagan cults would be the religion of the lower classes, those outside the cities, literally the country folk (*pagani* in Latin). Now Christianity was embarrassed to speak in the name of the God who "hath put down the mighty from their seats, and exalted them of low degree. He hath filled the hungry with good things; and the rich he hath sent empty away" (Luke 1:52–53), because it had become the religion of the powerful. However, within certain elements of the Church, a reaction against this newfound power and status set in. This was Monasticism, described by one writer, A.M. Allchin as "*the silent rebellion*". This was a rebellion against the direction in which the Church was moving i.e. becoming a large-scale and inclusive organisation. In its early years, the Church was a small community which found it easy to guard its character as a distinct body consisting of spiritually minded, devout believers. This stance however became increasingly hard to maintain as Christian communities grew and all sorts of people started flocking in; even the long process of instruction and preparation for baptism and admission to the communion of the saints which was then customary could not prevent this process. One answer however was found and that was in the birth of Monasticism.

> The history of Monasticism is a long one and may be regarded as almost unbroken from the fourth century to the present. In the sixteenth century, Monasticism was very seriously affected by the Reformation, and, in the eighteenth century, by the French Revolution and the prevailing scepticism. In the beginning of the nineteenth century, there was a great revival in France of the monastic spirit, while later on there was a reaction amongst monastic bodies, both in France and in the Italian and Spanish Peninsulas. A system of such long existence and so widely spread can scarcely be said to be entirely void of good, and to have served no purpose at any stage of its history. It may reasonably be supposed that it has its lights

as well as its shades, but perhaps any good purpose it has served has been in its earlier rather than its later stage.

From the impurity of the Christianity of the fourth century there was a recoil. The gaiety, the fashion, the thirst for show and pleasure in the Christian Church were felt to be too much for many earnest Christian minds, and so many retired into solitude for meditation and communion with God. The action of those stood as a warning against the worldliness and immorality of the great cities, and as a mighty call to repentance and conversion. Monasticism thus offered a quiet refuge to souls weary of the world and led its earnest disciples into the sanctuary of undisturbed communion with God.

The Monasticism of the early ages placed the rich and the poor, the high and the low upon the same level. It showed kindness to the wayfarer, and liberality to the poor and the needy. As a source of education and discipline, it sent forth most of those missionaries, who, inured to all hardships, planted the standard of the cross among the barbarian tribes of Northern and Western Europe, and afterwards in Eastern Asia and South America. It gave the Church many of her best bishops and popes. It produced saints like Anthony and Bernard, and trained divines like John Chrysostom and Jerome, and the long succession of good men during the Middle Ages. Some of the best writings came from the cloisters of Monasticism, such as the tracts of Anselm, the *Summa Theologica* of Thomas Aquinas, and the *Imitation of Christ*, by Thomas à Kempis.

In the west, Monasticism promoted the cultivation of the soil and the education of the people, and produced valuable transcriptions of the Bible, of the works of the Church Fathers, and of the ancient classics. This is the best and the brightest side of Monasticism. Let us look also at its dark side.

Those Monastic devotees adopted many views of the truth. They imagined that real piety consisted in subjecting themselves to trial, and enduring self-imposed penance. This indeed was at the root of the whole movement.

A quiet Christian youth at the village of Coma, on the borders of Thebais, diligently attended divine worship with his parents. Gifted with a splendid memory, he retained all that he received, but, unfortunately, he made a too literal use of it. In his eighteenth year, through the death of his parents, the care of his sister devolved upon him. One day, meditating over Christ's command to the young man,

"If thou wilt be perfect, go, and sell that thou hast and give it to the poor, and thou shalt have treasure in heaven, and come, follow me" (Matthew 19:21), he resolved to sell his estate, three hundred acres of fertile land. He divided it amongst the people of his village; he sold his personal property and entrusted his sister to a society of pious virgins. He then betook himself to the desert, where he lived with the utmost rigour for thirty years. He lived in the ruins of a castle near the Red Sea, where an old cloister still preserves his name and memory. His food consisted of bread and salt, sometimes dates, his drink of water. This was St. Anthony (251–356), the founder of the Monastic system, and the originator of its extreme rigours. Anthony was much adored, and closely imitated by thousands. The Emperor himself wrote him a letter, and begged an answer from him, but the letter the hermit would not at first receive. When told that the Emperor was a Christian, he read it and dictated an answer, for he could not write. "Show that thou worshippest Christ, be not proud of thy earthly power, think of the future judgment, and know that Christ is the only true and eternal King; practise justice and love for men, and care for the poor". To his disciples he said, "Wonder not the Emperor writes to me, for he is a man; wonder much more that God has written the law for man and has spoken to us by His own Son". Athanasius, who wrote his life, pays a high tribute to his memory. His fame spread over the whole Roman Empire. What gave him his renown was not learning, not worldly wisdom, not human art, but alone his piety toward God. And yet this same Athanasius tells us without apology that this prodigy of his never changed his raiment nor washed himself. Compared, however, with many of his followers and imitators, Anthony was a model Monastic. As in the case of many other movements, the propagators were much more extreme than the originators. Multitudes flocked to the desert solitudes to gain a reputation for piety, till thousands and tens of thousands became hermits of different degrees and kinds over Asia, Africa, and Europe.

Towards the end of the period now under consideration, a new type of hermits sprang up, called the Pillar Saints. Their piety was reckoned elevated and great in proportion as they denied themselves the semblance of the comforts of life and tortured themselves in every conceivable way. St. Simeon, the Stylite, originally a shepherd in Africa, became famous by his invention of various kinds of torture

> as means of attaining holiness. He spent some time as a hermit upon a mountain, with an iron chain upon his feet; thousands came to see him. He started a new plan near Antioch. He lived for thirty-six years, until his death, upon a pillar which at the last was nearly forty cubits high (for the pillar was raised as he approached nearer heaven and perfection). On this pillar he could neither lie nor sit, but only stand or lean upon a post, or devoutly bow, in which last exercise be nearly touched his feet with his head, so flexible had his back become with fasting. A spectator one day counted 1,244 of these bows before the Almighty and gave up counting. Simeon wore a covering of the skins of beasts and a chain about his neck. He lived to the age of sixty-nine, preached repentance twice a day to the crowds that gathered around the base of the pillar, and, as his historian Theodoret tells, converted thousands of heathen to the Christian faith. Tennyson makes him graphically describe his experiences:
>
> Although I be the basest of mankind,
> From scalp to sole one slough and crust of sin
> Unfit for earth, unfit for heaven, scarce meet
> For troops of devils, mad with blasphemy;
>
> I will not cease to grasp the hold
> Of saintdom, and to clamour, moan, and sob,
> Battering the gates of heaven with storm of prayer
> Have mercy, Lord, and take my sin away.
>
> No doubt this Monasticism nourished religious fanaticism. For the simple, divine way of the Gospel it substituted an arbitrary, eccentric, ostentatious, and pretentious sanctity. For Monasticism there is no foundation either in the teaching or in the life of Jesus and his Apostles. If the Christian Church followed the example of those extreme desert hermits, there would and could be no obedience to the Divine command, "Go ye into all the world and preach the Gospel to every creature" (Mark 16:15). This Monasticism superseded the all-sufficient merits of Christ by the glitter of the over meritorious work of man . It measured virtue by the quantity of outward exercise instead of the quality of inward disposition, and disseminated self-righteousness and an anxious, legal, mechanical religion.
>
> Cameron, 2016, pp. 67–71

It needs to be said that Greek Monasticism preserved many more links with the surrounding culture. One of its leaders, Basil, Bishop of Caesarea, discouraged solitary monks, and founded the monastic communities. These monasteries were not cut off from society, but educated children, nursed the sick, and gave hospitality to travellers.

In the West, monasteries were chiefly founded by Martin of Tours (335–397). These monks streamed out through the French countryside, evangelising pagans and founding churches. Also in the West, the idea of withdrawing from the world in order to cultivate the aesthetic life came to include cultivating the mind through the study of literature. This was an old Roman aristocratic ideal, and one of the reasons why Western Monasticism attracted converts from the ranks of the Roman aristocracy. It was these monasteries that, after the collapse of the Roman Empire in the West, became the guardians of Western European culture and civilisation. They became the vital centres of education in the Western Catholic world and their monks carried the Gospel into the pagan lands of northern Europe.

Christianity—its stabilising influence after the collapse of the Roman Empire

With the disintegration of the Roman Empire in the fifth century, much of the civil administration fell, by sheer necessity, upon the leaders of the Catholic Church. [see p. 19 under Attila]

The French Protestant historian, M. Francois Guizot states:

> From the commencement of the fifth century, the Christian clergy had a powerful means of influence. The bishops and clergy had become the first municipal magistrates. Of the Roman empire there remained, strictly speaking, nothing but its municipal government; by the vexations of despotism, and the ruin of the cities, the curiales,[6] or members of the municipal bodies, had fallen into apathy and discouragement. The bishops, on the contrary, and the body of the clergy, full of life and zeal, naturally came forward to superintend all and to direct all. It would be injustice to reproach them with it, to accuse them of usurpation; it was the natural course of things; the clergy alone had moral strength and energy; they became powerful everywhere; such is the law of the world.

6 Under Constantine, the curiales became a class of urban landowners who were responsible for the normal functioning of the city's institutions (finance, food supply, public works, entertainment).

> This resolution is manifest in all the legislation of the emperors in those ages. Open the Theodosian or the Justinian code, and you find an immense number of laws referring municipal affairs to the clergy and the bishops. Thus, the Christian Church has from that epoch powerfully influenced the character and the development of modern civilization. Let us sum up briefly the elements which she introduced into it.
>
> And, in the first place, in the midst of that deluge of material force which at this period overwhelmed society there was an immense benefit in the presence of a moral influence, a moral power, a power which derived all its force from convictions, from belief, from moral sentiments. Had there been no Christian Church, the whole world would have been abandoned to mere material force. The Church alone exercised a moral power: she did more—she kept up and diffused the conviction of a rule, a law, superior to all human laws. She professed that belief so essential to the well-being of mankind, that there exists, above all human laws, another law, at different times, and from a difference of morals, sometimes called reason, sometimes the divine law, but which everywhere and always is the same law under different names.
>
> As quoted in Gosselin, 1853, 2 vols. i. 42–43

Christianity—its civilising influence

That Christianity is accompanied by a civilising influence, can be seen from the following teaching of the early Church.

> At the time of the departure of the Romans lived Fastidius, bishop, as it is supposed, of London, who is the only Christian teacher among the ancient Britons of whom any doctrinal work yet remains. He has left a short treatise on the character of a Christian life, addressed to a pious widow named Fatalis, in which, after modestly excusing his own want of knowledge and little skill, and begging her to "accept his household bread, since he cannot offer her the finest flour," he shews, with very plain and good arguments, that Christians are called to imitate Him whom they worship; that without a life of piety and uprightness, it is vain to presume on the mercy of God, or to boast of the name of Christian; that it was always the rule of God's dealings with mankind to love righteousness and hate iniquity.
>
> "It is the will of God," says he, "that his people should be holy, and

apart from all stain of unrighteousness; so righteous, so merciful, so pure, so unspotted by the world, so single-hearted, that the heathen should find no fault in them, but say with wonder, Blessed is the nation whose God is the Lord, and the people whom he hath chosen for his own inheritance.

"We read in the evangelist that one came to our Saviour and asked him what he should do to gain eternal life. The answer he received was, 'If thou wilt enter into life, keep the commandments.' Our Lord did not say, Keep faith only. For if faith is all that is required, it is overmuch to say that the commandments must be kept. But far be it from me that I should suppose my Lord to have taught any thing overmuch. Let this be said only by those whose sins have numbered them with the children of perdition.

"Let no man then deceive or mislead his brother: except a man is righteous, he hath not life; except he keep the commandments of Christ, he hath no part with him. A Christian is one who shews mercy to all; who is provoked by no wrong; who suffers not the poor in this world to be oppressed; who relieves the wretched, succours the needy; who mourns with mourners, and feels the pain of another as his own; who is moved to tears by the sight of another's tears; whose house is open to all; whose table is spread for all the poor; whose good deeds all men know; whose wrongful dealing no man feels; who serves God day and night, and ever meditates upon his precepts; who is made poor to the world, that he may be rich towards God; who is content to be inglorious among men, that he may appear glorious before God and his angels; who has no deceit in his heart; whose soul is simple and undefiled, and his conscience faithful and pure; whose whole mind rests on God; whose whole hope is fixed on Christ, desiring heavenly things rather than earthly, and leaving human things to lay hold on things divine."

Churton, 1878, pp. 15–17

Many examples could be cited from this time. In our own country, much could be said about the influence of King Alfred and his influence for good on the character of Great Britain. However, we will take a broader view and glance at events on the continent, culminating in the reign of Charlemagne.

Towards the close of the seventh century the Mohammedan religion had become a great and threatening power. It had swept out from beyond the borders of Arabia and gained many converts in the East;

it advanced westwards over North Africa, Spain, and Southern Gaul, and seemed to be unstoppable in its progress westward. (The Western world, however, was saved from the all-conquering Mohammedans by the great victory of the Franks at Tours, under the leadership of Charles Martel (*c.* 688–741).

But first, we need to mention the great kingly dynasty that had taken possession of Gaul or France about the year AD 486.

The Franks (or Free Folk), were a mixture of Teutonic tribes led by their king, Clovis, who had embraced Christianity. This opened the way to the evangelisation of his territory by missionaries from Rome and England. Clovis' territory became the huge Merovingian realm stretching from the Pyrenees to Bavaria. It was said of him, "*Without knowing it, he had founded not a nation, but a historical force*" (Anton Lavisse quoted in Davies, 1997, p. 234). It was a force which was destined to give rise both to France and to the German Empire.

The Merovingian dynasty however gave way to the Carolingian dynasty. The Pope claimed the right of transferring the crown of France from the old dynasty of Franks (the Merovingian) to that of the Carolingian, or the family of Charles Martel. It is difficult to estimate all the consequences flowing from this to the Church and to Western Europe in subsequent years.

Amongst Martel's notable achievements was that he stopped the Muslim advance into France at the Battle of Tours in October 732—also called the Battle of Poitiers.

When the Muslims turned towards Provence, Charles Martel sent several expeditions against them and not only drove them back but, at the same time, succeeded in re-establishing his authority over the dissident provinces in the south-east of France.

> The victory of Charles—whose quaint surname of *Martel*, or "the Hammer", is derived from the iron weapon which he wielded on the day of Poitiers with the personal prowess of a hero of romance—had an obvious effect in strengthening his own dominion and perpetuating the grandeur of his family.
>
> Smedley et al., 1845, p. 289

He further re-established his influence in Germany, and his numerous military campaigns succeeded in driving the Saxons across the Rhine, and returned the Bavarians under Frankish control, at the same time annexing Frisia and Alemagne. He also encouraged missionary activity, which, as some say, was a means of consolidating his power.

Amongst the missionaries that came into his kingdom at that time was Boniface (English name Winfrith), an English monk, who is sometimes referred to as the apostle of the German nation. Boniface is known for hacking down the old and venerable Donar's oak, which was dedicated to the pagan god Thor. It is said that he approached the tree with an axe and began, in the presence of its devotees, to cut it down and split it up. The ancient tree offered little resistance to Boniface's energetic blows and in the felling of the tree the pagans bowed before the superior might of the God of the foreign missionaries. From the wood of the tree Boniface built a church for Christian worship. Tradition says that from the place where the tree stood, there sprang up a small fir tree which ever since in Europe was known as the Christmas tree.

Through the energetic and devoted ministry of Boniface literally thousands were converted and baptised; heathen temples were destroyed, and Christian churches built in place of them.

> It must not be forgotten that Germany was visited by missionaries from Scotland and Ireland before the time of Boniface. These were not subjects of the Roman Church, nor did they approve of all her tenets. For this reason, Boniface, who was a loyal subject of the Pope, condemned them as heretics. These missionaries did great service but lacked a most important help to which Boniface owed a large amount of his influence. The reigning king of the Franks, the son of Charles Martel, threw in his military power to aid Boniface, and to conquer the German nation. There was no effort of moral or spiritual persuasion with him. He employed material force, believing that people became Christians by water baptism. In the same manner, he tried to convert the Saxons to Christianity. His policy was either to Christianise or to kill them. Great and shameful atrocities were thus perpetrated in the name of religion.
>
> Cameron, 2016, p. 103

The great English scholar Alcuin who resided at the court of Charles Martel protested against this wholesale conversion by force. He held that the heathen should first be instructed, because baptism without faith is meaningless. Moreover, moral persuasion, love and self-denial are the only proper means by which to confirm true faith.

However, in spite of this great blemish in the method of Christianising, the grandson of Charles Martel, Charles the Great, better known as Charlemagne, rendered significant service in further opening up amongst the Teutonic tribes the way for the spread of the Gospel.

> The great tradition of the *Orbis Terrarum* or of the unity of the world, formerly the political end and aim of the Roman Empire of the Caesars, which arose contemporarily with Christianity, was revived in the age of Charles the Great. This age transformed the ancient Imperium into the Western monarchy, which found its inmost bond of cohesion in the principle of the Christian religion. Charles was the Moses of the Middle Ages, who successfully led mankind through the deserts of barbarism and bestowed on them a new code of political, ecclesiastical, and civil constitutions. In his theocratic Empire was exhibited the first attempt to establish the new federation of nations in the form of a Christian republic.
>
> Gregorovius, 1895, pp. 18–19

His ambition was to unite the Teutonic and Latin races on the continent in close union with himself under the spiritual dominion of the Pope. He saw himself, in a sense, as a new Constantine. His dominions extended from the Baltic and the Elbe in the north to the Ebro (a river on the Iberian Peninsula) in the south; from the Bristol Channel to Rome and even to the Straits of Messina, taking in France, Germany, Hungary, and the greater part of Italy, and Spain.

In some ways Charlemagne was the father of the Middle Ages, and like Constantine his influence was both good and bad.

> The name of the "blessed Charles" is enrolled in the Roman Calendar for his services to the Church and gifts to the Pope. Heathen Rome deified Julius Caesar; Christian Rome canonized Charles the Great. His life, however, public or private, cannot be said to justify all this honour. To his towering ambition and passion for conquests he sacrificed thousands of human lives. He converted the Saxons by force of arms, crushed out their spirit of independence, and, in order to prevent a future revolt, removed ten thousand from their homes on the banks of the Elbe to different parts of Germany and Gaul. His war was one of annihilation of heathenism conducted on the Mohammedan principle—submission to the Faith or death. And, when we come to his private life, we find no excuse for his disregard

> of the sanctity of the marriage tie. In this respect, he was not better than an Oriental despot or a Mohammedan caliph. He married several wives, and divorced them at pleasure. It is very much to the discredit of the Popes that they never rebuked him for a vice which they were ready to condemn in the case of weaker and less devoted monarchs. Like many other great men, his brilliant character is stained with many vices that, in modern and better days, would have excluded him from a place among the faithful, and debarred him from the privileges of the Church. But no one will deny that a man of such religious tendencies, such giant intellect, and such unbounded influence, presiding as he did over the vast territories of the new Roman Empire, could not but help forward the interests of Christianity.
>
> Charles seemed to have had implicit faith in the preaching of the Word as a means of consolidating the Church. He was specially impressed with the conviction that her safety depended largely upon the performance of the preacher's office. He admonished the clergy to prepare their sermons well, to be diligent in the study of the Bible in order to the better discharge of their sacred duties. In this view of things, he was strengthened by his faithful adviser, Alcuin. "There is no knowledge of God", says this man, "without the Holy Scriptures, and if the blind lead the blind, both will fall into the ditch. Provide yourselves with teachers of the Holy Scriptures that there may be no want of the word of God among you, that men capable of guiding the people may not fail, that the fountain of truth may not become dry among you". In the opinion of this excellent man, it was considered most important that Christian knowledge should be diffused among the laity, and that they should be led to take an intelligent share in the services of the Church. He was impressed also by the conviction that the promotion of the kingdom of God was not a work for the clergy only, but that it ought to be the care of all Christians in common.
>
> Cameron, 2016, pp. 106–107

One of the greatest blots on Charlemagne's reign was the massacre at Verden, where it is said that 4,500 Saxons were massacred in one day in October 782. The Nazis, in the 1930s, in their efforts to discredit Christianity, attempted to portray this as being part of Charlemagne's Christianising programme, and actually built a monument to mark the event. Though we cannot condone Charlemagne's action, it does seem to have had something to do with his misguided Christianising policy by force as well as an action to put down a rebellion in that region.

Alcuin further wrote in regard to Charlemagne:

> Behold our Solomon, resplendent with the diadem of wisdom imitated his most noble traits. Cherish his virtues but avoid his vices.

We may continue to enumerate a number of other virtues possessed by Charlemagne. We could add that he was a great reformer of the Church. It never entered his head that this was not his business. Alcuin called him "*Pontifex*" and later another churchman called him, "Bishop of the Bishops".

He counted himself responsible for the Church's good order. His self-chosen designation was in this respect "Protector and Corrector". He certainly found the Church of his day in need of both. Boniface described the state of the Church at this time as follows.

> For the most part, in the cities, the Episcopal sees are given over to the possession of avaricious laymen, or to wicked and worldly clergy to enjoy in a merely secular way
>
> Watt, 1927, p. 117

Nothing pleased Charlemagne better than to encounter a capable and serious bishop, devoted to his proper work. Such of these were few and far between at the beginning of his reign. We know that he put on record his intention to right this wrong. He pointedly addressed this question to the bishops and abbots in words after this effect: "Declare to us truly what these words mean which you use so often, 'to renounce the world', and by what sign one can distinguish those who renounce the world from those who are still occupied with it. Whether it is only by the fact that they do not bear arms, and are not publicly married? Further how can it be that a man can say he is renouncing the world and yet labouring each day, no matter how, to increase his wealth?"

Once on another occasion in conversation with Alcuin, Alcuin was extolling the virtues of learning such as the learning of Augustine and Jerome. Charles impatiently interrupted, "Why can I not have twelve clerks such as these"? Alcuin was astounded at the demand, and replied, "The Lord of heaven and earth had but two such, and wouldst thou have twelve?"

In comparison with the Popes of his day Charlemagne had far more concern for the spiritual well-being of the Church then for its temporal wealth and power.

Another strong characteristic of the reign and influence of Charlemagne was his zeal for education. This leads us now to our next heading where we will seek to consider the Church and its influence upon education.

Charlemagne was very much concerned for education and also very much aware of his own lack of it. He saw his Church and his people handicapped by ignorance. His land must possess the most efficient educational agencies. There had been a Palace School before, but, as Charles himself said, "The study of letters had been well-nigh extinguished by the neglect of his ancestors". Such reputation as Christian Gaul had for learning had disappeared in the wild Merovingian days. The lands where the torch of learning was still alight being Northumbria and Ireland prominent among the scholars of Northumbria was Alcuin of York. Charles encountered him in 768, the very year of his accession, they met again in Italy in 781, and this time Charles invited Alcuin to settle at his court. The Palace School was reinstituted. Charles set a good example by attaching himself to it as a pupil. As his appreciation for learning grew, he began to feel keenly the need for an educated Church. In 787, this most important observation and declaration, some have said the most important document of the early Middle Ages was made. It stated thus:

> During the past years we have often received letters from different monasteries informing us that at their sacred services brethren have offered up prayers on our behalf; and we have observed that the thoughts contained in these letters, though in themselves most just, were expressed in uncouth language, and while highest devotion dictated the sentiments, the unlettered tongue was unable to express them aright. Hence there has arisen in our minds the fear lest, if the skill to write correctly were thus lacking, so too would the power of rightly comprehending the sacred Scriptures be far less than was fitting, and we all know that though verbal errors be dangerous, errors of the understanding are yet more so. We exhort you, therefore, not only not to neglect the study of letters, but to apply yourselves thereunto with perseverance and with that humility which is well pleasing to God: so that you may be able to penetrate with greater ease and certainty the mysteries of the sacred Scriptures.

We need to note that within this statement there was the intention that not only the Church apply itself to its own education, but that it might also take up its responsibility for the teaching of the nation. The same proclamation desired that each monastery identify "men who are both able and willing to learn, and also desirous of instructing others".

Further, two years later "*A General Admonition*" was devoted to the subject of schools in each Cathedral and monastery. In 796, Alcuin was released from his labours in the Palace School to take charge of the foremost monastic institution in France, the great Abbey of St Martin at Tours. It was from this institution that there dawned a whole new culture, an educated culture that we call the Carolingian Renaissance.

It has been said that his emphasis on education, and an educated Church, has been one of Charlemagne's most lasting legacies.

He died on 28 January 814, in the 71st year of his age, and the 47th of his reign. He was buried on the same day in the Cathedral of Aix-la-Chapelle, amidst the great lamentation of the people. (Watt, 1927, p. 115ff.)

Christianity—its early role in establishing universal education, and the development of western literature

> It is without dispute that our Lord Jesus Christ was the greatest teacher the world has ever known. It has been said, "Had Christ left this world without making any provision for carrying on his work, he would still have been the greatest teacher of all time, and his life and example would have influenced profoundly the whole development of educational theory.
>
> L. Millar *Christian Education in the First Four Centuries*—quoted by Schmidt, 2004, p. 170

We might also add that Christ's teaching was not an end in itself, for he taught that those who followed him might teach others. Further on the death of the apostles, ministry and teaching continued in the Christian Church and one of its early literary productions was the appropriately called *Didache* from the word didactic meaning teaching.

Catechetical instruction has been a constant feature of Church life throughout the centuries. Justin Martyr around the year 150 established catechetical schools in Ephesus and Rome. And soon these schools appeared in other regions.

We might also add that while Christians were not the first to engage in formal teaching activities in school-like settings, they appear to have been the first to teach both sexes in the same setting. The instruction of both men and women, as the early Christians did, was seen as something revolutionary. The renowned scholar William M. Ramsay states that Christianity brought in "*universal education*, not education confined to the rich, as among the Greeks and Romans … and it made no distinction of sex".

Augustine writing in the fifth century said that Christian women were better informed on divine matters than the pagan male philosophers.

> In the 1330s, there is an interesting report from a chronicler in Florence that between eight and ten-thousand children in his city were attending the city's grammar schools. These also he notes included girls and boys.
>
> Rosenthal, 1990

Looking forward in history for a moment, we glance at the time of the Reformation. It was required of all clergymen, to hold catechetical classes on the Lord's Day afternoon. Into these were gathered all the children and youths, and in the case here in England, the teaching of the catechism of the Church of England was the beginning of universal education.

Patrick and Ireland

Here in Britain, though there were schools established by the Romans, as far as schools for the indigenous population were concerned, it is the ancient Celts we find ourselves looking at, in particular individuals, such as the well-known St. Patrick. Patrick is not only renowned as the apostle of Ireland, but he also occupies a significant niche in the origins of Celtic literature. He is in fact the earliest known pioneer of letters in Ireland—the first of whose work we have definite records to attest their authenticity. Certainly, from his missionary advent in Ireland a knowledge of letters seems to have spread rapidly over the land. Patrick wrote his own autobiography, particularly the account of his own conversion.

Besides his autobiography there are three pieces of literature assigned to him, namely the "*Confession*", and the "*Epistle to Coroticus*", both in Latin, and the "*Deer's Cry*" in Gaelic.

These are still in existence in the British Museum, Bodleian Library, Oxford and one copy in the public library of Arras.

The "*Deer's Cry*" is a hymn; it is written in a very ancient dialect of the Irish Celtic.

It has come down to us via a book of hymns collected in the eleventh century, which, like the *Book of Armagh*, contains several of Patrick's pieces. It is perhaps best known to us as the hymn *St. Patrick's Breastplate* beginning with the words:

> I bind myself today to the virtue of Christ's birth with his baptism,
> To the virtue of his crucifixion with his burial,
> To the virtue of his resurrection with his ascension,
> To the virtue of his coming to the Judgement of Doom …

The reason for the composition of this was to protect himself and his monks against his deadly enemies. The King at that time had sent for Patrick to explain the new religion to the nobles at Tara. On his return, an ambush was laid, apparently by the King's orders, to kill Patrick and his companions; they assumed, however, the form of the deer in the eyes of the would-be murderers, and thus escaped. Hence the title of the hymn "*The Deer's Cry*".

We may also add these remarks from Arthur Compton-Ricket in his *History of English Literature*:

> With the conversion of Ireland to Christianity came the introduction of the Latin alphabet and Latin literature, and the establishment of monastic schools. These soon became famous. Great numbers of foreigners—Gauls, Teutons, Swiss, Italians—crowded into these schools in which a wonderful standard of scholarship was maintained. Greek, Hebrew and Latin were taught in addition to grammar, philosophy, theology, etc. Moreover, this instruction was given to the foreign students through the native language. A number of the very oldest Irish texts are contained in the glosses to be found written in the margins between the lines of a Latin commentary on the Psalms, and a Latin sermon written in the eighth century, now in the libraries of Milan and Cambrai. The margin of the manuscript of St. Priscan of St Gall in the Milan codex contains these several little Gaelic poems such as:
>
> A grove surrounds me,
> The swift lay of the blackbird makes music to me,
> I will not hide it,

> Over my much-lined little book
> The song of the bird makes music to me.

Matthew Arnold made this comment:

> If I were asked where English poetry got these three things: its turn for style, its turn for melancholy, its turn for the natural magic, the catching and rendering the charm of nature in a wonderfully near and vivid way, I should answer, with some doubt, that it got much of its turn for style from a Celtic source; with less doubt that it got much of its melancholy from a Celtic source; and with no doubt at all, that from a Celtic source it got nearly all its natural magic.
>
> Compton-Rickett, 2018, p. 16

Though the influence of Celtic literature has been mainly indirect, the fusion of the races has led to the qualities and characteristics of Celtic and Teuton becoming intermingled. The earliest direct influence of the Celtic spirit may have been exercised on the Northumbrian school of poetry—Northumbria was Christianised in the seventh century by Irish missionaries. Men from the Irish monasteries came to Whitby, and there is in the poetry of the Cynewulfian school a love of colour, and a feeling for nature, and the strong personal note that bespeaks the Celt.

Columba and Scotland

Magnus McLean in *The Literature of the Celts: Its History and Romance* tells us:

> There is no evidence that the northern Picts had a knowledge of letters before Columba taught them. There is even doubt as to what language these tribes spoke. Yet in AD 710, little more than a hundred years after his death, a knowledge of letters was common in Pictland. With reference to subsequent ecclesiastical changes, it is known that King Naitian sent a proclamation "by public command throughout all the provinces of the Picts to be transcribed, learned, and observed". This we have on the authority of the Venerable Bede, a statement which shows that learning must have made considerable progress among the people even at that early date so that in this respect we may very well endorse the opinion of Professor Mackinnon, when he says that, "We have not yet perhaps fully realised the part which the School of Iona had in shaping the destinies of the Scottish nation". The same writer adds: "When in

> Scotland we discuss the past history of our national education, the figure of John Knox invariably rises before us as prime inaugurator of the first real system, but the great Abbot of Iona was at it 1000 years before him". (MacLean, 1902)

The same writer also affirms that the Celtic poets in the Columban period taught Europe to rhyme. It is pointed out that the Latin verses of Columcille (that is, Columba), and other early saints, either rhyme or have a strong tendency to rhyme. Scholars maintain that the use of rhyme in the literature of Scotland, England and the Germanic nations can be traced back to the influence of the Irish saints on the Island of Iona.

After this, we may identify Adomnán's *Life of St. Columba*, written in Latin but containing some parts written in Gaelic.

Interestingly, the original manuscript of this work still survives and is held by the public library of the town of Schaffhausen on the Rhine in Switzerland.

This fact again illustrates how widespread was the influence of the Christian teaching emanating from the Isle of Iona, and how well it deserves its name as the "Light of the Western World".

Wales

Wales is famous for its four ancient books.

- The Black Book of Carmarthen.
- The Book of Aneurin.
- The Book of Taliessin.
- The Red Book of Hergest.

From the book of Taliessin, there is a poem concerning the creation of Adam and Eve.

> The Almighty made
> Down the Hebron Vale,
> With his plastic hands
> Adam's fair form.

These books all have Christian influence. In the case of the Black Book of Carmarthen, some maintain that the identity of one Myrddin who is engaged in dialogue with another by the name of Yscolan, is none other than that of St Columba. This book originally belonged to the Priory of Black Canons at Carmarthen, from whom it passed to St David's.

Later in Welsh literature, we have of course the famous *Geoffrey of Monmouth's Chronicle*. Geoffrey of Monmouth was in actual fact a Welsh priest born in 1128. In this work, he professes to have translated into Latin from an ancient Welsh manuscript the history of Britain from the days of Brutus, the great-grandson of Aeneas, and on through the whole period of King Arthur's Round Table to the days of Cadwallader, a king who died in 689.

The influence of Christianity upon English literature

Amongst the earliest forms of English literature, we must include the historic writings of Gildas, known as the English Jeremiah. He is supposed to have been born in the year 520 of a bardic family and connection, and to have studied at the college of Llantwit Major, Glamorganshire. His *History of the Britons* is all we have of his works.

Later, there are the poems of Caedmon. The Venerable Bede puts Caedmon's date of death as 680 and describes him as being one who was given the gift of poetry from God. Bede says that he was wont to make pious and religious verses, so that whatever was interpreted to him out of Scripture he soon after put the same into poetical expressions of much sweetness and humility in English, which was his native language.

> Caedmon was a simple, unlettered man, an inmate of St. Hilda's monastery, near Whitby, to whom fell the task of looking after the cattle. Leaving the feast of the singers because he could not take part, he fell asleep among the cattle. While he slept, he dreamt that one came to him and commanded him to sing. "Of what am I to sing?" said Caedmon. "About the beginning of created things", came the reply. He then fashioned a song about the Creation and awakened from his dream. The song he remembered and composed many more like it. After this he became a monk. The Bible was read to him because he could not read, and he would turn into verse those passages that appealed especially to him.
>
> These stories in verse—Caedmon's *Paraphrases*—were written about 670 and became very famous. Of these poems only a fragment has survived. They were at that time copied and carried from monastery to monastery. The influence of Caedmon upon his

> successors was great. So we may say of Caedmon that he founded a new school of religious poetry, and it is probable that his verse served as a model for many subsequent writers.
>
> Compton-Rickett, 2018, p. 6

One of these subsequent writers was Cynewulf who was in the line of succession from Caedmon. It is not improbable that he was the author of "*The Christ*" and "*The Dream of the Rood*".

He was a Northumbrian who lived at the close of the eighth century. It is not surprising that it has been said that Anglo-Saxon poetry resembles Hebrew poetry, indulging in parallelism and metaphorical phrases. It is not in rhyme and as we have noted above this influence came later from the Irish Celtic tradition.

The two great writers of English history of course were the Venerable Bede (671–735), in the north and Aldhelm (d. 709), Abbot of Malmesbury, then Bishop of Sherborne, in the south. Bede was the abbot of the monasteries of Weirmouth and Jarrow.

> At the request of his friend Acca, he undertook to write a large commentary on the greater part of the books of Scripture, selected from the writings of the Christian fathers, and, with many additions of his own, a work of great labour and value. Besides this, he wrote many treatises and letters to friends on religious and moral subjects, on the nature of the world, on the art of calculating time, and on metre; a great number of sermons or homilies; and a history of the Church of England from the mission of Gregory to his own time
>
> Churton, 1878, pp. 148–149

Aldhelm wrote mainly in Latin, but his English verse was esteemed highly by Alfred the Great, who was also an esteemed figure in the unfolding story of English literature.

According to tradition, when Alfred was about four years old, just before his mother died, she showed him an illuminated Saxon manuscript with the promise that the first of the children who was able to read it should become its owner. Alfred won the prize and thus the foundation was laid of that knowledge and love of learning with which his name has been associated ever since. His mother died when he was five and his father when he was eight.

When he later became king, he had a great burden for the Christian education of his people. He invited scholars from the continent of Europe to assist in establishing schools and it was his especial desire to instruct his people in the elements of the Christian faith. Alfred himself translated Bede's *Ecclesiastical History*, originally written in Latin, into Anglo–Saxon, as well as portions of the Psalms and the Ten Commandments. He is also reputed to have begun the work on the *Anglo-Saxon Chronicle*. In order to encourage the clergy in the performance of their duties, Alfred presented each of them with a copy of Pope Gregory's book, *Pastoral Care*. He made the Ten Commandments the basis of English law, and at the same time he informed his judges that Christ came into the world not to destroy but to fulfil the law of God.

Amongst the significant books that King Alfred translated or had translated into English besides those mentioned above we may include:

The Consolations of Boethius.

The History of Orosius.

Gregory's Dialogues.

The Soliloquies of Augustine of Hippo.

Various translations of Holy Scripture.

Tradition asserts that Alfred founded the University of Oxford although this is challenged in these days.

It is important to remember that Christianity:

> Offered itself without reservation to all individuals, classes, and nations; it was not limited to one people, like Judaism, nor freed men of one state, like the official cults of Greece and Rome
>
> quoted in Schmidt, 2004, p. 176

This openness existed not just in regard to those whom the Church sought as members, but also in its educational activities. Unlike the Greek and Roman practice of teaching only boys from the privileged class of society, Christianity taught individuals from all social classes and ethnic backgrounds, especially in its preparation for Church membership. There was no bias to any particular class or peoples. The poor and lower classes were not excluded from membership nor from the educational activities of the churches. One of the remarkable features of the early Church was that from the highest to the lowest all were welcome. In a manuscript called the "*Acts of Peter*", compiled in the second century, Roman senators, equestrians, and women of high social standing were members of the apostle Peter's congregation alongside of whom and on an equal footing were slaves.

We have already noted that the monasteries in the early days were places of education. These monasteries, particularly the Benedictine monasteries, placed great value on the literary treasures of antiquity. It has been said that Benedict was the "*godfather of libraries*". In the "*scriptoria*" of the monasteries we might see in embryonic form the origins of universities.

Some say that the University of Oxford is the oldest university, others the University of Bologna and yet others the University of Paris. What cannot be denied is that these institutions were founded as Christian institutions, regardless of whether they taught law, theology or medicine.

> Not too long after the first universities arose, some schools engaged in empirical research. By 1300, for example, the University of Bologna dissected human cadavers for forensic purposes to settle legal suits. The dissecting of human bodies soon spread to other universities that functioned as medical schools, for instance, Montpelier and Padua. By 1396, Charles VI of France ordained that each year a cadaver of a criminal be delivered to the faculty of Montpelier for anatomical study. The King's action was preceded by the University of Montpelier statutes of 1340, which provided for dissection of human cadavers every two years.
>
> That empirical research, first confined to medical schools, occurred relatively early in the existence of the mediaeval universities should not come as a surprise if one remembers that it was the monks who were the university lecturers and who came from a long-standing tradition of doing both physical and intellectual work. Monks were used to getting dirt under their fingernails. Doing empirical research was simply an extension of their physical work; it was the Christian way of combining manual and intellectual activity.
>
> Prior to this era, with the minor exception of Archimedes (287–230 BC), who built a water screw and a device to study geometry, and Galen (131–200), who dissected animals and some human cadavers, the great thinkers never tested their empirical theories. Educated Greeks and Romans saw all manual activity as only fit for slaves, and since empirical research required manual activity, the brilliant theories proposed by the ancient Greek philosophers were left untested. For instance, Pythagoras (*c.* 560–489 BC) argued that the earth was spherical and that it revolved; and Anaxagoras (*c.* 500–428 BC) theorised that the moon received its light from the sun and the moon's eclipses were the result of the earth's impeding a portion

> of the sun's light. Archimedes put forth the theory of the sun centred (heliocentric) universe and thought that the earth revolved around the sun, which was stationary. Thus, the empirical research, which really first appeared in the mediaeval monasteries where intellectual and manual activities were not seen as incompatible, was a major innovation and revolutionary contribution to the world of learning and bequeathed to posterity a method that today's universities, secular or Church-related, could not do without. The world of knowledge would be greatly enhanced if scholars and scientists were to make this major legacy of Christianity known.
>
> Schmidt, 2004, pp. 189–190

Christianity's influence on the development of science

Undoubtedly biblical Christianity is the mother of modern science because it insists that the God who created the universe has revealed himself in the Bible to be the kind of God he is. Consequently, there is a sufficient basis for scientific study of the universe. This must be emphasised as much current popular opinion would hold that science grew thanks to the classical and in spite of the biblical tradition.

Much is made of the so-called retarding influence of the mediaeval Church on the development of science. The role played by mediaeval biblical exegesis in offering resistance to the new scientific spirit on the movements of the earth and planets has been emphasised again and again. In the first place, we might say that just as it would be wrong to blame Aristotle for all the prejudiced, dogmatic and even silly interpretations of his philosophy put forward by his mediaeval scholastic followers, so it would be wrong to lay to the account of the biblical authors the short-sighted interpretations of those who used the Scriptures to oppose legitimate scientific opinions and discoveries.

The first point being made here however is that because God has made an orderly universe, with laws and principles that can be measured, and deductions, derived from the observation of the orderly movements and patterns of the universe, there can be such a discipline as science. The first chapter of Genesis makes it very plain that God is a God of order. The separations of the first days served the cause of order, they permit classification by categories. The repetition of the formula "according to their kind" reinforces the theme. Everything is in its place, God assigns to the great luminaries their exact function. Isaiah chapter 45:18 says:

> *For thus saith the Lord that created the heavens; God himself that formed the earth and made it; he hath established it, he created it not in vain, he formed it to be inhabited*

> The universe has order. It is not a chaos. One is able to proceed from the particulars of being to some understanding of its unity. One is able to move ever deeper into the universe and yet never come upon a precipice of incoherence. We find this emphasised in Genesis 1 which points out that God has made all these things to produce after their own kind. Here is order. And so it is with the God of Scripture. He is not the philosophic other, nor the impersonal everything, nor that which is chaotic or random. He is a God who is (and I use this word carefully and worshipfully) a *reasonable* God. Moreover, the universe speaks of God's character. God not only is and is the God of order and of reason, but God is good. He created a universe that is totally good, and, as it originally came from God by fiat, this too speaks of him.
>
> Schaeffer, 1972, p. 58

Moreover, God has from the beginning encouraged man to observe and to classify the created order. The opening chapters of Genesis speak of God as the author of light, the days are numbered and measured, and Adam is given the task of naming or we could say classifying the various species of creatures and giving them names.

God has called man "to multiply, and replenish the earth, and subdue it: and have dominion over the fish of the sea, and over the fowl of the air, and over every living thing that moveth upon the earth" (Genesis 1:28).

Here we are delivered from the pagan view that nature and creation in some way are to be worshipped. Paganism would deify nature, and hence not make it a subject to be analysed, categorised or dissected.

> By contrast with the nature worship of its neighbours, the religion of Israel was a unique phenomenon. The God of Israel, by his word, brings forth all things out of nothingness. He is truly all powerful: He was not opposed by any matter that had to be forced into order, and he did not have to reckon with the eternal forms; his sovereign will alone created and sustains the world. In the first chapter of Genesis, it is made evident that absolutely nothing, except God, has any claim to divinity; even the sun and the moon, supreme gods of the neighbouring peoples, are set in their places between the

> herbs and the animals and are brought into the service of mankind. The personal gods of the Greeks had an origin, in spite of their immortality. The God of the Bible is the only God who is immutable and eternal, unlike all created things which are liable to change and final destruction. Nothing else has divine power, not even by delegation: "The LORD is one; there is none other."
>
> The New Testament proclaims again the message that there is no eternal cycle of nature or cycle of history. The history of the world moves towards its final destination and heaven and earth are destined to fall back into the nothingness from which once they emerged. Not only the creating, but also the upholding of the world belongs to God alone; that is to say, Jehovah is not a deistic supreme being who, after the creative act, leaves everything to the innate laws of nature, and he does not withdraw, like a Platonic demiurge, into "the way of being that belongs solely to him". He remains forever the will and power behind all events—Christ "upholds all things by the word of his power".
>
> Hooykaas, 2008, pp. 7–8

The Christian believes that the natural world is to be admired as God's work, and as an evidence of its Creator, but it is never adored. Nature can arouse in a person feelings of awe, but it is not to be worshipped; rather mankind is given the task of studying its beauty, coming to understand its laws and principles, and manage them, and harness them, to derive from them the good and useful purposes for which end God has made them and given them to mankind.

> The scientific and technological enterprises still comprise God's mandate to man relative to the earth and its inhabitants, and man would find himself immeasurably more productive and effective in such pursuits if he would only approach them in the reverent and believing attitude of an honest and good servant of his Maker.
>
> Morris, 2009, p. 77

We cannot emphasise too strongly that modern science has arisen entirely within the borders of Christendom; all other religions have lacked the sensitivity, curiosity, daring and love of truth, the sense of order and the unity of spirit which have combined to produce it. It is true that five centuries before Christ the philosophers of Athens began to seek for truth and order, but they lacked the biblical background giving them the understanding of the nature of things, and the impetus to follow these things through.

"It is true to say," said Dr Charles Singer the renowned British historian of science:

> It was with the Ionian Greeks that the scientific idea was born, and it can be traced back among them with some clearness to the sixth century BC … It was thus not the *practice* of science which the Greeks invented, but the *scientific idea*, the conception that the world was knowable inasmuch and in so far as it could be investigated.
> So the Ionian Greeks got science started. They believed you could understand the world by investigating it. However, the idea that everything in the world operated by fixed laws was not a Greek idea. It was a Christian idea.
>
> Quoted in Wile, 2011

It was because of this that the ancient Greeks failed to build on their legacy.

The Romans were lacking in a similar way, in that while they pursued the ideals of law, order, and military strategy, true science was not on their agenda.

We may look at the ancient civilisations of Persia, China and India, and though they produced many great works of literature and art, and pondered deep philosophies, they were never much moved in the direction of scientific enquiry or discovery.

When we consider the ancient civilisation of China, with its fantastic wealth, population, technological prowess during the ancient and mediaeval periods, it is natural to wonder why science did not occur there first.

The answer is that there were science-hindering metaphysical concepts in Chinese philosophy and religion, that frustrated and blocked its development.

One Buddhist monk attacked the Christian doctrine of creation as follows:

> Space, worlds, and beings have no beginning nor end if we consider them not in themselves and individuals but in their totality. They are eternal in this global point of view. They will proliferate without end and during incalculable cosmic periods progress through successive stages of formation, stability, degradation and then return to nothingness.

> Such ideas were no mere individual eccentricity of this monk, but were part and parcel of Chinese intellectual life, having apparently been strengthened by the entrance of Buddhism from Hindu India, and were assimilated into Neo-Confucian thought. What are the problems caused by acceptance of such cycles of thousands of years in which the world and its civilisations are repeatedly created and destroyed only to be created again? Such views create a sense of metaphysically-induced hopelessness and passivity since no matter how hard humans may struggle to achieve, work, and think, the result of all efforts will be destroyed. Also, a non-linear view of time makes careful, precise quantification (measurement using numbers) of time irrelevant. It also makes people tend to confuse the order of cause and effect since the idea of this—after—that (succession) is weaker …
>
> Christianity: A Cause of Modern Science.
> https://www.rae.org/essay-links/jaki/

Cause and effect did not matter to the Chinese, and this undercutting of the idea of succession in time therefore obviously destroyed their concept of applying the law of cause and effect.

We can add to this the Taoist belief that one should not actively investigate nature but rather apply a "*mystically-inclined contemplation and inactivity concerning it. He who practices the Tao, daily diminishes his doing; it diminishes it and again diminishes it, till he arrives at doing nothing. Having arrived at this non-action, there is nothing that he does not do*". Taoism teaches that man is totally weak and impotent compared to the majesty of nature, with which he should see an intimate organic unity. But these outlooks kept him from developing the idea of natural law in the modern sense. Such ideas have a negative effect in developing an active mind-set towards nature, which is of course necessary to the development of modern science.

In short, both belief in eternal time cycles and in nature as one huge organism encouraged passivity as opposed to mental activity and the investigating spirit of science. This was the total opposite of the view of Aristotle and Leonardo da Vinci, and indeed the Christian view of nature.

Again it was not that there was no order in nature for the Chinese, but rather that it was not an order ordained by a rational personal being, and hence there was no conviction that rational personal beings would be able to spell out in their lesser earthly languages the divine code of laws which he had decreed at the beginning.

We may now turn to the Islamic world and ask the same question; Why did not the Islamic world develop science before Christendom?

Islam was not hindered by the cyclic views or the orgasmic views of the universe as in the case of the Chinese and far Eastern philosophies. Islam believed in one God, who created the universe at a definite point in time, with time linearly proceeding towards judgement day. Islam did not deny the reality of the external world, nor was it apt to think the heavens were divine. Therefore, we are not surprised that amongst the early followers of Islam there were significant figures who made important contributions towards the development of science.

Mention could be made of the early medical works of al-Raci and Avicenna (980–1037) and these works were used in Christendom deep into the 16th century. Moreover, such English words as alcohol, algebra, algorithm, almanac, assassin, chemistry, coffee, mascara, etc., are derived from the Arabic. Islamic mathematicians made very important contributions in the realms of algorithm, algebra, trigonometry and analytical geometry.

However, various factors need to be added to this. We need to remember that Islam gained its knowledge of the Greek writings via the Eastern Church which it overran and which had preserved these Greek manuscripts. Moreover, the early Islamist Caliphs employed Nestorian Christians very much in their administrative organisation. It is certainly a fact that Eastern Christians introduced the Muslims to Greek learning in the Ummayad and the Abbasid periods by translating the works of Greek philosophers into Syrian and then afterwards into Arabic. The same Nestorian Christians also excelled in philosophy, science, theology and medicine. It is said that eight generations of Nestorian Christians served as private doctors to Caliphs and sultans between the 8th and 11th centuries. Many Christian medical textbooks were translated into Arabic at this time. Hunayn ibn-ishaq was a famous and influential Christian scholar, physician and scientist of ethnic Arab descent, in the service of some of the early Islamist Caliphs and Sultans.

Rodney Stark comments on the fact that the Moslem invaders overran many previously Christian civilisations in the Middle East and North Africa. Jews and Christians in these regions who refused to convert to Islam were known as *dhimmis*. It was official policy that such people should "*feel inferior and know their place*". Various restrictions were placed upon them such as they could not ride horses, only mules, and that they should wear certain marks of their religion on their costumes. This involved dressing in black and hanging wooden crosses from their necks, half a metre long, and half a metre wide when amongst Muslims. In some places non-Muslims were prohibited from wearing clothing similar to that of Muslims nor could they be armed. Invariably such people were more severely taxed than the Muslim population. (*The Triumph of Christianity*, p. 208.)

However, the Muslims recognised that there were many among the *dhimmis* population who had extremely valuable gifts in the realm of administration, as well as considerable scientific, mathematical, and medical knowledge. Many of these were Coptic Christians. They were especially trusted in the handling of funds and were valued for their trustworthiness in carrying out administrative duties. They retained their posts because very often Muslim replacements simply could not be found.

The irony was that during this period science was somewhat neglected by the Christian Church. It flourished for a while under early Islam, who took advantage of the Christian influence it inherited in regard to these scientific disciplines, but however in time, the deadening effect of Islamic theology eventually quenched the flame.

Rodney Stark quoted above has commented on the fact that the total number of books translated into Arabic during the thousand years since the age of Caliph Al-Ma'moun (a ninth-century Arab ruler who was a patron of cultural interaction between Arab, Persian and Greek scholars), to this day is less than those translated in Spain in one year. He further claimed that the "*inability of Muslims to keep up with the West occurred because Moslem Arab culture was largely an illusion resting on a complex mix of dhimmi cultures, and as such, it was easily lost and always vulnerable to being repressed as heretical. Hence when the 14th century Muslims in the East stamped out nearly all religious nonconformity, Muslim backwardness came to the fore*".

However, as the Middle Ages progressed a new interest in science was rekindled in the Christian West. The University of Padua began to study Aristotle in the light of the Arabian commentator Avarroes. In England Robert Grosseteste is regarded as the founder of science at Oxford, in the early thirteenth century. He produced a work entitled *Compendium Scientiarum*, in which he introduced the concept that "*it is impossible to understand Nature without experiment or describe her without geometry".*

C.A. Coulson comments:

> [Grosseteste's statement:] "it was impossible to understand Nature without experiment or describe her without geometry" (or, as we might say now, theoretical physics); and by this he implied the unity of science and faith, just as much as did his distinguished pupil, the Somerset Friar Roger Bacon, whose *Opus Maius*, written at the request of Pope Clement IV, was designed to show that the new knowledge, so far from being an enemy of Christian faith, was actually an aid, even in the business of evangelising mankind. This was because it could "assist the Church … by leading the mind through a study of the created works to a knowledge of the Creator". Indeed, arithmetic, even in the new Arab notation just coming into vogue, was something in the nature of a necessary study for theologians, who, he says, should, "abound in the power of numbering".
>
> Coulson, 1958, p. 22

Returning to why science did not continue to flourish in the Islamic world we must answer summarising our answer in the words of Robert Moray:

> Because the God of the Bible is limited by his own righteous nature and there are certain things he cannot do, he is completely consistent and trustworthy. When we turn to study the actions of Allah in the Koran, we discover that he is totally capricious and untrustworthy. He is not bound by his nature or his Word.
> Hence the metaphysics of the Koran, by emphasising God's arbitrary and changeable will, as opposed to his reason, help to sink Islamic science through creating a weak view of the laws of nature and an orderly universe.
>
> Christianity A Cause of Modern Science
> https://www.rae.org/essay/jaki/

It is also necessary for us in this section to try and debunk some of the popular ideas in regard to Christianity's opposition to science in the Middle Ages.

It is popularly thought that Columbus took years to raise funds needed to launch his famous voyage of discovery because of the unanimous opposition by Church scholars and officials, all of whom were certain that the world must be flat. This interpretation of the Columbus story was reported by the famous Andrew Dickson White (1832–1918) founder and first president of Cornell University, and author of the very influential two volume work, *A History of the Warfare of Science with Theology in Christendom*. Here is an extract from that work:

> The warfare of Columbus with religion, the world knows well: how the Bishop of Ceuta worsted him in Portugal; or sundry wise men of Spain confronted him with the usual quotations from Psalms, from St Paul, and from St Augustine; how even after he was triumphant, and after his voyage greatly strengthened the theory of the world's sphericity … The Church by its highest authority solemnly stumbled and persisted in going astray … The theological barriers to this geological truth yielded but slowly … Many conscientious men opposed the truth for 200 years longer.

In actual fact nearly every word of White's account is either misleading or untrue—as are so many of the other stories he wrote about conflicts between religion and science in his now discredited and no longer esteemed work.

A considerable time before the 15th century, every educated European, including Roman Catholic prelates, knew that the Earth was round. A book with the title *Sphere* was the title of the most popular mediaeval textbook on astronomy, written in the early thirteenth century. In fact, the opposition encountered by Columbus was not about the shape of the earth, but about the fact that he was wildly wrong about the circumference of the globe. He estimated it was about 2,800 miles from the Canary Islands to Japan. In reality it is about 14,000 miles. His opponents knew how far it was and opposed his voyage on the grounds that Columbus and his men would all die at sea. Had the Western hemisphere, i.e. America not been there, and no one knew it existed, the *Nina, Pinter*, and the *Santa Maria* might as well have fallen off the earth, for everybody aboard would have died of thirst and starvation.

There is in fact no hint about Columbus having to prove that the earth was round in any contemporary accounts, and not even in his own *Journal*, nor that of his son's *History of the Admiral* is it even mentioned.

According to Rodney Stark the story was entirely unknown

until more than 300 years later when it appeared in a biography of Columbus published in 1828, by the author Washington Irving (1783–1859) who is best known for his fictional writings for example *The Legend of Sleepy Hollow*.

Although the tale about Columbus and the flat earth is equally fictional, Irving presents it as a fact.

We might next turn to the example of Galileo (1564–1642) and his being called before the Roman Inquisition in 1633 to recant his acceptance of the Copernican theory that the earth circles the sun. We might put the thing into its historical context by reminding ourselves that Pope Urban VIII had earlier written a poem on the glories of astronomy and was not hostile to scientific investigation.

We need also to remember that Nicholas Copernicus (1473–1543) was a Canon of Frauenberg Cathedral in East Prussia.

It would seem that because of the tumultuous nature of the times, the Roman Church was just in the midst of the Counter Reformation, in which she was being accused (we would say rightly) of going against Scripture. In view of all this Pope Urban VIII advised Galileo to simply present his conclusions as hypotheses, and not be too definite in his statements that the earth was the centre of the universe in a physical sense. Galileo blatantly refused to take this advice, and made this unmistakeably obvious in his work of 1632, entitled *Dialogue Concerning the Two Chief World Systems*. The dialogue involved three speakers, two of them philosophers and the third a layman; the layman was given the name "*Simplico*". Galileo did include the disclaimer suggested by the Pope, but he put it into the mouth of *Simplico*, with all the derogatory connotations that name implied.

However, as William Shea notes, "Had Galileo been less devout, he could have refused to go to Rome and face the Inquisition; Venice offered him asylum". (William Shea, *Galileo and the Church*, 1986, p. 14, quoted by Stark, p. 291).

But Galileo did not flee to Venice and often expressed his personal faith to his daughter and friends after his trial was over.

> We may also bear in mind, going back to the originator of this theory of Nicholas Copernicus that though he remained a loyal Roman Catholic to the end of his days, it was his Lutheran friends that made his publication possible. It was the Lutheran Duke Albrecht of Prussia who subsidised the publication of Copernicus's work. It was the Lutheran theologian Andreas Osiander who arranged for

> the printing of the work, and the Lutheran mathematician Georg Joachim Rheticus who arranged the printing.
>
> Schmidt, 2004, p. 226.

We might also mention at this point that it is often said that Martin Luther reportedly called Copernicus a "*fool*". However, it has been shown that this frequently cited remark lacks reliable scholarly support. First of all, it comes from Luther's Table Talks, a late redacted copy, published twenty years after his death, of what some thought he said. Secondly, Copernicus is not named in the remark, so even if Luther said it, it is not certain that he had him in mind. Thirdly, if he did make a comment, it was in Luther's un-guarded, often light-hearted, jovial conversation. Fourthly we may bear in mind that this is the only such remark in all of Luther's writings, which total nearly 100 volumes. Fifthly, Philip Melanchthon, Luther's closest colleague, who initially was suspicious of Copernicus, stated publicly in 1549, "*We have begun to admire and love Copernicus more*".

We might also remind ourselves that the Calvinists did not condemn the Copernican theory.

Indeed, in the 16th and early 17th centuries Lutherans and Calvinists, mostly Puritans, did much to advance science. For example, men of Calvinistic persuasion founded what became the Royal Society in London 1645, with seven of its ten scientists being Puritans. After royal recognition 1662 this became the world's most prestigious scientific association.

We may conclude by reminding ourselves also that the modern notion that the Church significantly held back the development of science can be traced back to the secularist writings of individuals like Voltaire who in the 18th century reported, "*The great Galileo at the age of fourscore groaned away in the dungeons of the Inquisition because he had demonstrated by irrefutable proofs the motion of the earth*".

Or again quoting the Italian Guiseppe Baratti (1719–1789) who stated that Galileo was "put to torture, for saying that the earth moved".

Further we can affirm that science arose only in Europe because only mediaeval Europeans believed that science was possible and desirable. The basis of their belief was that man was made in the image of God and had created all things. This affirmation was made by the philosopher and mathematician Alfred North Whitehead (1861–1947) whilst giving the 1925 Lowell Lectures at Harvard University, USA. He explained that science developed in Europe because of the widespread "*faith in the possibility of science*" and this being derived "*from Mediaeval theology*".

Further weight is given to the unbiased nature of this statement when we remember that Whitehead was the co-author, with the atheist Bertrand Russell, of the widely acclaimed *Principia Mathematica*. (1910–1913).

Whitehead may not have been a Christian but he knew that Christianity was not as some have claimed "*the unrelenting enemy of science*".

Stark's comments on these insights of Whitehead and the connection between Christian theology and the rise of science are well worth repeating in full:

> Whitehead had recognised that Christian theology was essential for the rise of science, just as non-Christian theologies had stifled the scientific enterprise everywhere else. He explained that "the greatest contribution of medievalism to the formation of the scientific movement was the inexpugnable belief … that there was a secret, a secret which can be unveiled. How has this conviction been so vividly implanted in the European mind? ... it must come from the mediaeval insistence on the rationality of God, conceived with the personal energy of Jehovah and with the rationality of the Greek philosopher. Every detail was supervised and ordered: the search into nature could only result in the vindication of faith in rationality". Whitehead was, of course, merely summarising what so many of the great early scientists had said—René Descartes justified his search for the "laws" of nature on the ground that such laws must exist because God is perfect and therefore "acts in a manner as constant and immutable as possible". That is, the universe functions according to rational rules or laws. As that great mediaeval scholastic Nicole d'Oresme put it, God's creation "is much like that of a man making a clock and letting it run and continue its own motion by itself". Furthermore, because God has given humans the power of reason it ought to be possible for us to discover the rules established by God.
>
> Indeed, many of the early scientists felt morally obliged to pursue these secrets, just as Whitehead had noted. The great British philosopher concluded his remarks by noting that the images of God and creation found in the non-European faiths, especially those in Asia, are too impersonal or too irrational to have sustained science. Any particular natural "occurrence might be due to the fiat of an

irrational despot" god, or might be produced by "some impersonal, inscrutable origin of things. There is not the same confidence as in the intelligible rationality of a personal being. It should be noted that given their common roots, the Jewish conception of God is as suitable to sustaining science as is the Christian conception that Jews were a small, scattered, and often repressed minority in Europe during this era and took no part in the rise of science—albeit Jews have excelled as scientists since their emancipation in the 19th century.

Stark, 2012, p. 285

Chapter 7
Christianity and the Crusades

TURNING NOW TO WHAT SOME HAVE CONSIDERED TO BE A STAIN ON the history of Christianity, we might make some remarks on the period of the Crusades.

To rightly appreciate this period of Christian history we need to go back a few centuries to the time of the Roman destruction of Jerusalem, when many of the Christians in that region fled and took refuge in the East. But at an early date there were Christians present in Syria, Persia, parts of Arabia, Mesopotamia, Turkestan, Armenia, and on even into India, with some even claiming a Christian presence in China at this early date. Due to further missionary expansion North Africa was very much Christianised and later gave to the Church some of its greatest leaders such as Tertullian, Cyprian and Augustine.

There were therefore many Christian and Jewish people and communities living in Arabia by AD 570 when Mohammed was born. For example, there were Christian towns in what is now modern Yemen, and large Jewish settlements in towns like Mecca and Medina.

At first Mohammed expected that the Jews and the Christians would accept him as the Prophet sent from God.

At first he was patient towards them but soon became frustrated when they rejected him. When he had gained enough strength to impose his will upon them, he attacked the Jews in Mecca and Medina; and eventually forced the male members of the last Jewish families in Medina to dig their own mass grave, whereupon all six to nine-hundred of them were beheaded and the women and children sold into slavery.

Eventually Mohammed expanded his influence into Byzantine Syria and into Persia. These attacks were in keeping with what came to be known as Mohammed's farewell address during which he said: "I was ordered to fight all men until they say, '*There is no god but Allah*'". Again in the spirit of the Koran which says, "*slay the idolaters wherever ye find them, and take them (captive) and besiege them, and prepare for them each an ambush*". Muslim armies launched a century of successive conquests throughout the Middle East. These forces eventually reached to Armenia and into the Indus Valley which is now modern Pakistan.

Moving westwards they first of all took what is now known as the Holy Land, at that time the most westerly part of Byzantine Syria. Caliph Umar, the second successor of Mohammed, began the invasion of Egypt which at that time was a major centre of Christianity and also at that time a Byzantine colony.

Attacks were made on Alexandria, and eventually the Muslims took all the main centres along the north coast of Africa and in AD 711 they invaded Spain, a century later taking Sicily and southern Italy.

We have already noted how the Muslims oppressed the indigenous populations, but also plundered their knowledge and even used some of the intelligentsia of the population in administrative capacities, rather as was the case with Daniel and his friends in Babylon. Likewise, some of these members of the intelligentsia were given new names, in this case, Moslem names.

In 1009 at the direction of Fatimid Caliph al-Hakim the Church of the Holy Sepulchre in Jerusalem was destroyed. This was the splendid basilica Constantine had erected over what he believed to be the site of our Lord's tomb where he lay before the resurrection. Worse still the Muslims attempted to destroy the tomb itself, leaving only traces of the hollow in the rocks.

Later in the same century the Sejuk Turks, who had been recently converted to Islam, became the new rulers of Asia Minor. Their expansionist policy soon brought them within a hundred miles of Constantinople.

Some awareness and understanding of this rapid and brutal expansion of Islam is necessary to rightly understand the rationale behind the Crusades.

It was in this climate that Alexes Comnenus the Emperor of Byzantium requested help from his fellow Christians in the West to come to their rescue. In his impassioned plea he described in gruesome detail the tortures inflicted on pilgrims on their way to the Holy Land and the relentless destruction and desecration of churches by the Moslem forces.

This cry for help resonated with Pope Urban II who is generally regarded as the first instigator of the Crusades.

He preached a famous sermon in the French city of Claremont on 27 November 1095. An immense crowd gathered from all quarters and listened to what some have regarded as one of the most effective speeches of all time. The response of the crowd was the famous shout of "*Dieu li Volt!*" ("*God wills it*"). (Note: some say this sermon was preached in the Italian town of Piacenza).

It is generally regarded that there were seven Crusades in all stretching over a period of about five hundred years.

The first Crusades were waged against the forces of Islam, while a second series of Crusades was raised against the Albigensians in southern France, and a third against the Hussites in Bohemia.

We certainly cannot countenance these Crusades, though we may to some degree challenge some of the prevailing wisdom which interprets the Western Church's challenge to the rise of Islam as no more than an expansionist, imperialistic, brutalised Christendom, looting and colonising a tolerant and peaceful Islam.

We have to bear in mind with all that can be said negatively about the Crusades, that the Western condemnation of the Crusades originated at the time of the "*Enlightenment*" in the 17th century. Again mentioning Voltaire (1694–1778) who called the Crusades "*an epidemic of fury which lasted for 200 years and which were always marked by every cruelty, every perfidy, every debauchery, and every folly of which human nature is capable*". Another enlightenment figure David Hume (1711–1776), said the Crusades were "*the most signal and most durable monument to human folly that has yet appeared in any age or nation*". Denis Diderot (1713–1784), labelled the Crusades as "*a time of the deepest darkness and of the greatest folly … To drag a significant part of the world into an unhappy little country in order to cut the inhabitants' throats and seize a rocky peak which was not worth one drop of blood*".

The idea that the Crusades were early Western imperialistic endeavours, waged under the cloak of a religious excuse to seek land and loot treasure, was most probably originated by Edward Gibbon (1737–1794), who claimed that the Crusaders really went in pursuit of "*mines of treasures, of gold and diamonds, of palaces of marble and jasper, and of odoriferous groves of cinnamon and frankincense*". (*The Decline and Fall of the Roman Empire*, 6. 58, quoted by Stark, p. 215).

These sorts of views have been built on during the latter part of the 20th century, and labelled as crimes against Islam, as the source of the present conflict between Islam and the West. In 1999 to mark the 900th anniversary of the Crusader conquest of Jerusalem, hundreds of "Christians" took part in a "Reconciliation Walk" begun in Germany and ended in the Holy Land. All along the way the walkers wore T-shirts bearing the message "*I apologise*" in Arabic. In the same year the *New York Times* proposed that the Crusades were comparable to Hitler's atrocities or the ethnic cleansing in Kosovo. Karen Armstrong, the popular writer on "*religious*" subjects, described the territory taken by the Crusaders as "*our first colonies*".

It is true that there were great elements of folly in the Crusades; there was certainly greed and there was certainly cruelty. The so-called Children's Crusade was undoubtedly a tragic folly.

However, speaking of the motivation behind the Crusades in general it is important to note that they were precipitated by Islamic provocations, and Islamist expansionism, by cruel and grossly inhuman acts.

Those who went on the Crusades did not do so to get rich. It is true that many went because of the mistaken delusion that by going they would cancel their debt of sin. But it is a fact that those who went paid an immense price in going. The rich often knowingly bankrupted themselves; others paid at the expense of their lives.

It is simplistic to picture the situation of the Crusaders as bloodthirsty barbarians in contrast to the more civilised and tolerant Muslims. There were many gentlemanly acts displayed in the character of Saladin, but these have been overplayed to hide some of the darkest atrocities committed under his authority and by him in person.

It is easy to see the manifestation of man's corrupt nature in the actions of both the Crusaders and their Muslim protagonists.

It is sometimes raised that the Crusaders eventually attacked Constantinople itself. This seems to be clear evidence that the real motive behind these military campaigns was greed.

The story is far more complex and it involves the fact that it was agreed that once the victory was won the Byzantine forces would maintain the peace. However, the Byzantine leaders, seemingly having asked for help, reneged on their subsequent responsibilities. Moreover, the Byzantine Emperor Alexes Comnenus seemed to lose interest in retaining the Christian hold on the city of Jerusalem, and at the same time took offence at the presence in his country of crusading armies passing through. No doubt some of these undisciplined armies created trouble for him in the country, but his loss of interest in the campaign, and the failure to contribute to the cause created widespread resentment, and the sack of Constantinople has been seen by some as a rather crude way of exacting from him what they considered to be their due.

It will be debated for years to come whether or not the Crusades should have taken place or not, but we must not be completely blinded by modern interpretations, and see things in the context of the day and age in which they were carried out. Our present times owe a great deal to historic Christianity but there are many today who will take every opportunity to overdo their criticisms of our cultural forebears.

In one sense it could be said that the Crusades were a failure, and one of the consequences was the ultimate fall of Constantinople and the Byzantine Empire.

On the other hand, they succeeded in turning back the intended rule of Islam in Europe and lost to its influence only the furthest fringes of the East. A further advantage can be seen by a comparison of the conditions of the peoples under the Sultans and Caliphs of the Moslem world with that of the general populace of the Christian West.

Prior to the Crusades, for some time Europe was in a state of mental torpor. Ignorance was widespread and general. Even kings and emperors in many cases had scarcely acquired the art of reading. Science was almost exclusively confined to the cloisters while the mind of the people quietly slumbered. The Crusades in a sense shattered this mental torpor. They were, as one called it, "*the sound of a trumpet to a sleeping host*". (Allan Cameron in *Great Men and Movements of the Christian Church*, p. 132). Further positive results were the general extension of ideas. In their progress towards the Holy Land, the followers of the cross marched through countries often better cultivated, and more cultured than their own, such as Italy in which cities, such as Venice, Genoa, Pisa, etc., had made significant advances towards wealth and refinement.

A special place of rendezvous on the march to Palestine was Constantinople. Before the disaster of the 4th Crusade this city was regarded as the most beautiful city in Europe, and the only one in which remained any remnant of the true sophistication and elegance of the old Roman Empire.

In spite however of the conquest of Constantinople the long-term result was that of widespread commercial contacts with this city, and the cities further east.

Another result was that the Crusaders on their return brought with them from Asia to Europe specimens of products unknown in the West. This created a desire in the market for such goods and thus a further enlargement of commerce was developed.

As we have noted many of the noble families who went on Crusade expended large sums of money for their expedition. The barons and great landowners tended to sell off their land in order to raise this money. The monarchs of the great kingdoms took advantage of these circumstances and bought those lands, adding to their own territories. This facilitated the ability of governments to better rule their territories. Also many of the barons who perished in the Crusades left no heirs and thus again land fell to their respective monarchs who used those lands to more effectively develop the economy of the nation. This same decline in the number of Barons also enabled the monarchs to centralise their power. This in turn led to a more consistent and uniform administration of justice, eventually leading towards the establishment of regular government in the modern sense. Also these things led to the advanced importance of towns, which up to this point had been held back by feudal tyranny and opposition.

In respect to common individuals, serfs on their return were declared free men, and this led to the development of a middle class in society, bridging the wide chasm which had until this point existed between the highly wealthy and powerful and the poor and powerless.

The Christian Martyrs' Last Prayer by Jean-Léon Gérôme

King Alfred presenting Runcorn Church to his daughter, Ethelfleda

Magna Carta

The Landing of the Pilgrim Fathers

Hopwood sculpsit.

JOHN WICLIF, D.D.

From a Picture in the Possession of the Duke of Dorset.

Published by R. Edwards, Crane Court, Fleet Street, Jan.y 1st 1810.

John Wiclif

1859

Novum
Organum
or
True Suggeſtions for the
Interpretation of
Nature
By
FRANCIS LORD VERULAM
Newly Tranſlated by the
REV. ANDREW JOHNSON
M. A.

LONDON
BELL & DALDY FLEET STREET

Francis Bacon and the Christian Foundation of Scientific Investigation

Cromwell outside the Mother of Parliaments

William Carey's 'An Enquiry'

Lord Shaftesbury

William Wilberforce and the Abolition of Slavery

Sunday School Banner

Chapter 8
Christianity's Contribution to Civilisation: The Middle Ages

A very good assessment of the impact of the Church in the Middle Ages is given by Archibald Robertson in his Bampton Lectures for 1901 on the subject of The Kingdom of God in Christian Thought. In the following I am quoting selectively from his summary.

Whatever our estimate of the moral or religious character of the Middle Ages, there can be no question of their ecclesiastical character, nor of the immense influence of the papacy in impressing the ecclesiastical stamp upon the civil and social life of the time. Christian people will differ as to the spiritual value of ecclesiastical organisation, institutions, and interests, in themselves, and as to the degree to which they may wholesomely predominate in the individual or the common life.

However, without their ecclesiastical character the Middle Ages would have been a barbarous time indeed. The Church brought the discipline of character, the summons to that absolute self-effacement which alone raises mankind wholly above the brute, brought comfort to the suffering, (and it was a time of suffering for the mass of men), binding up of wounds to the penitent, terrors to the hardened and the tyrannical.

Louis IX, a most typical product of mediaeval Christianity, would do honour to any Christian age or country. It is no doubt to the Church, not to the papacy, that the credit of these and such-like moral triumphs is due; but it may be questioned whether, at the beginning of the Middle Ages, the Church without a papacy would have had the coherence necessary for the task or the power necessary to enforce elementary Christian duties, to make headway against the numberless petty tyrannies of feudal Europe. Thus much may be fairly claimed for the Gregorian system.

But although the carrying out of that system was entrusted to a succession of Popes of exceptional character and ability (not to say that there were others who ought never to have occupied the papal throne), the point however being that it never really succeeded; nor so far as it did succeed did it wholly further the spiritual good of mankind.

The attempt to enforce the temporal claims of the Popes filled Italy and Germany with war and misery, and set Guelf against Ghibelline, city against city. (The curia was the den where Dante's "*Wolf of Avarice*" had her securest home. *Inferno* i.51).

It imposed upon the Popes the position of a territorial sovereignty inconsistent with the example of the Apostles and with the spiritual character of the Church and ministry. This again drew the Popes into territorial wars and intrigues, and into growing need of money. Though the Crusades were at first a movement of great idealism, headed by the Pope as the spiritual leader of Europe, they eventually were turned against Christians, and eventually embarked upon Crusades against the Albigensians, and later the followers of John Huss.

Hildebrand (1023–1085) during his pontificate had hoped, by the vigorous centralisation of power in his own hands, to cleanse the Church from simony and usury; his successors merely succeeded in concentrating both evils at Rome. The papal supremacy was employed above all as a means for extorting money. At the Council of Lyons in 1245, Innocent IV, bent on hurrying forward the imposition of and the support of the tottering Latin Empire of Constantinople, was obliged to listen sullenly while amid painful silence the English delegates to the council represented the disasters he was inflicting on their Church. "We gave long since," they said, "to our mother the Roman Church an honourable subsidy, namely, St. Peter's pence. But she, not content with that, asked, by her legates and nuncios, for further help; and that too we freely gave. You know, too, that our ancestors founded monasteries which they richly endowed, and to which they gave the patronage of many parish churches. But your predecessors, wishing to enrich the Italians, whose number has become excessive, gave to them these cures, of which they take no heed, neither in caring for the souls, nor in defence of the houses in whose patronage they are. They no longer fulfil the duty of hospitality nor of almsgiving, nothing of anything but to receive the revenues, and take them out of the kingdom, to the hurt of our kinsmen who ought to hold these livings and who would do the duty in person. Now to tell the truth these Italians draw from England more than 60,000 silver marks a year, which is a larger revenue than that of the King himself. We hoped that at your promotion you would reform this abuse, but on the contrary our charges are increased".

After giving details of the most recent extortions they concluded, saying; "We pray you promptly to remedy this; otherwise we could not any longer endure such vexations".

At the beginning of the Middle Ages, the papacy had almost wholly on its side all that was good and true in the life and mind of Christendom. By the end of the thirteenth century this was far from being the case. The Popes had, indeed, by judicious homage to an ideal of life in glaring contrast with their own practice, gained the support of the great movement of the Friars, which did much to regenerate the Mediaeval Church, and which secured to the support of the Church and papacy the ripest fruits of the new theological and speculative activity in the universities. But, the signs of the times:—Arnold of Bresca, Frederick Barbarossa, the growing popular liberties of England, the parishes of England and Germany suffering spiritual neglect in order that Rome might be rich—are so many reminders that the papacy was beginning to be a disruptive force, unable to hold together all the good that belongs to Christ as of right, a force that enlists on its side much moral and religious enthusiasm, but also repels much that is noble and good and true.

The one supposed Christian duty in which an advance was made was that of persecuting heretics. Before the end of the 11th century this was by no means common in the Church, though a few examples undoubtedly occurred. But Innocent III was the first to preach a crusade against the so-called heretics, and shed as much innocent blood as lies at the door of any human being.

There were of course better Popes and it is only fair to award to them credit for the blessings for which they were responsible, than for the evils, which attended their efforts to rule the world in Christ's name. Some of the evil consequences of their actions perhaps they were unaware of at the time. Others however were less than noble, and used their office to further their own ends, and surround themselves with luxury and opulence.

Archibald Robertson remarks that the mediaeval papacy did achieve something for the Kingdom of God, but it went on to make the disastrous mistake, or we may call it the most presumptuous of sins, of claiming that it was the Kingdom of Christ on earth, the Kingdom in which Christ reigned through his Vicar, the Pope.

It took Augustine's teaching on the Kingdom of God, or as he called it the City of God, and completely externalised it. Augustine spoke of government in the lap of the Church, the Church influencing for good the government. This however became under Hildebrand the Church seeking to control all governments in outward form.

This went way beyond Augustine's concept, and developed into an ecclesiastical constitution whereby the papacy sought to exercise supreme authority over all peoples and kings. This could only be achieved by employing methods directly in conflict with the Church's essential character and the injunctions of our Lord himself. "*The kings of the Gentiles exercise lordship over them, and their great one's exercise authority upon them; but ye shall not be so*" (Luke 22:25–26).

There are two alternative ideals of a Kingdom of Christ on earth and the method of its realisation: righteousness by means of government, and government by means of righteousness. The latter is the real and fundamental idea of Augustine; it is that of St. Paul, and of Christ himself. There is room for the other, but in strict subordination to it. In the education of the young, in the infancy of a civilisation or of Christendom, righteousness must come from without, by means of government. But government must know its own limitations and must realise the need for its gradual supersession, or rather transformation. External pressure, in the ideal healthy growth of individuals and societies, must give place to self-government which comes with maturing character.

> In God's providence, with much apparent retrogression and conflict and dissolution, the history of modern Christendom has run and, as we may believe and hope, will continue to run, some such course as this. Each stage of the process has its characteristic dangers and mistakes. We do not despair of freedom because its progress is beset with licence and indiscipline, nor need the record of tyranny and corruption blind us to the indispensable service which external authority has done in preparing us for the exercise of liberty. The papal monarchy in Christendom, like the monarchy in Israel, belonged to a necessary stage in the divinely ordered history of our Christian faith. In both cases its establishment was at once an advance and a decline; in neither case was it to remain for ever. But both alike served the will of God in their generation, and both alike have bequeathed for all time the ideal of the reign of Christ over the unruly will and affections of sinful but redeemed mankind.
>
> Adapted from *Regnum Dei*, Archibald Robertson,
> Bampton Lecture, 1901, pp. 276–282

Before we leave the Middle Ages, having acknowledged their many defects and inadequacies, which were soon in history to be rectified by the Reformation, we must identify at least three principal legacies and bequests received from this period of Christian history.

They are first of all the concept of Christendom—that is, a society ordered on Christian principles and unified by the pursuit of an ideal.

Next is the concept of chivalry—that is, the dedication of physical force to the service of spiritual objects, the consecration of soldierhood.

And thirdly the concept of justice embodied in law, grounded on liberty—that is, the conception of an ordered democracy.

If we consider the first of these legacies, we may say that human society has been held together by many forces during the course of time. Physical factors have counted for much in the rise and fall of nations. Political fortunes accounted for more. The invisible, immaterial forces of the human spirit, supremely expressed in religion, have counted for most in the process. For the human spirit preserves its mysterious potency through all the changing scenes of time, and remains the most stable factor in the protean problem of history. There is a reason why the mediaeval concept of human society as Christendom has long held a persistent and attractive hold even in the modern world. It pictures a society built on the rock of the Christian religion, accepting the Christian version of human nature, human obligation, human destiny, holding men therefore to their inherent and inalienable responsibilities, thrusting across the many-sided pageant of human life, in all its myriad phrases, the sobering certainty of Divine judgement.

With the simple concreteness of boyhood, the mediaeval mind insisted on giving immediate and apparent expression to the ideal. Christendom must, for it be the kingdom of this world, be a political unity governed by a visible head, Pope or emperor, as the situation seemed to suggest and require, and ruled by his laws and commissioned agents. The thirteenth century witnessed the completest expression of this naïvely boyish dream, and also its complete and most dramatic exposure. Its record includes the glory and failure of the two mighty rivals, Church and State, represented by their greatest exponents, Innocent III and Frederick II. It opened with the tradition of Canossa, and ends with the assured prospect of Anagni.

In our present century we no longer turn to Popes and emperors for

> the symbols and guarantors of Christendom. No more do we "*put our trust in princes or in any child of man*". History has done us this service, but the imperialisms of the past, sacred and secular alike are seen to rise and pass away whereas Christendom is otherwise pictured. We ground our hopes on the gradual establishment in men's minds of those beliefs, standards, and ideals which are the essential content of morality, as Christ presents it, and which, as they are understood and honestly accepted, will release men from the base customs and measures of the past, and set their feet on an ascending path. That profound word of Christ to the Pharisees when they would know "*when the Kingdom of Heaven cometh*", is, we can see, as we read it in the light of experience, both a warning and a promise: "*He answered them and said, The Kingdom of God, cometh not with observation: neither shall they say, Lo, here! Or, there! For lo, the Kingdom of God is within you*". Christ bids us be patient, for men are reluctant and prejudiced, so that his Kingdom does not find easy entrance into their minds; but he allows us to hope, for it is his Kingdom, and in the long run its establishment is assured.
>
> "*For thine is the kingdom, the power and the glory, for ever and ever. Amen.*"

The above words were spoken by Hensley Henson in Westminster Abbey during the early and dark days of the Second World War. He adds that this conception of European civilisation as unified by Christianity and militant in its defence has survived, and today has leapt into unchallengeable pre-eminence. Here again are echoed the words of Winston Churchill that we quoted in our introduction to this book.

The second legacy of the Middle Ages identified by Hensley Henson here is the principle of chivalry.

He remarks, Christianity in prescribing the object of warfare, could not leave the method unaffected. In the service of Christ, even war, that terrifying enigma which still wounds the heart and insults the reason of civilised mankind, could not lie wholly outside the cleansing influence of religion. Chivalry is the meeting point of physical force and moral purpose, the consecration of soldier-hood to be the symbol and servant of spiritual conflict. We may add, whether or not we are pacifists or believers in the just war principle, we must agree that the concept of chivalry fostering self-restraint, regard for women and children, compassion even to our enemies, a discerning justice, and a noble humility are valuable precepts and qualities to sustain and guide us in every aspect of the battle of life. There is a spiritual battle, and as Milton reminded us, even in those periods we call peacetime, *new foes arise threatening to bind our souls with secular chains.*

In all the battles of life it behoves us to seek to observe those old concepts of chivalry as we fight the good fight of faith.

The third precept identified by Hensley Henson is the precept of justice embodied in law, grounded on Christian morality, accessible to all, impartial, discerning, merciful, expressing the deliberate will of a free democracy.

This was the ideal towards which mediaeval Christendom was moving; pre-eminently in this country, notable progress was made. The Europe of thirteenth century was the age of the great mediaeval legislators, civil as well as ecclesiastical. Frederick II, St. Louis, Edward I, the "*English Justinian*", Alphonso the Wise were matched by the great popes and canonists. Moreover, it was in that century that the English Parliament took definite shape. The shield of Simon de Montfort stands beside that of Henry III on the walls of Westminster Abbey. At the time of the Middle Ages Westminster Abbey passed into the possession of the ancient and learned societies who still possess it and guard it with pious and intelligent vigilance. Throughout the civilised world, "*The Temple*", its name when it was the Church of the Hospitallers, has become a synonym for the training and practice of Law as we know it in England. Henson says, "*I shall not be guilty of exaggeration if I say that English Law commands the homage of all civilised peoples, as providing by its provisions, its procedure and its official exponents the noblest expression of essential justice known to human experience*". (He was writing in 1941).

Incidentally in another sermon found within this same book entitled *Christianity and Peace*, Henson identifies five distinctive features that from a social point of view should mark genuinely Christian society.

Its sexual morality.
Its assumption that there are inalienable rights of the individual man.
Its assertion of the greatness of social service.
Its insistence on the responsibility of power.
Its achievement of the union of mercy and justice.

See H. Hensley Henson, *Last Words in Westminster Abbey*, pp. 73–82, also p. 126

Chapter 9
Christianity at the Time of the Reformation

As we have seen, in the providence of God the period we know as the Middle Ages had now run its course. As is clear from the Old Testament and from the subsequent history of the Church, God in his great mercy periodically revives his Church. In the eyes of some (as recorded by Kenneth Scott Latourette) in 1500 it was doubtful whether the Church would survive another generation. However, it was to be seen that God's promises hold true, that Christ shall build his Church and the gates of hell shall not prevail against it.

A movement towards reformation had long been growing, and we could supply a long list of forerunners of the Reformation who lived several centuries before it truly came to pass.

Principally the Reformation was a desire for a fundamental return to a Bible-based Christianity, a return to a primitive purity of doctrine, worship and organisation, a cutting free from the multitude of accretions and unhelpful distortions that had fastened themselves onto the Church during the period of the Middle Ages.

It is not the purpose of this present volume to go into the lives and ministries of all the great figures of the Reformation. My purpose here is to mark the effect which certain features of the Reformation had upon individuals and society at large. One of the most far reaching of these was the translation of the Bible into the common tongue. It brought before men's minds again the great doctrines of Christianity, the sovereignty of God, the scriptural view of man made in the image and likeness of God, his fall, his redemption by grace alone, his purpose in this world and the hope of the life everlasting. These things had a profound effect upon individuals and society at large.

We may briefly mention John Wycliffe (*c.* 1320–1384), known as the Morning Star of the Reformation, his translation of the Bible into English and its being preached, with its subsequent beneficial consequences.

> Wycliffe's influence extended through Huss to Luther and through Luther back to England. This has been known for many years, but his direct influence through his followers upon the English Reformation

> has been greatly underestimated. Even more significant is his influence upon English Puritanism and 17th-century Nonconformity.
>
> Fountain, 1984, p. 86

It cannot be denied that Wycliffe made a very great contribution to the development of Christianity in England and beyond. One of his themes very relevant to our current study was that of *dominium* or lordship, on which he wrote two treatises. The first dealt with the Lordship of God himself, *De Dominio*; the second with the lordship as exercised by human beings, *De Civili Dominio*. These themes had already been explored by Archbishop Richard Fitzralph (1295–1360).

This is a very important theme because as soon as the Lordship of God is set forth, all human forms of lordship are relativized. The concept of the Lordship of God limits all other lordships. It de-legitimises dictatorships.

God is supreme Lord but he is also supreme reason, so his Lordship will be rational, not an arbitrary despotism. Furthermore, God's Lordship is not only above all others, it is also the measure or model for all other lordships. The paradox of God's Lordship is that his service is perfect freedom. We find our true being in his service and discover as he says, "*My yoke is easy and my burden is light*".

In the latter part of this work Wycliffe deals with specific problems, such as the limits of papal power, the conditions of a just war, and the power of the State in relation to the Church (especially in matters of property).

For Wycliffe, God is no arbitrary monarch; he is no oppressor, but one who works with and for his creatures.

The notion of "*being set over*", for example, presupposes a world in which there are relations of super-ordination and subordination, and to be subordinate is to owe some service to one superior. Already in his definition Wycliffe includes the claim that every creature owes service to God whom he calls the "principal Lord", the Lord *par excellence*. In recognising that there is a universal obligation of service to God, Wycliffe is also asserting that any obligation to a human superior can only be a limited obligation. In fact, he speedily introduces a distinction between *servitium* (service) and *servitude* (servitude or slavery) and between *serviens* (servant) and *servus* (slave). Service is honourable, and is ennobled by Christ himself, who came not to be served, but to serve, and who is described as the "*most efficient servant of the Trinity*". Slavery, on the other hand, is a degrading condition, springing from human sinfulness. It is significant that Wycliffe uses the words meaning "*servant*" and "*service*", not "*slave*" and "*servitude*", for the human relation of subordination to God, making it clear that man is a rational creature and therefore has some affinity to God, and so God's Lordship can never be mere despotism or tyranny.

Furthermore, God's Lordship is not only above all others, it is also the measure or model for all other lordships, and if a human being has also a share in rationality the demand that human lordship should measure itself against the Lordship of God is not impossible. "*The Lordship of God is the measure, anterior and presupposer, of all other lordships that may be allotted*".

Wycliffe goes on to state that God is the most exalted of Lords, yet it is also said that he is the easiest to please. "*My yoke is easy and my burden is light*" (Matthew 7:30).

Wycliffe also says that "God is supremely liberal, and therefore supremely giving". Here we may add John 3:16. "*For God so loved the world, that he gave his only begotten Son that whosoever believeth in him should not perish but have everlasting life*".

Further Wycliffe's doctrine of Dominion considers the command in Genesis 1:28, to subdue the earth and exercise dominion over the other creatures. Wycliffe taught as other mediaeval thinkers, such as Aquinas, that all human dominion derives from God and is therefore stewardship, and further that mutual service among the rational creatures of God demands a just sharing of earthly goods, and hence the exercise of Dominion as stewardship highlights man's responsibility to deal with God's gifts in an unselfish and responsible way.

> We neglect these great theologians of the past at our peril, they have a massive amount to teach us today, and their neglect is an example of the shallowness and lack of depth so prevalent in so many aspects of modern life. As the American sociologist Peter Berger once remarked: "*The denial of metaphysics may be identified with the triumph of triviality*".
>
> *A Rumour of Angels*, p. 94, quoted by McQuarrie, 2003, p. 18

Wycliffe condemned by the Council of Constance

Wycliffe, though condemned by the Council of Constance, was still able to continue his work because he was protected by John of Gaunt, uncle to the King, and by the University of Oxford, and supported by many thinkers eager to see reform. He escaped all punishment, and died in peace in his own parish of Lutterworth, on 28 December 1384.

Thirteen years after his death the papal authorities disinterred his body and burnt his remains and had them cast into the River Swift.

The following inscription is to be found on a tablet erected to the memory of Wycliffe in Lutterworth Parish Church:

SACRED TO THE MEMORY OF JOHN WYCLIFFE
The earliest champion of ecclesiastical reformation in England.
He was born in Yorkshire in the year 1324.
In the year 1375 he was presented to the rectory of Lutterworth:
Where he died on the 31st December 1384.
At Oxford he acquired not only the renown of a consummate schoolman
But the far more glorious title of the evangelical doctor.
His whole life was one of perpetual struggle against the corruptions,
And encroachment of the Papal Court.
And the impostures of its devoted auxiliaries, the mendicant fraternities.
His labours in the cause of Scriptural truth were crowned by one immortal
Achievement, his translation of the Bible into the English tongue.
This mighty work drew on him, indeed, the bitter hatred of
All who were making merchandise of the popular credulity and ignorance.
But he found an abundant reward in the blessings of his countryman of
Every rank and age, to whom he unfolded the words of eternal life.
His mortal remains were interred near this spot; but they were not
Allowed to rest in peace. After the lapse of many years, his bones were
Dragged from the grave and consigned to the flames; and his ashes
Were cast into the waters of the adjoining stream.

Martin Luther (1483–1546): by grace alone through faith alone

Martin Luther was the leader of the Reformation in Germany. He was the son of a Saxon miner, graduated in arts at Erfurt, and in 1505 left his studies in law to become an Augustinian monk. After a deep and thorough conversion experience he became a lecturer in the newly formed University of Wittenberg. Here he began to reflect upon and teach his growing belief that "justification by faith" rather than by "works" expressed the Church's true and biblical faith.

Luther maintained with all his might that it is grace alone through faith alone that saves us.

It was one single text that particularly opened his eyes.

> For therein is the righteousness of God revealed from faith to faith: as it is written, "The just shall live by faith".

The text, found once in the Old Testament in Habakkuk 2:4, and three times in the New Testament, Romans 1:17; Galatians 3:11; Hebrews 10:38, so moved the soul of Luther, to the extent that he became under God "the monk that change the world".

F.W. Boreham in his classic *A Bunch of Everlastings* said of Martin Luther:

> It goes without saying that the text that made Martin Luther made history with a vengeance.
>
> When, through its mystical but mighty ministry, Martin Luther entered into newness of life, the face of the world was changed.
>
> It was as though all the windows of Europe had been suddenly thrown open and the sunshine came streaming in everywhere.
>
> The destinies of empires were turned that day into a new channel.
>
> His light was to flame as a beacon over long centuries and epochs of the world; the whole world and its history was waiting for this man!
>
> The moment in which Luther defied the wrath of the Diet of Worms was the greatest moment in the modern history of men. Here then, was the man; that was the text that made him.

We may say that it was this text and the experience of salvation that it brought him that took Luther on and forward to take the next decisive step from the Christian humanism of Erasmus and Dean Colet to a fully evangelical understanding of the Gospel. The truth which equipped him with a power and a theology, a system of theology we might say, which in a spiritual and moral sense shook Europe as Columbus and Copernicus shook it in another way.

There can be no doubt about the fact that the Protestant Reformation was a revival of true religion. The way of salvation had been lost in the main by the body of the mediaeval Church. There were notable exceptions as we know—Robert Grosseteste (1175–1253), Thomas Bradwardine one of our own archbishops of Canterbury (1290–1349), John Wycliffe (1320–1384), and of course the example of John Staupitz who so profoundly influenced Luther.

The way of salvation had been replaced with a ritual that had very little to do with biblical worship or Gospel truth. Rather than teaching that sinners are justified by faith, the Roman Church prior to the Reformation was teaching that salvation was to be had by doing what the Church taught. In particular, submission to baptism, confession, penance, and attendance at the Mass, were means by which grace is conferred enabling us to lead a holy life. As was revealed in the Indulgence scandal, grace and forgiveness could even be bought at a price. Alongside this, application could be made to the exalted saints for assistance, and to the treasury of merit which the Roman Church taught had been built up by exceptionally godly people now in glory, which was available to make up for any shortfall in the amount of grace needed to counterbalance the shortfall of other less saintly individuals. All this falsehood was swept away, and the sinner was pointed to the Lamb of God who alone can take away the sins of the world.

Luther's doctrine of justification is best summed up in the words of the Augsburg Confession of 1530. Though drawn up by Melanchthon, they perfectly sum up Luther's biblical position.

> Men cannot be justified before God by their own strength, merits or works, but are justified freely through Christ by faith, when they believe that they are received into grace and their sins forgiven through Christ, who made satisfaction by his death for sins. This faith God imputes for righteousness before him. See Romans chapters 3–4.
>
> Martin Luther, *Documents of Modern History*, ed. Rupp and Drewery, 1970, p. 145

Luther and the doctrine of the Mass

Luther's spiritual enlightenment enabled him to see that the doctrine of the Mass developed over the period of the Middle Ages had become a tremendous and detrimental barrier to the true understanding of the Gospel, clouding and distorting as it did the doctrine of grace.

The simple ordinance of the Holy Communion, the memorial and pledge of our Saviour's great once-and-for-all sacrifice for sin, instead of focusing our attention on God's abounding in free grace in Christ, had degenerated in the Mass to a work man performed for God.

Luther particularly took exception to such expressions in the Mass as, “this holy sacrifice”, “this oblation”, “these offerings”.

1. These expressions indicated and gave the impression that the Mass was something man did by way of a sacrifice and offering to God. The

Holy Communion is a remembrance and realisation of what God has done for us.

> Luther laid the theoretical groundwork for the most significant changes. This principle was that the Mass is not a sacrifice but a thanksgiving to God and communion with believers. It is not a sacrifice in the sense of placating God, because he does not need to be placated; and it is not an oblation in the sense of something offered, because man cannot offer to God but only receive.
>
> Bainton, 1963, p. 156

2. Furthermore, the Mass confined the partaker to be utterly dependent upon the organisation of the Church through its priests and hierarchy who alone had the "*power*" to turn the elements of bread and wine into the body and blood of Christ.

> Only the Church possessed the Mass, and only the Church could offer the Body and Blood of Christ.
>
> Murray, writing in Hammerton, p. 3346.

3. Another aspect of this was that it tended to make the ordinance objective, a mere physical partaking of the elements, (we may remember that the wine was withheld because of belief in the doctrine of transubstantiation which raised the fear of spilling some of the "blood of Christ").

The mere objective element grew at the expense of the subjective, the material rather than the spiritual. The partaking of the elements, it came to be believed, conveyed grace automatically in the life of the believer (the Latin phrase used was *ex opere operato*).

Furthermore, the priest absolved the penitent sinner: this also was objective. Could the priest be sure that the sinner was truly penitent? It was the subjective aspect which appealed to Luther. It seemed to him that instead of Christ being the one Mediator between God and man the human priesthood intervened.

The Mass therefore was the tremendous obstacle to true religion, and it had come to be thought of as the central aspect of the worship and devotion of the Church. The Lord's Table had become the altar and all the worship of the Church centred upon it.

Luther came to see that if the Mass and all that surrounded it could be swept away, then all mediation save that of Christ could be swept away with it. If this could come to pass, then there would be none to interfere. God would be seen to bestow upon the guilty sinner the gift of pardon and peace through Christ; this also made the partaker a member of the priesthood, to whom all the faithful belonged.

A need for reformation of the Church had long been acknowledged. From the Council of Vienne, 1311, there had been recognised the necessity of reform in the Church. Christian Humanists like Erasmus and Dean Colet had aimed at freedom for learning and reform in its organisation, and a greater thoroughness in removing irregularities. However, the Conciliar Movement, as it came to be called, failed in its task. The Church refused to reform and there was not the power in this movement to challenge that stubbornness.

Luther's reform was thorough, and truly empowered by the Spirit of God. It addressed the very root of the problem, and his insistence on the doctrine of salvation by grace alone through faith alone threw light upon every aspect that needed reform, and effectively undermined the whole structure and system of the Roman Church as it had developed through the Middle Ages.

Luther and the Supremacy of Scripture and the right of private judgement

Luther restored three great biblical truths that had been lost sight of.

1. The first is, as we have indicated above, the fact that righteousness is the gift of God, Christ's righteousness imputed to us, by God's grace through faith alone.
2. The second being that the Bible is the sole authority in all matters of faith and practice.

Luther went on to challenge the mediaeval Church's concept of authority in religious matters. For many years the Roman Church had taught that the hierarchy of the Church, with the Pope as its head, occupied the place of supreme authority in such matters. Now Luther began to emphasise the fact that the Bible alone is the source of all authority in religious matters.

3. The third is the right of Private Judgement.

Luther further came to challenge the concept that the Church alone had the authority and knowledge of how to interpret the Bible. He emphasised the fact that the Bible in its main principles was able to be understood by any Christian man or woman with the aid of the Holy Spirit.

He held to the fact that the Bible was clear and plain in its principal points. He also believed that Scripture could be used to interpret Scripture; if any portion were found to be unclear, the plainer sections could be used to enable us to understand those which were more difficult to understand.

Luther believed that the Bible was one book, and each part complemented the other … There were no contradictions in the Bible. If the reader took the chief doctrines as his pattern or guide, these would also enable him to understand the book as a whole.

Luther pointed out that the priests and the hierarchy of the Church had usurped the role of the Holy Spirit. He freely recognised the need of teaching, as was obvious by the institution of the ministry, but this did not contradict the right of private judgement nor the need for the illumination of the Holy Spirit to rightly understand the Scriptures. Luther also pointed out that this had been the understanding of the early Church Fathers, just as much as they had also emphasised the priesthood of all true believers.

The Reformation and democracy

These rediscovered theological truths also had wider moral and social applications and consequences.

If ordinary people were able to interpret the sacred Scriptures, could they not also be entrusted with playing a more significant role in the affairs of the state?

Could they be debarred from a voice in regard to the way that their everyday affairs were handled and managed? If they were fit to be entrusted with internal affairs could they not also be entrusted far more with temporal affairs? We see here the beginnings of universal suffrage and democracy.

The Reformation restored a right view of the justice and mercy of God.

As the doctrine of justification by faith bestowed a free pardon on guilty sinners, and said "*that God so loved the world that he gave his only begotten Son, that whosoever believeth in him should not perish but have everlasting life*", their eyes were opened at the same time to the Fatherhood and gracious character of God.

Mediaeval Catholicism had rightly portrayed the august nature of God, and his awful justice, but this emphasis had been distorted to the extent of becoming a misrepresentation of God's true character. Many simple souls came to think of him as a cruel despot, whose demands upon the children of men were excessive and crushing in the extreme.

We know that Martin Luther himself had this impression of God, and that he even went so far as to say that he hated God.

> I greatly longed to understand Paul's Epistle to the Romans and nothing stood in the way but that one expression, "the justice of God", because I took it to mean that justice whereby God is just and deals justly in punishing the unjust. My situation was that, although an impeccable monk, I stood before God as a sinner troubled in conscience, and I had no confidence that my merit would assuage him. Therefore, I did not love a just and angry God, but rather hated and murmured against him. Yet I clung to the dear Paul and had a great yearning to know what he meant.
>
> Night and day I pondered until I saw the connection between the justice of God and the statement that "the just shall live by his faith". Then I grasped that the justice of God is that righteousness by which through grace and sheer mercy God justifies us through faith. Therefore, I felt myself to be really born again and to have gone through the open doors into paradise. The whole Scripture took on a new meaning, and whereas before the justice of God had filled me with hate, now it became to me inexpressively sweet in the greater love. This passage of the dear Paul became to me a gate to heaven …
>
> If you have a true faith that Christ is your Saviour, then at once you have a gracious God, for faith leads you in and opens up God's heart and will, that you should see your grace and overflowing love. This is to behold God in faith, that you should look upon his fatherly, friendly heart, in which there is no anger nor ungraciousness. He who sees God is angry does not see him aright but looks only on a curtain, as if a dark cloud had been drawn across his face.
>
> Bainton, 1963, pp. 50–51

This true picture of God had in turn the effect of bringing into question the concept of an absolute pope, and the legitimacy of absolute rulers.

It was said that a correct view of the grace of God was the hammer that broke the power of the absolute Pope, and in turn was the hammer that broke the concept and the spell of the absolute Prince.

As Chateaubrand (1768–1848) the French author and statesman, pointed out:

> The man who seeks the fundamentals in his creed does not delay long before investigating the principles of the government under which he lives. When the spirit demands its freedom the body wishes it too. It is an absolute natural consequence.

We can certainly say that free religious and free political life are ultimately inseparable.

The Reformation highlights a line of succession from John Wycliffe to Martin Luther, to John Calvin, to Philippe Du-Plessis-Mornay the great Huguenot leader, to John Knox, to John Milton to John Locke whose work in turn led to the concept of universal suffrage.

Luther of course did not challenge the principle of authority as such, but in the context of his day, he challenged the authority of the Pope and set in its rightful place the authority of Scripture, *The entrance of thy word giveth light, thy word is truth*, and truth must be the basis of all true freedom, and all just society.

The Influence of John Calvin (1509–1564)

John Calvin the French Protestant Reformer was born in Picardy, and as a young man studied theology in Paris and law at Orleans and Bourges. In 1533 after his conversion he felt called of God to work alongside those seeking to restore the Church to its original purity.

Forced to flee from Paris, he settled in Basle where he published in 1536 the *Institutes of the Christian Religion* in Latin. Intent on a life of study his intentions were disrupted when passing through Geneva in 1536. He somewhat unwillingly agreed to become William Farel's colleague and helper in establishing the Reformation in that city. After a while he was expelled by the authorities and found refuge in Strasbourg, but later returned to Geneva where his great life's work was carried out.

The practical aspects of Calvinism

Calvin's doctrine of predestination might well have issued in a fatalism which induced a paralysis of ethical endeavour. It actually did the very reverse—it braced men's wills. It saturated them with aspiration. It inspired them to a strenuous and heroic activity which brought about a very miracle of moral revolution in all spheres of life in all quarters of the world.

Calvinism indeed worked as a moral purgative and stimulant

wherever it gained any influence at all—and that is its greatest glory. It cleansed the Augean stables of Geneva. It entered licentious courts and touched reckless cheeks there to a strange, unwanted shame. Everywhere it awakened and made sensitive lethargic consciences. It created a refined, if vehement, piety, which blossomed into a strength and frequent beauty of high character that has since been the world's most valuable asset. Calvin's religion was reflected in his crest—a hand with a burning heart, and the words "I give Thee all". That is what it meant to him, and what it meant to him he taught to others. Calvinism in a word stood for consecration, a consecration that found its ideal and example in the Christ whose tired feet climbed Mount Olivet to pray and the hill Calvary to die.

> It is this fundamental and ultimate aim of Calvinism to moralize life by religion which interprets and explains the character of Calvin's own activities. It instructed his legislation. It determined his views on the relation between Church and State. The Church should be the conscience of the State, the State the organ of an evangelized conscience. As a reminder of the spirit that should infuse all life, private and public, Calvin had the letters I. H. S. carved or stamped on all public buildings, coins, and standards in Geneva. (Iesus Hominum Salvator—Jesus Saviour of Men, sometimes interpreted to stand for I have suffered or, In His Service though this is not strictly a correct interpretation).
>
> In his famous Bible commentaries, it is notable how closely he keeps to everyday life. That is one of the reasons why these expositions still retain their value. They are instinct with a constant concern for the attunement of life to the divine precepts. This fundamental principle, too, explicates his attitude to heresy. He was wonderfully patient for those days and for one in his position with all kinds of creedal vagaries around him. It was only when these threatened (in his view) the foundations of morality and orderly government, and therefore of that society, he became severe. But (excepting in the case of Servetus) his severity limited itself to expulsion of the offender from Geneva as a threat to the public peace, as a discordant element in the community whose continuance there might be fraught with insidious and perilous potencies of evil.
>
> Hunter, 1950, p. 300

Calvin's teaching on the providence of God

The doctrine of Providence teaches us that all things are under the control of a good and wise God and that all things work together for good to them that love him. This teaching creates a tremendous impetus towards a life that is noble, good and self-sacrificing.

Julian Huxley, grandson of Thomas Henry Huxley the Victorian evolutionist, claimed that belief in God's providence was a kind of opiate that bred fatalism and sapped the strength out of human endeavour. He wrote,

> The release of God from the anthropomorphic disguise of personality also produces release from that vice which may be termed Providentialism. God provides for the sparrow, we are told; how much more for man? And so this beneficent power will always provide. Divine Providence is an excuse for the poor whom we have always with us; for the human improvidence which produces whole broods of children without reflection or care as to how they shall live; for not taking action when we are lazy; or, more rarely, for justifying the action we do take when we are energetic. From the point of view of the future destiny of man, the present is a time of clash between the idea of providentialism and the idea of humanism—human control by human effort in accordance with human ideals. If providentialism wins, even if it wins only in the domain of the soul and the religious life, humanity is doomed either to stagnation or else to distortion, the material and the spiritual sides of his life being in disharmony. And in spite of the old proverb, "The Gods help them who help themselves," the conception of a personal divine being is the chief asset on the side of Providentialism.
>
> Huxley, 1945, pp. 18–19

If Huxley is correct it is reasonable to expect it to be borne out and confirmed by the history of Calvinism. The question is, does that story bear out the thesis that faith in God's providence paralyses man's vital energies in seeking that which is good, or Marx's theory that *religion is the opiate of the people*? It is manifestly clear that it does not. We may use as an illustration the great Calvin Memorial in Geneva. The idea of that monument is that out of the faith of Calvin were born all the free governments of the modem world. Right and left of the figure of John Calvin are the figures of William the Silent of Holland, Coligny of

France, John Knox of Scotland a Pilgrim Father of New England and Oliver Cromwell, Calvinists all.

When we think of such men we do not think of pietistic acquiescence, or of their faith as *an opiate of the people*. We think of firm endurance on the very edge of despair against overwhelming odds and of their Herculean activity for the City of God.

> So far is Calvinism from producing slackness of will and feebleness of character, that Calvinists have been among the most strenuous of men. … [The] true Calvinist feels himself to be an instrument of the Omnipotent Will, and bends to whatever toil he undertakes in the unshakable conviction that he is on the side of God. How copious a spring of energy lies in this thought I need not tell you; nor is it without a power of moral consecration too.
>
> [Calvinism] was the form of faith in the strength of which the Dutch Republic was sustained and the American Republic founded: to propagate which, Tyndale gave to the English people the Bible in their own tongue, and with it his life: which formed the royal intellect of Cromwell, and inspired the majestic verse of Milton.
>
> Beard, 1883, pp. 257, 261

Calvinism and Politics

A.M. Fairbairn the famous Congregationalist writing in *The Cambridge Modern History* series commented:

> Calvin's chief title to a place in history rests upon his success as a legislator. As a theologian he was a follower, as a legislator he was a pioneer. His system of doctrine was derived, while his political economy broke new ground and based the social edifice on new principles. Certainly he is entitled to the credit of having established a political and legal system on a model of its own, which has profoundly influenced, directly or indirectly, all subsequent democratic institutions.
>
> Quoted by Meeter, 1990, p. 72

It is true to say that Calvinism is a much greater influence upon modern political history than is commonly supposed. Calvin himself never developed a theory of the State, but future Calvinists, and those who while not Calvinists in theology, were profoundly influenced by his Democratic ideas, such as Hugo Grotius and John Locke.

As far as Britain is concerned; the work of the various Puritan groups at the time of the Civil War were deeply influenced by Calvin's teachings. Cromwell's influence on the Mother of Parliaments, the Glorious Revolution of 1688 and the Act of Settlement of 1703 all bear the marks of that influence.

> We have an important and vexing problem to consider in determining the task of the state: the extent of the territory over which the state has jurisdiction and in which it must administer justice. In the solution which it offers to this problem, the Calvinist system occupies the middle ground between all theories which advocate state absolutism and the theories which advocate consistent individualism, as those of the old-time liberals.
>
> The tendency of state absolutism is to bring everything under the domination of the totalitarian state. According to this view the state's task would be to govern everything within the territorial limits of the state—a man's personal life, his home, his religion, and the internal affairs of all groups in society would then only have as much liberty as the state would allow them. There never existed a thoroughly totalitarian state. But the various forms of state absolutism hold that if the state should choose, it would have the right to direct all matters of all citizens residing within its territory.
>
> The individualistic view of liberals goes to the opposite extreme. The ideal condition under this system would be reached if the state could almost cease to exist and leave the individual himself to run things as he might choose.
>
> In opposition to the first of these two propositions, the Calvinist maintains that there are very definite limits to the state's authority. The state is not absolute; it cannot do anything it pleases. First of all, its territory is limited to the province of the natural common good. It may not presume to regulate such spiritual matters as the religion of a man's heart, sometimes defined as his conscience. In this area, conscience has not improperly been termed the limit of the Sates authority.
>
> A second boundary of the state's authority arises from the nature of the individuals who inhabit the state. The individual is not the mere creature of the state, existing only by and for the state. As God's image-bearer he has duties and responsibilities in his private life beyond the duties he owes to the state for which he must be allowed

> the necessary freedom and upon which the State may make no encroachment.
>
> A third boundary limiting the state's authority lies in such natural spheres in society as the home, the school, the church, and economic and social organisations, which do not owe their origin or mode of existence to the state, and have their own task entrusted to them by God. These are sovereign within their own boundaries. Only insofar as any of these should overstep its limits, or endanger the welfare of other spheres, or of individuals, or the state, or insofar as by neglect of its duty it should endanger the well-being of the state, has the state here a duty to perform.
>
> A case in point would occur when parents neglect the proper training of their children, or when the husband abuses his wife, or one group in society tyrannises another group.
>
> Meeter, 1990, p. 101

Calvinism and the Virtues

The virtue of reverence was emphasised by Calvin and this carried with it a horror of all kinds of profanity. This meant also the obligation to go to church regularly and remember the Sabbath day and to keep it holy.

> The supreme virtue, Calvin says, is holiness, this means that above all else, God's honour must be exalted, and God's will obeyed. To break in any least detail one of God's commandments is to offend God. To defraud one's neighbour of his rightful due is to offend God. To give rein to one's natural impulses towards pride or avarice or lewdness is to offend God. Any deviation whatsoever from the strict path of model rectitude is a direct affront to the Almighty.
>
> Harkness, 1931, p. 78

Sobriety

When Calvin referred to sobriety he meant by the term both moderation in the use of intoxicants and a general simplicity of living. To live soberly meant to avoid excess of any kind. Following Paul, he summarised the virtues of a well-regulated life as sobriety, righteousness and godliness (Titus 2:11–14).

> "Sobriety" undoubtedly denotes chastity and temperance, as well as a pure and frugal use of temporal blessings, and patience under

> poverty. "Righteousness" includes all the duties of equity, that every man may receive what is due. "Godliness" separates us from the pollutions of the world, and by true holiness unites us to God. When these virtues are indissolubly connected, they produce absolute perfection.
>
> Calvin's *Institutes*, Book III, Chapter VII, 3 quoted in Harkness, p. 160

Frugality

Calvin noted that the sins of the drunkard, the spendthrift and the adulterer are often closely intertwined. The pure and frugal use of goods is constantly enjoined. Economy was the dominant trait of the Calvinist conscience. Calvin lived simply and frugally himself, and laid on his followers an aversion to extravagance, the effects of which still persist for example among the Scots and many others of Calvinistic lineage. Calvin had a deep insight into the perils of prosperity. We cannot blame God for sending scarcity and want, he said, for when he sends us plenty we misuse his gifts.

Industry

The question of whether Calvin was the originator of the capitalist system (as Max Weber maintained) I think must be answered in the negative. Calvin however worked very hard himself and took it for granted that people ought to work hard.

It is taught by the Scripture and recognised even by the heathen that man was created to do something. Paul's principle is wholly reasonable, that idleness is not to be encouraged by supplying the lazy with food. Calvin elsewhere enjoins almsgiving as a religious duty, but never the feeding off the shiftless. For "*idle bellies that chirp sweetly in the shade*" he had no sympathy. (Harkness, p. 172)

Protestantism and Capitalism: Honesty

Among the Florentine traders, where arguably capitalism had its rise, the virtue of honesty came as early as the 14th century to be highly prized. Calvin certainly contributed to an emphasis on the virtue of honesty but he was not the first to give it religious or popular sanction.

The Calvinists and Puritans accepted and accentuated this view of the sinfulness of chicanery and avarice. Fair dealing toward master, servant, or peer was a virtue highly prized. Honesty of spirit—not simply the appearance of honesty as an economic asset—characterise the Calvinistic and Puritan conscience. Though covetousness existed, it was condemned. It was not respectable to be avaricious or to defraud one's neighbour.

Calvinism a bastion against the spread of Islam

It is often forgotten that Islam made massive progress, putting her to the forefront of human power during the Middle Ages. John W. Robbins writes:

> As the greatest political, military, economic, and religious power on earth, Islam's global triumph seemed inevitable. The battles of old that the Europeans thought so decisive, such as Charles Martel's victory at Tours in Northern France in 732, only a century after Muhammad's death, were regarded as minor setbacks by the Muslims. Rather, they saw their inexorable advance reflected in the ignominious expulsion of the Catholic Crusaders from the Levant in the 13th century, the capture of Constantinople in 1453, and their triumphant march through the Balkans in the early 17th century.
>
> Quoted by Raymond, 2004, p. 141

But for some reason Islam did not absorb these backward peoples of the West. And the answer to why that was the case is that God revived his Church at the Reformation and humanly speaking the man foremost in being responsible for that revitalisation of the West was John Calvin.

Calvin has left a massive legacy to the Western world, though few today seem to be aware of it

David Hill in a recent work on Calvin lists ten areas on which this outstanding Christian man has made a lasting impact.

1. He was one of the forerunners of modern public education. He was the only Reformer to found a university that would last for centuries, i.e. The Academy of Geneva.
2. He contended for the freedom of the Church from state interference.
3. He opposed the idea of totalitarian government, arguing that the powers of government should be limited.

4. He began a system of social welfare which provided for the needs of the deserving poor.
5. He maintained that the Ten Commandments were the foundation of public morality.
6. He established in Geneva one of the earliest forms of democratic society.
7. He believed that one could serve God in every legitimate area of life. He dignified work and said that whether we eat or drink we are to do all to the glory of God.
8. He encouraged enterprise in business, but warned against the danger of riches and mere materialism. He warned against the squandering of money and said that all work should be done without fraud or deception.
9. He introduced congregational singing into public worship.
10. He encouraged the printing of Christian literature and the widespread reading of good Christian books.

Summing up

> "There are people" [remarks Paul Wernle] who are certainly under the influence of no glamour for Calvin or Calvinism. There are people who have been told at school that Servetus was burned through Calvin's fault, and are therefore done with this man. They ought to remember that had they lived at the time, they would in all probability have joined in burning him. It is not so easy to be done with the man who was the most luminous and penetrating theologian of his time and the source from which flowed that power which Protestantism showed in Scotland, France, England and Holland. We are all glad, no doubt, that we did not live under his rod; but who knows what we would all be had not this divine ardour possessed him? Concentrated, well-directed enthusiasm—that is his essence, it was himself, first of all, whom he consumed in his zeal; his rule at Geneva was no more rigorous than the heroism was glorious with which he compacted half the Protestantism of Europe into a power which nothing could break. Calvin was in very truth the soul of the battling and conquering Reformed world; it was he who fought on the battlefields of the Huguenots and the Dutch and in the hosts of the Puritans. In scarcely another of the Reformers is said to be seen such thoroughness, absoluteness. And yet what moderation, what real dread of every kind of excess; with what deference and

> tact did he know how to speak to the great! If you would know the man, how he lived with and for God in the world, read first of all in the Institutes the section On the Life of the Christian Man. It is the portrait of himself. And then for his religious individuality add the sections On Justification and On Predestination, where will be found what is most profound, most moving in his life of faith.
> Such a man was John Calvin; and such was the work he did for God and his kingdom on earth. Adolf Harnack has said that between Paul the Apostle and Luther the Reformer, Augustine was the greatest man God gave to his Church. We may surely add that from Luther the Reformer to our day God has given His Church no greater man than John Calvin.
>
> Warfield, 1981, p. 25

Chapter 10
The Reformation: Further Enumeration of its Benefits

The benefits of the Reformation to the Church and Society at large were manifold.

In regard to the Church the Reformation restored the true concept of Christian worship

Ryle comments on the Church services prior to the Reformation:

> The service of God's house must have been to most Englishmen a mysterious performance, which left them entirely in the hands of the priests. If they were present at any Church service, they could only be present as sleeping partners, or passive, ignorant spectators. It was of mere formal, histrionic worship, to which the laity could only bring their bodies, but in which their minds, and reason, and spirit, and understanding could take no part at all.

He quotes the 24th Article of the Church of England which states:

> It is a thing plainly repugnant to the Word of God and the custom of the Primitive Church to have public prayer in the Church or to minister the sacraments in a tongue not understood of the people.

The Reformation taught the true notion of the office of the Christian minister. Not a sacerdotal ministry like that of the Jews of the Old Testament. A minister did not hold the keys of heaven, or to be practically the mediator between God and man. A minister was to have as his chief business that of preaching the Word, to be diligent in prayer and reading the Scriptures, and to lay aside the study of the world and the flesh.

The Reformation restored a right standard of Christian holiness

Under the monastic way of life or that of an imposed celibacy, myriads of men and women were continually becoming monks and nuns, in the vain idea of becoming "*religious*". The Reformers cut up by the roots this most fallacious idea. Henry VIII and the civil power dissolved the religious houses and dispersed the inhabitants. This thing was done roughly, and the property of the abbeys and monasteries in many cases fell into the hands of greedy individuals. Monasteries had begun well, as places of learning and training for the ministry. In the Middle Ages some of them had been the means of bringing about many inventions for the improvement of farming, and indeed of industrial production. In many cases they served as hospitals and hospices of their local region. However, they had sadly become corrupt and when they were dissolved few objected.

As Ryle further comments:

> The great scriptural principle was established, that true religion is to be seen, not in retiring into holes and corners, and fleeing from difficulties, but in doing our duty in every position to which God calls us, and manfully facing our foes. It is not by running away from the devil, and giving up the management of the world to him, but by manfully resisting the devil, and overcoming him, that true holiness is to be exhibited. The Reformers ordered the Ten Commandments to be set up in every parish church and taught to every child, and our duty towards God and our neighbour to be set forth in the old Catechism.

The Reformation put the emphasis on the Word above that of the image. Luther had reworked his faith through the exacting text of Paul's Epistle to the Romans, and opening up the mysteries of the Bible to the people. The exposition of the Word has always been at the intellectual core of the Protestant faith. Unsurprisingly, Protestant communities—especially Puritan ones—were amongst the most literate and educated in their day. Reading and learning were central components of Protestant existence.

The Reformation furthered the development of Science

Undoubtedly biblical Christianity is the mother of modern science because it insists that the God who created the universe has revealed himself in the Bible to be the kind of God he is. Consequently, there is a sufficient basis for science to study the universe.

Herbert Butterfield, Regius Professor of history at Cambridge wrote in his *The Origins of Modern Science*:

> Modern scientific investigation is firmly rooted in the Reformation. Scientific thinkers amongst the French Huguenots, the Dutch and English Protestants and the later Puritans believed that they should come to the book of God's works with the same reverence as they came to the book of God's words.

They believed that as God had made all things in order, so the natural laws of creation are orderly, and therefore the subject of scientific investigation.

Just as God at the beginning of the Bible in Genesis caused Adam to name the animals and creatures, so all living things can be classified and studied in an orderly fashion.

As in the Bible we see moral cause and effect: so the natural laws of creation can be studied as to their cause and effects.

As God has promised the stability of natural laws in his Word, therefore, the natural laws are stable and can be the subjects of rational study.

Finally, God the Creator is revealed in Scripture as good, so the creation is for the benefit of mankind and we should learn therefore all we can about the laws of nature and use this knowledge for the good of man in his earthly condition.

C.S. Lewis summed this up well when he said:

> Men became scientific because they expected Law in nature, and they expected Law in nature because they believed in a Legislator.
>
> Quoted by Prior, 1975, p. 77

It is of the utmost significance, and to be well noted, that the era of modern science coincided with the period of new translations of Scripture from the original tongues. Also the widespread reading and discussion of Scripture culminating in the opening of the human mind at this time.

As R. Hooykaas observes:

> In the epoch when modern science arose, religion was one of the most powerful factors in cultural life. What people thought about God influenced their conception of nature, and this in turn influenced their method of investigating nature; that is their science.
>
> Hooykaas, 2008, p. xiii

The essential difference between the ancient Greek concepts of science which dominated the world up until the time of the

Reformation was largely that scientific thinking was bound up within the confines of human reason. Whilst human reason plays an important part in scientific investigation, the process of bringing all observations to the bar of human reason tended to put a straitjacket of traditional thinking and circularity on all scientific investigation.

Francis Bacon who is often called the father of modern science expressed this difficulty as follows. In Bacon's opinion the root of all evil in science is the violation of the truth of nature by rationalistic prejudice.

> "We copy the sin of our first parents … they wished to be like God, but their posterity wished to be even greater. For we create worlds, we direct and domineer over nature; we will have it that all things are as in our folly we think they should be, not as it seems fittest to the divine wisdom, or as they are found to be in fact … we clearly impressed the stamp of our own image on the creatures and the works of God, instead of carefully examining and recognising in them the stamp of the Creator Himself". Thus we lost our dominion over nature, "because we desire to be like God and to follow the dictates of our own reason". And then Bacon implores his readers to "discard these preposterous philosophies which have led millions captive, and triumphed over the works of God; and to approach with humility and adoration the works of God, to reverently unroll the volume of creation and read what it says". Bacon criticized the inadequate intellectual reasoning of the Greeks, their neglect of experiments and their premature construction of theories, as spinning out of laborious webs of learning upon a too narrow basis of facts.
>
> This way of thinking exactly parallels the way that the Reformers looked upon God's revelation in Scripture. In true religion we are obliged to accept the way in which it pleased God to reveal himself, that is, in Jesus Christ, without whom no communion with God is possible. This way may not correspond to the ideas about the Godhead which human reason has produced but if we are ever to break free from the confines of our own fallen nature and limited powers of reason we must accept the authority of Scripture.
>
> Hooykaas, 2008, p. 39.

This was recognised by the English physicist Robert Boyle, a founder of the precursor of the Royal Society 1645.

> Boyle considered science to be an excellent school for religion. He pointed out that both science and religion are based on fundamentals that are incomprehensible, and that both are founded on facts "historical" rather than rationally cogent. The scientist finds much in nature that he does not thoroughly understand and he has therefore a special aptitude for accepting things that seem to be beyond belief to the "vulgar philosopher", the man who thinks that he understands all things and that nothing which does not conform to his philosophy could be true. The scientist is prepared to learn even from unlearned people; just as it would be possible to learn more about the natural history of America from a companion of Columbus than from a hundred Schoolmen, so too one could learn more about God from those unlearned men, the Apostles, who were in close contact with "Him who was at the heart of the Father", than from any philosopher.
>
> Hooykaas, 2008, p. 48

The fact that a Christian understanding of the world has made true scientific advance possible is well summed up as follows:

> Our modern understanding of the structure of the physical world originates in the scientific revolution of the 17th century. It has been argued persuasively by Michael Foster and others that it was the Christian doctrine of creation which enabled this step to be taken in Western Europe, a step which had not proved possible in the equally technically advanced setting of, say, Chinese culture. To the Christian, God is reasonable and so the works of the Creator are intelligible and open to rational inspection. Yet, because God is free, there is a contingency in creation which means that its order cannot be determined by a priori thought but must be discerned through experimental observation. Torrance puts this very well when he says: "The intelligibility of the universe provides science with its confidence, but the contingency of the universe provides science with its challenge". The separation which Christian theology maintains between Creator and creation de-sacralises the world and so makes its contingency open to empirical inquiry, free from the danger of impiety. Because the universe is God's creation, it is a fit subject for study. Thus it was that in the 17th century Christian theology

> provided the ideological setting in which science could embark on its task of investigating the pattern and structure of the physical world.
>
> John Polkinghorn, "Creation and the Structure of the Physical World" in Gill, 1995, p. 25

As people like Herbert Butterfield and A.N. Whitehead have shown convincingly, science grew up within a Christian tradition: and for many years it was in no sense distinct or separate. The founder of science and Oxford, in the early 13th century, was Robert Grosseteste, author of a *Compendium Scientiarum* and later Bishop of Lincoln. He had no hesitation in saying that it was "impossible to understand Nature without experiment or describe her without geometry". By this he clearly implies the unity of science and faith, just as much as his distinguished pupil, the Somerset friar Roger Bacon who in his *Opus Maius*, sought to show that the new knowledge, so far from being an enemy of Christian faith, was actually an aid, even in the business of evangelising mankind.

This same wholeness of outlook lasted well into the beginning of modern science. A precursor to our Royal Society was founded in 1645, and to its growth in importance much of the dissemination of knowledge, without which science cannot live, is due. Among its members were John Wilkins and Seth Ward, both bishops; John Wallace doctor of divinity and mathematician; Robert Boyle the chemist bequeathed the sum of £50 a year to found a lectureship for "proving the Christian religion against notorious infidels", and "chiefly recommending to his sister" (his executor), to the laying of the greatest part of his estate "for the advance or propagation of the Christian religion among infidels", John Rae, the founder of systematic botany and zoology, whose great book, *The Wisdom of God Manifested in the Works of Creation*, exercised a profound influence among thinking people and was even used in a shortened form by John Wesley in training his travelling preachers, Christopher Wren, astronomer and architect of St Paul's Cathedral, as well as the greatest figure of them all, Isaac Newton, who claimed that his theological studies were at least as important as his strictly scientific ones. It may be true that religious discussions as such were not permitted at meetings of the Society, but in their second charter, the Fellows were commanded to direct their studies to the glory of God the Creator, and the advantage of the human race. And any doubts regarding the relation between the Society and Church was dispelled by its first historian, Sprat, who wrote:

> I do here in the beginning most sincerely declare that if this design (of a Royal Society) should in the least diminish the reverence that is due to the doctrine of Jesus Christ, it was so far from deserving protection that it ought to be abhorred by all the polite and prudent, as well as by the devout, part of Christendom.
>
> Coulson, 1958, pp. 22–23.

We may also add the following:

Adam was thought to have possessed a perfect knowledge of all sciences, a knowledge lost to posterity when he fell from grace and was expelled from the Garden of Eden. The goal of 17th century scientists such as Francis Bacon and his successors in the Royal Society (founded 1660) was by God's good grace to attempt to regain some of that knowledge.

The Reformation, the great Voyages of Discovery

Even prior to the Reformation proper we might remember that Columbus's great voyage of discovery, as he himself testifies, was very much inspired by his Christian beliefs.

He saw his voyages as a fulfilment of what Isaiah prophesied about the heathen turning to the true God. He wrote:

> It was the Lord who put into my mind (I could feel his hand upon me) to sail to the Indies. All who heard of my project rejected it with laughter, ridiculing me. There is no question that the inspiration was from the Holy Spirit, because he comforted me with promises of marvellous illumination from the holy Scriptures … Our Lord Jesus Christ desired to perform a very obvious miracle in the voyage to the Indies.
>
> *The Vision of Sir Humphrey Gilbert* about 1575

Sir Humphrey Gilbert and Sir Walter Raleigh, stirred by the spirit of this exciting age, saw the need to expand the trade of Britain through the mastery of the seas. Sir Humphrey Gilbert, a Devonshire man who had a taste for learning and travel as well as skill in armed combat, had devoted himself to the study of geography and navigation. In 1565 he began to devise a scheme to search for a North-West passage to the East, or as it was described in those days, to Cathay. A few years later in 1575 he summed up his arguments for;

1. The practicality of the route.

2. Its political and commercial advantages to the State.

His work was entitled *Discourse to prove a passage by the North-West to Cathay and the East Indies.*

Gilbert set himself to prove that such a route was possible. He also set out to show what he felt would be the advantages of opening up sea routes to the East.

These were as follows:

1. The discovery of a sea route free from interference of "any prince living, Christian or heathen", will enable England to secure a share of the infinite wealth of the East.
2. The North-West route from England to the East, being so much shorter than any open to other countries of Europe, will enable us not only to compete with the Portuguese or Spanish traders, but further …
3. We should be in a position to trade with regions not yet reached by Europeans.
4. Also we might inhabit part of those countries, and settle there such needy people of our country which now trouble the Commonwealth, and through want here at home are forced to commit outrageous offences, whereby they are daily consumed with the gallows.
5. Such trade and settlement would be aided by the comparative nearness of these regions:
6. Which would provide a market for the launch and production of English cloth, making us less dependent on the demand from European countries.
7. English shipping and seamanship will be greatly benefited to the advantage of national defence.
8. New industries may spring up at home to supply articles suitable to the needs of Eastern nations and various peoples to be found on the voyage thither; thus providing employment "for vagabonds and such like idle persons".

Pecham, later, in 1583 also brought forward a scheme for developing an English colony in Newfoundland.

Also in 1583, Hayes brought forth a scheme for the colonisation of the American continent north of Florida.

He argued his case on religious grounds saying: "*which must be the chief motive of such of all I shall make any attempt in that way*".

He urges that the obligation not less the privilege lies with England to colonise this part of the American continent, on grounds of prior rights of discovery, of geographical situation, of the fitness of national character, arising from the over-plus of population due to long continued peace: "*it seeming probable of the countries lying north of Florida God hath preserved to be brought to Christian civility by the English nation*". He especially rebukes "the fault of foolish sloth in many of our nation choosing rather to live indolently (i.e. dependent upon others) and very miserably to live and die rather than to adventure as becometh a man to obtain an habitation in those remote lands in which Nature very prodigally doth minister unto men's endeavours".

We may sum up the reasons set forth for the policy of settlement, or plantation, as it was then called, under the following headings:

First. *National policy.* This country by rights of discovery and geographical situation has a natural claim to the settlement of the temperate regions of the West, which are present un-occupied by Europeans. Such possession will secure to England a counterpoise to the power of Spain; will tend to an increase in the number of mariners and ships, and to greater skill in seamanship; and further strengthen the nation by rendering it independent of European supplies of timber, cordage and all other raw materials of shipbuilding. So deeply is the conviction implanted that the wealth of England and her safety must be sought upon the seas.

Second. *The economic condition of England.* A century of comparative peace tended to growth of population outstripping that of manufacture. And settlement will provide employment for the sons of well-to-do houses, as well as for peasantry and an increasing class of "sturdy" vagrants, paupers and even criminals.

Third. *Commercial advantages.* All classes of the community will find plentiful occupation in a new home. A demand will spring up for English goods, notably for woollens, and the needs of native populations may even create new trades in the mother country, which will naturally retain the monopoly of such commerce. Precious metals may be confidently looked for, the store of gold and silver in the mother country increased rather than diminished. Articles such as hides, spices, silks and sugar now imported from our rivals may be produced by English subjects settled in English lands, while the produce of the Newfoundland fishery will be secured to English fishermen.

Fourth. *Religious motive.* The "*compassion of poor infidels*", who should be brought to Christianity and settled industry, was in this first age of colonisation a more prominent motive than it was later. It was not less necessary that the native should be saved from the errors of Rome, which would be his inevitable fate if England were forestalled by Spain.

In 1587, Hakluyt, an English clergyman who was deeply interested in encouraging English voyages and the extension of the British name, in a dedicatory letter to Sir Walter Raleigh of an edition of Peter Martyr Angleria's *De Orbe Novo*, spoke of one object of such adventures as bringing those not knowing God to a reverence for the divine name. In the famous fleeting settlement on Roanoke Island, in Pimlico Sound off the coast of North America, one of its members, Hariot, expound the contents of the Bible to the Indians, and we hear of them asking for Christian prayer in time of illness, possibly because they thought that its magic, added to their own, might assist in recovery. The first charter, by James I, for the plantation in Virginia (1606) said that one purpose of the enterprise was the propagation of "the Christian religion to such people who as yet live in darkness and miserable ignorance of the true knowledge and worship of God". The Second Virginia charter, granted by James I in 1609, declared that "the principal effect which we desire and expect of this action is the conversion and instruction of the people in those parts unto the true worship of God and the Christian religion". Early in the history of Virginia, a project was set afoot for the establishment of a college at Henrico for the education of the children of Indians in the Christian faith. James I issued a letter asking that collections be taken in England for the proposed institution. Several hundred pounds were received, and in 1620 George Thorpe was sent out as the college's superintendent.

It was to be expected that if in New England, in whose earliest settlements the religious motive was potent, missions to Indians would be especially strong. The first charter of the colony of Massachusetts, granted in 1628, spoke of the royal desire that the settlers by "their good life and orderly conversation" might "win and invite the natives of that country to the knowledge and obedience of the only true God and Saviour of mankind and the Christian faith". It is not surprising that the most famous of the early missions by British Protestants, that of John Eliott, should be near Boston. To support the work of John Eliott and to carry on other missions among the Indians of New England, there came into existence what seems to have been the first Protestant Missionary Society. It was, indeed, without exact counterpart in the earlier spread of Christianity or of any other religion.

Through it the Christian impulse was giving birth to a new type of organisation. This was The Society for the Propagation of the Gospel in New England. It was incorporated in 1649 by the Long Parliament and the act ordered that a collection be taken through the counties, towns, and parishes of England and Wales for the Society's purposes. Nearly £12,000 was thus received. It was invested and the income was expended for the purpose of the organisation. On the Restoration, the charter lapsed, but in 1661 it was renewed by Charles II under the title of the "Company for the Propagation of the Gospel in New England and the parts adjacent in America" And the celebrated and deeply religious Robert Boyle became its first Governor.

Moreover, Robert Boyle left by bequest a sum for the "propagation of the Christian religion among infidels". For many years the income was remitted to William and Mary College in Virginia for the education of Indian children. After the independence of the Thirteen Colonies, the fund was administered by a new society formed for this purpose, usually known briefly as the "Christian Faith Society", which supported missions of the Church of England in Mauritius and in the British possessions of the West Indies.

Latourete, Volume Three, 1941, pp. 43–5.

The Reformation and Further Developments towards Universal Education

Alvin J. Schmidt comments on the influence of Martin Luther on the concept of universal education.

The most significant move in the direction of universal education occurred with the Protestant Reformation in the 16th century. The early Church catechised individuals from all social classes and ethnic backgrounds in preparation for membership. But this practice had greatly deteriorated by the time Luther hammered his ninety-five theses to the door of the Castle Church on the campus of Wittenberg University in 1517. In the autumn of 1528 when he visited the churches of Saxony, to his dismay he found widespread ignorance. In order to

> improve this deplorable condition, he wrote his Small Catechism in 1529. In his catechism's preface, he notes that he found the common people had little or no knowledge of Christian teachings and that many pastors were incompetent to teach. Countless members of the Church did not even know the Lord's Prayer, the Creed, or the Ten Commandments. He addressed the bishops and asked how they would some-day answer for this lamentable state before Christ.
>
> Luther's concern for education did not stop with his writing the Small Catechism. He was not an esoteric theologian. Mark Noll notes that to Luther cultivating the human mind was absolutely essential because people needed to understand both the word of Scripture and the nature of the world in which the word would take root. He once said that parents who fail to teach their children were "*shameful and despicable*" and that he would write a book against such parents.
>
> Even though Luther sometimes mentioned only boys when he talked about teaching the youth, there were times when he specifically included girls in his discussion. For instance, he wanted mendicant houses "*converted into good schools for boys and girls*". On another occasion, when he urged parents to send and keep their children in school, he also mentioned girls. William Boyd is right when he notes that "*Luther, in fact, wanted a system of education as free and unrestricted as the Gospel he preached, and indifferent, like the Gospel, to distinctions of sex or of social class*". And although he never denied that one of the purposes of education was to train pastors for the Church, he also wanted children to be educated as God-fearing and law-abiding lay citizens who would serve God and society in all stations of life. Schools, to him, were to train and prepare more than just clergy. He criticised the Popes of the late Middle Ages for having done just that.
>
> John Calvin, another leader in the Protestant Reformation, also advocated universal education. In his *Geneva plan* he included a system of elementary education in the vernacular for all, including reading, writing, arithmetic, grammar and religion, and the establishment of secondary schools for the purpose of training citizens for several positions in ecclesiastical leadership.
>
> Schmidt, 2004, p. 176.

What we may note here is that the examples of Luther and Calvin clearly demonstrate the fact that to educate everyone is not the product of the modern secular world, but rather a concept that was the logical outgrowth of Christianity.

Time fails us to speak of this concept of education in the 18th century rising to a concern to educate the deaf, and the blind. It was out of Christian conviction that the Abbe Charles Michelle de l'Épée, Thomas Gallaudet and Laurent Clerc joined forces to develop a sign language for school use in Paris in 1775. It was specifically in the mind of Épée, that the deaf should hear the Gospel of Jesus Christ. It was Gallaudet who became a Congregational minister who emigrated to the United States and opened the first school for the deaf in Hartford, Connecticut.

It was again in France in the 13th century, that King Louis IX, often known as St. Louis, had built the famous *Hospice des Quinze-Vingts* for the blind in Paris.

We may recall that in the Greco-Roman world infants born blind, as in the case of other physical defects, were commonly abandoned. In Greece blind babies were often cast into the sea. Blind boys who survived childhood often became galley slaves and blind girls were commonly destined for a life of prostitution. Again in the 4th century Christians were operating asylums for the blind and in the 6th century the *Typholcomium* (literally a place for taking care of the blind) was opened by the Church in Jerusalem.

In the 16th century attempts were being made to teach the blind by using raised letters on wax or wood. But it was a devout Christian, Louis Braille in the 19th century, who had lost his sight at the age of three by accidentally puncturing one of his eyes with an awl in his father's harness shop, who developed the system of raised dots now known as Braille.

Louis Braille said on his deathbed:

> I am convinced that my mission is finished on earth; I tasted yesterday the supreme delight; God condescended to brighten my eyes with the splendour of eternal hope.

The Reformation's influence on national character

Sense of duty

Stanley Baldwin (1867–1947), three times Conservative Prime Minister between the wars, writing in *British Life and Thought* …, comments on the fact that leaving aside the many defects in our national character there is one notable and persistent and worthy characteristic i.e. the instinct of the English mind to find out what is unjust among us and undo it, to know what is our duty and to do it, as God's bidding. He traces some of its origins in Caedmon,

> *For us it is very right that we praise with our words, love in our minds the Keeper of the Heavens, Glory King of Hosts.* It was the same spirit that worked in Chaucer's time, that worked in the Vision of Pier's Ploughman and spoke through the voice of Gower the poet and contemporary of Chaucer, who called him "*Gower the Moral, a voice crying in the wilderness, 'Prepare ye the way of the Lord*'". It needed not in those days that a man should be a Wickliffite to see the griefs of the Church and people, and to trace them in their root to duties unperformed.
>
> Baldwin, 1928, pp. 442–3

In Britain this sense of duty manifested itself in many ways through literature and prose, for example in Nelson's famous words at Trafalgar, "*England expects that every man will do his duty*". We have it in Tennyson's Ode on the death of the Duke of Wellington. *Not once nor twice in our rough island's story the path of duty has been the road to glory*. Also in Wordsworth's *Ode to Duty*. In Mrs. Heman's famous *Casabianca*, and in Baldwin's affirmation that *where an Englishman sees his duty, he will follow to the gates of hell.*

> "It would hardly be too much to say", wrote W. MacNeil Dixon, "that into this one word, duty, the English have distilled the whole body of ethics". The merits of this notion, he argued, lies in its simplicity, it strikes no high-pitched or rhapsodical note; it applies as well to daily drudgery as to the heroism of war. It makes no claim at all for the person who obeys it, but on the contrary records his acts as something expected implying that anything else would be an aberration.
>
> Scruton, 2006, p. 56

The concept comes up time and again in the writings of the Puritans. Matthew Henry said; "We must do our duty and leave the rest to God".

Arthur Bryant called Britain the Protestant Island.

> During her first century as a fully committed Protestant nation, out of our native stock, schooled by a thousand years of Catholic civilisation, England produced the world's greatest seaman, Drake,

> its greatest poet, Shakespeare, and its greatest scientist, Isaac Newton. Under a Queen descended on her father's side from a line of petty Welsh squires, and on her mother's side from East Anglian clothiers, her people laid the foundations of their future maritime ascendancy and, under her Stuart successors, founded beyond the Atlantic the thirteen colonies which were to become the United States of America. What is remarkable is how much, with their material limitations, this little nation of five million achieved.
>
> Bryant, 1967, p. 12

At the time of the Reformation the Scriptures were personally and individually taken to the hearts of ordinary people; in thousands of homes the Bible was read and re-read and great portions of it known by heart. Through this reading of the Scriptures and the hearing of them expounded, Britain's natural propensity towards Protestantism was re-born and strengthened and woven into the concept of nationhood and national identity.

> The Bible played a large part in moulding English nationalism, in assessing the supremacy of the English language in a society which from the 11th to the 14th century had been dominated by French-speaking Normans. In the 17th century the Bible was central to all spheres of intellectual life … the Bible was foundational to all aspects of English culture.
>
> Hill, 1992, p. 7

The Reformation, and Political Liberty and Justice

The Bible, as we are seeing, certainly played a gigantic part in securing the political liberty which has characterised these islands over the years. As men, women and children read the great themes of Scripture, justice (Abraham at Sodom and Gomorrah, *let not the innocent be punished with the guilty*), liberty, (the Exodus), righteousness (the Ten Commandments) mercy, forgiveness, self-sacrifice, service, loyalty and many other great precepts were fixed in the hearts and consciences of the population.

Alexander Hodge writing on Reformation Christianity makes a valuable contribution to our thinking on this subject.

> The Christian doctrine of predestination is the antidote to the Darwinian doctrine of determination. Alexander Hodge in the

> 19th century was quick to see that the concept of freedom, and with it the concept of responsibility, was under threat because of Darwinian deterministic thinking. People were beginning to say that human beings could not help the way they behaved. Their behaviour was the result of various glands and other biological factors. The historian Paul Johnson has also commented on this, saying; Marxist and Freudian analysis combined to undermine in their different ways, the highly developed sense of personal responsibility, and duty towards a settled and objective true moral code, which was at the centre of 19th century civilisation. Sociology, criminology, technology and psychology are largely based on the assumption that environment, education and generic inheritance not only influence, but determine human behaviour, and that individuals are therefore only minimally answerable for their own conduct. In the light of this, it is of paramount importance for us to grasp this synthesis that we find in theologians such as A.A. Hodge and William Cunningham and also in "Rabbi" Duncan between fore-ordination on the one hand and freedom and responsibility on the other. They remind us that the Westminster Confession teaches that foreordination does not destroy liberty. I am free because God has foreordained my freedom. I am not a plaything of pressure and circumstance, or even of internal and endocrinological factors. I am free, I make my own decisions, I am the cause, the ultimate answerable cause, the responsible cause of my own decisions.
>
> Based on Macleod, 2010, p. 44

The Reformation's influence on national character

The Reformation fostered a spirit of humility and dependence on God. Regular Bible reading produced in the people a spirit of humble obedience towards God.

> What was the effect of the Bible on the character of the Englishman? To us, looking back, it is not difficult to see. To those living in the 16th, 17th, and 18th centuries ignorant of what lay ahead, it was impossible to pierce through the mists. I should describe the effect on the common Englishman, as generation after generation that amazing language of the Bible fell on his ears, Sunday after Sunday, the effect was something like this. He became soaked unconsciously

> in the Hebrew tradition which in some strange way accorded with his native temper and disposition.
>
> The Hebrew spirit was always conscious of the mystery of life, and of human weakness. From that consciousness necessarily arose the sense of dependence on a higher power, God, whose ways were past finding out. Given that attitude to a Creator, unless a man is completely indifferent, he seeks to reconcile his conduct to what he believes is the will of God; that is to reckon his conduct by a standard of right and wrong … the generations which received this impress have long been dust, but consciously or unconsciously we of today are still their children and their heirs.
>
> Stanley Baldwin, Conservative Prime Minister 1923, writing in *British Life and Thought, An Illustrated Survey* by various contributors, p. 443

The Reformation encouraged a sense of personal responsibility

Built into this biblical outlook on life was also the firm belief that individuals must take responsibility for their own lives and suffer the consequences of their actions. Staying on the right side of the Law was not merely a duty therefore, it was also a liberation. For it guaranteed that you were safe, that no busybody could give you orders or force you to comply with a routine that you had not chosen. The Law was there not to coerce you or to shape you into regiments obedient to the state. It was there to free you from the state and its officials, and to allow you to "get on with your own life" in private. Those who minded their own business and attended to their duties were rewarded with inalienable rights. The most important of these was the right to do what you ought.

The Reformation bred a spirit of freedom and independence

The extraordinary result of this was that, while the English believed in law and authority, they despised officialdom and distrusted the State. English society was the creation of amateur initiatives; its most valuable institutions were the result either of private patronage or people making common cause in clubbing together. Such networks of mutual self-help are natural and are the fruit of the Christian conscience; they exist wherever the State does not extinguish them—as it extinguished them in Revolutionary France and later in Nazi Germany and Communist Russia. In England, however, private foundations, amateur circles, clubs and friendly societies sprang up not merely from the normal superfluity of social energy, but in response to social problems, calling upon the resources and consciences of Christian men and women to resolve them. It was not the State but Friendly Societies and Building Societies which provided industrial workers with housing. It was not the State but People's Dispensaries and Volunteer Hospitals which first brought the benefits of modern medicine to the poor. Schools, universities and colleges began as private foundations and, when it came to leisure, every village was a centre of spontaneous institution building, with its football club and cricket club, its Boy Scouts and Girl Guides, its Women's Institutes and its circles of amateurs devoted to needlework, music, photography, theatricals, brass bands, jam making etc. almost always centred on the village church. (Based on Scruton p. 58).

Bible reading made individuals sensible, concerned and active towards the needs of others, i.e. The Good Samaritan principle.

Even Thomas Huxley the biologist and Darwinian evolutionist writing in his *Educational Essays*, 1874 draws attention to the powerful influence of the Bible on our national life.

> The great historical fact is that for three centuries this book has been woven into the life of all that is best and noblest in English history; that it is become a national epic of Britain, and is familiar to noble and simple, from John O'Groats to Land's End; that it is written in the noblest and finest English, and abounds in exquisite beauties … By the study of one of the books could children be so much humanised, and made to feel that each figure in the vast historical process fills, like themselves, but a momentary space in the interval between the eternities; and earns the blessings or curses of all time according to its effort to do good and hate evil.
>
> The Bible was and is the Magna Carta of the poor and of the oppressed; down to modern times no state has had a constitution in which the interests of the people are so largely taken into account, in which the duties so much more than the privileges of the rulers are insisted upon, as that drawn up for Israel in Deuteronomy and Leviticus; nowhere is the fundamental truth that the welfare of the state, in the long run, depends on the uprightness of the citizen so strongly laid.
>
> Quoted by Sivan, 1973, p.77

John Milton said: "There are no songs compatible to the songs of Zion; no orations equal to those of the prophets; and no politics like those which the Scriptures teach."

The Reformation and democracy

The translation of the Bible into English, culminating as it did in the publication of the Authorized Version of 1611, opened in every way the minds of those who read it. It facilitated and enabled true debate and discussion of all manner of topics religious, political and sociological.

This undoubtedly helped lay the ground for democracy. Now that this book was widely available, argument and debate were licensed and legitimated. A sermon from the book of Judges or Kings might stimulate debate on good and bad government, or the beneficial effects of a good monarch or the tyranny and oppression of a bad one. One might theoretically plan a revolution through debate on the Sermon on the Mount, or out of a sermon on a chapter from the Old Testament prophets speak of justice or oppression or the building of the New Jerusalem.

> In the English Civil War, a furnace of ideological conflict, Charles I was convinced that unrestricted access to the Bible, conjured up and enforced by his father, had nourished the discontent of the people. Throughout the Civil War, one extreme group after another sought and found the justification for its radical social views and political actions in the sacred pages of the King James Version.
>
> Yet after the Civil War, this began to change and change quite rapidly. The King James Version was now seen as the bedrock of monarchy and Englishness. And so it remained for more than three hundred years until, in a misguided fit of mere modernising, it was "revised", that is to say adulterated, diminished, stripped of everything that had made it last and made it count.
>
> It was a small step from the English Civil War to the American Civil Rights Movement; in both, the Bible was key as an inspiration against brutal and tyrannical authority. Yet in America, as in England three hundred years previously, once the blood was let, the King James Version reverted to its natural home, which is at the centre of a Christian state.[7]
>
> Bragg, 2006, p. 283

7 See also Terry Johnson, *The Case for Traditional Protestantism*, 2004, pp.153-5

> The grip Protestantism has on the United States is strong and fundamentally influential in its political practices. The majesty of the language so transparently established in America's great public spoken moments, such as Lincoln's Gettysburg address, informs and is embraced by the leading democratic nation on the planet. Through this Bible the Protestant voice in English became the ruling tongue of two successive world empires. It also said to the world that Christianity was the leading faith, the Christian God the one true God and Christ the true and only Redeemer. *This Bible has had more impact on the ideology of the last four centuries than any other creed, manifesto or dogma.*
>
> Ibid. p. 282

It was in Protestant England that democratic theory was first put to the test and in time the results of that experiment rippled out to the margins of the globe. Through the influence of the modern missionary movements and the influence of the Bible Societies it is perfectly legitimate to speak of the Authorised Version of the Bible as the Book that Changed the World.

> Daniel Webster once remarked that the tavern was the headquarters of the American Revolution—meaning, in part, that ideas of self-determination could only emerge in a setting where free discussion naturally took place. That discussion was free because the English Reformation had established the right to it, by virtue of the place the English Bible had in people's lives.
>
> Before the advent of the vernacular Bible, which was made available to the general public by printing, most people did not know what the Bible said. Thereafter, they could read it for themselves and decide, for themselves, what it meant. Their free discussions about the authority of the church and state fostered concepts of constitutional government in England, which in turn were the indispensable prerequisites for the American colonial revolt. Without the vernacular Bible—and the English Bible in particular, through its impact on the reformation of English politics—there could not have been democracy as we know it, or even what we call today the "Free World".
>
> Bobrick, 2003, p. 277

This popular Bible reading marked the origin of a culture belonging to the man in the street which increasingly reached towards popular and democratic institutions. This awakening of the minds of ordinary people brought about in turn the birth of the popular press. The popular press first began to develop in London in September 1513. Between 1590–1610 at least 450 English news-books, as they were first called, appeared.

The Influence of the Reformation on the moral ethos of British Society

Grotius the Dutch theologian, after returning home from a visit to England in 1613 wrote: "*Theology rules there*", Casaubon (the Swiss scholar 1559–1614) made a similar report after his visit to the court of James I. This was a period when the nation was saturated with biblical truth.

This was to have an extraordinary moral effect. It certainly manifested itself in the literature of Jeremy Taylor, George Herbert, Milton and Bunyan and many others. It certainly lay behind the high moral tone of Cromwell and his parliament and the ministers of the English and Scottish Puritans. At that time, it was said that ordinary men took their Bibles with them to the marketplace and to the work shop; they bought and sold with its words on their lips and in their hearts. It was their guide in every part of their life, and when duty called them to take up arms they charged the enemy as it were with "*the sword of the Lord and of Gideon in their hands, and David's psalms on their lips*". It made men like Faithful and Greatheart and Gaius, and women like Mercy and Christiana.

> From the very first the spread of the Authorized Version made for progress and freedom. It was the study of the English Bible which in a single generation raised so many in the 17th century from the puerilities, superstitions and prejudices of the Middle Ages, and made them strong, far-seeing men; tender, and heroic women. It raised the nation at one bound to the foremost place among the nations of Europe, and more than all else, kept it there. It taught us that the only enduring national prosperity is that which is based on loyalty and obedience to the Word of God. Piety which is nourished on manuals of devotion and the lives of the saints is of the hot-house order. It is those alone who are nourished on the Bible who can

> stand the storm and flourish in the open air. It is they who become explorers and reformers, colonists and pioneers of … truth.
>
> Muir, 1911, p. 178

It reappeared at the time of the 18th century revival.

It is well known that the Evangelical Revival brought about a moral transformation of Britain and, as we tend to forget, many other countries also. Canon Overton wrote of the faith and its effects as follows:

> Of the faith which enabled a man to abandon the cherished habits of a lifetime and to go forth ready to spend and be spent in his Master's service; which nerved a man to overcome the natural fear of death, and, indeed, to welcome the last enemy as his best friend who would introduce him to the better land he had long been living for; which made the selfish man self-denying, the discontented happy, the worldling spiritually-minded, the drunkard sober, the sensual chaste, the liar truthful, the thief honest, the proud humble, the thriftless thrifty and the godless godly.
>
> Overton, 1900, p.131

In the early and mid-Victorian era, the Reformation ethos held massive sway in our nation. On the Sunday of the 1851 census the records show that half the population were in church. On the same day over two million of the nation's children were in Sunday school and the figures for Sunday School attendance continued to rise throughout the century. From the 1850s the crime rate was also falling every year in spite of an increase in population.

Serious crime fell by 60% between 1850 and 1890. In 1888 three out of every four children attended Sunday School. Illegitimacy fell by the end of the 19th century to 4%, divorce was almost unknown, and single parent families in the modern sense virtually unheard of. Drunkenness was a decreasing problem due to the influence of the Temperance Movement.

The virtues of self-control, self-help, self-discipline, hard work, independence, thrift, propriety, the concept of cleanliness is next to godliness, temperance, honesty, promptness, regularity etc. were held in the highest regard.

Margaret Thatcher, reminiscing in 1983, summed this up when she spoke of the values (she ought to have said virtues) which made this country great.

> We were taught to work jolly hard. We were taught to prove yourself; we were taught self-reliance; we were taught to live within our income. We were taught that cleanliness is next to godliness. We were taught self-respect. We were taught always to give a hand to your neighbour. We were taught tremendous pride in our country.
>
> *Evening Standard*, April 15, 1983 quoted by Himmelfarb, 1994, p. 4

The way these precepts were worked out in everyday working-class Victorian homes has been described as follows.

> For men it meant having a job, however lowly, and for women managing a clean, orderly, and thrifty household; for children, being obedient at home and school, doing chores and contributing, if possible to the family income. For the family as a whole, it meant staying out of the workhouse and off the dole, belonging to a burial club or Friendly Society so as to be spared the ignominy of a pauper's burial, having a clean paid up rent book, wearing clean even if threadbare clothes and, for special occasions, Sunday best, giving no cause for disgrace (such as being arrested for drunkenness or having an illegitimate child).
>
> Himmelfarb, 1994, p. 32.

It was said of England of that time, "England is a domestic country; here the home is revered and the hearth is sacred".

Good behaviour/Christian behaviour was expected of high and low.

> We have come to regard the crown as the head of morality. The virtues of Queen Victoria or the virtues of George III have sunk deep into the popular heart. We have come to believe that it is natural to have a virtuous sovereign and that the domestic virtues are as likely to be found on the throne as they are in the humblest cottage.
>
> Karl Beckson, *London in the 1890s*, quoted by ibid. p. 55

It was to the eternal truths of God's Word and the unchanging law of righteousness that Arthur Mee turned the thoughts of his readers in the dark days of 1940. He wrote, "*If for one day the common people of these islands lose their faith in God the cause of freedom must perish*". (*1940 Our Finest Hour*, p. 27)

The Reformation and revival

We commented earlier that at the beginning of the 16th century,

Christianity had appeared to be on the wane. The renowned Christian historian Latourette commented.

> At the beginning of the 1500s the outlook for Christianity appeared unpromising. In many respects what remained of Christianity, seemed a diminishing force. Was Western Europe shedding its Christianity? Christianity, although driven out of much of the Mediterranean world by Islam, had been a tutor to bring civilisation to the barbarian peoples of Northern Europe. Were these peoples outgrowing their teacher? Now that they were coming to manhood's estate were these rude folk whom the Church had taught the rudiments of culture to regard Christianity as something outworn, as swaddling clothes which should now be cast aside? Were a thousand years of certainty to be followed by centuries of decisive and final decay? As the world had witnessed the decline and fall of the Roman Empire, was it now to see the decline and disappearance of the faith with which the Roman Empire in its latter years had been so closely identified? The facts proved to be quite the opposite to the gloomy prognosis. Never had the influence of Christianity been so pronounced and widespread as it was after AD 1500.
>
> K. S. Latourette, 1941, Introduction

Clearly it was the translation of Scripture into the common tongues of the European peoples that brought about the extensive revival and expansion of the Church in that period. We see here that the translation of the Authorized Version was one of the ripe fruits of that period of spiritual awakening. The widespread reading and the periods of the widespread preaching of the Authorized Version in the 17th, 18th and 19th centuries again brought extensive revival of the Church.

It is often remarked that this great era of Bible translation and the spiritual revival it produced also unlocked and stimulated all that was best and most noble in the human spirit. It was a revival of literature, science, art, music and discovery etc. to a most remarkable degree.

This is summed up by Arthur Bryant as follows:

> In this period England produced the world's greatest seaman, Drake, the greatest poet, Shakespeare, and its greatest scientist, Newton. In this period the foundations of Britain's maritime ascendancy were laid. There were founded the thirteen colonies which were to become the United States of America. What is remarkable is how much, with their material limitations, this little nation of five million achieved.

> Like their Catholic ancestors the English of the first Protestant generations believed implicitly that the world was governed by moral law. Released from the international bureaucracy and doctrinal straitjacket of Roman orthodoxy, they differed, often violently as to the character of that law, but they still believed that God, its embodiment and enforcer, was all seeing, and that men and nations who transgressed it would be punished. The civil wars which convulsed England in the middle of the 17th century, with all their heroism, nobility and tragic waste, were a witness not only to their pugnacity and factiousness, but to the intensity of their religious feelings and striving for moral betterment. And when their fanatic enthusiasms in religion and politics provoked, as they were bound to do, a reaction, they embarked with equal enthusiasm on the task of making human existence more comfortable and intelligible. By their energy, curiosity and good sense they helped to lay the foundations of the modern world.
>
> Arthur Bryant, 1967, p. 12

The Reformation and subsequent long-term social reform

It is not infrequent that we hear the charge levelled against Evangelicalism that it has no social concern and that its pursuit of the salvation of souls excludes any interest in the everyday problems of society. Those who level such a charge only reveal their ignorance of history. It has been said that social reform in our own and other countries owes more to biblical Christianity than to any other influence. Kathleen Heasman in her study, *Evangelicals in Action, an Appraisal of their Social Work*, states that in the 19th century a good three quarters of the charitable and voluntary societies which were set up were evangelical in character. Many of the functions of the Welfare State were recognised and met, not by social economists and Socialists, but by practical and practising Christians, whose action was characterised by an intensely personal concern for the individual and his family: for prostitutes, cripples, drunkards and even navvies and cabmen.

It was John Wesley, William Wilberforce, Thomas Clarkson, Granville Sharp, Fowell Buxton, who fought the slave traffic, and they were all evangelicals.

It was John Howard and Elizabeth Fry, both evangelicals, who championed the cause of prison reform.

To the memory of the great reformer, Lord Shaftesbury, a pioneer emancipator of industrial England, and also an evangelical, stands the Eros monument in Piccadilly Circus, purchased with the pennies of the grateful poor.

It was John B. Gough, Frances Willard, Fred Charrington and Sir Wilfred Lawson—all evangelicals—who attacked the entrenched interests of the drink traffic, and whose labours resulted in many Temperance Societies for both old and young.

It was Robert Raikes, an evangelical, who inaugurated Sunday Schools in this country, which, says J.R. Green the historian as noted above, "were the beginnings of popular education".

It was Benjamin Waugh, George Muller, William Quarrier, C. H. Spurgeon, J.W.C. Fegan, and T.J. Barnado, all pronounced evangelicals, who espoused the cause of the children, and established orphanages in England and Scotland, some of which continue to the present day.

It was William and Catherine Booth who brought into being the vast and worldwide organisation of the Salvation Army. Sir George Williams originated the Young Men's Christian Association. Arthur Broome founded the Royal Society for the Prevention of Cruelty to Animals (R.S.P.C.A.); and Florence Nightingale was the great reformer of hospital nursing. All of these were deeply rooted believers in the Word of God.

> What is not so often remembered is that particularly towards the end of the 19th century the individual churches and chapels engaged in a tremendous amount of social work in their immediate vicinities. A pamphlet published in 1883 by the Rev. W.C. Preston, a Congregational minister entitled *The Bitter Cry of the Outcast Poor*, did a great deal to stimulate this work.
>
> The publication of *The Bitter Cry* would probably have caused less concern had it not appeared at the time when the unemployment and under-employment of the 1870s was beginning to gain the attention of the public. Widespread discussion of social conditions was taking place both among the workers and the intellectuals, and socialist ideas were being revived. *The Bitter Cry* was the response of those evangelicals who appreciated the situation and who wished to apply similar remedies with an evangelical emphasis. This method of approach was quickly seized upon. William Stead made it the basis of an article in the *Pall Mall Gazette*, and it inspired the *Liverpool Daily Press* to publish some vivid accounts of "squalid Liverpool". It also

> suggested the lines which were followed in 1890 by William Booth's, *In Darkest England and The Way Out*—a book which was widely read in the last decade of the century and roused not only the Salvation Army but other groups of evangelicals to recognise their social duties.
>
> Heasman, 1962, p. 49

Some of this work was very innovative, for example the societies set up to rescue women from prostitution were established by men such as the Rev. Baptist Noel and Theophilus Smith. The London Female Mission with a home in White Lion Square, London, held periodic midnight mission meetings of which hundreds of prostitutes attended to hear the message of the Gospel and receive practical help.

If there had been no Word of God little of this work would ever have started. Britain would have remained in the condition it was in the early part of the 18th century as described in great detail in Dr Bready's famous book, *England Before and After Wesley*. Here is Baldwin's summary:

> It was just about 200 years ago that one of the great spiritual revivals of Christian history broke over England. Two men Whitefield and Wesley, devoted themselves to the evangelistic work. From early morning to late at night, in fields and byways, amongst crowds of miners, in the roughest quarters of our towns they preached and taught and organised. Their lives put an end to apathy, the Church had been liberated and there was a stirring of the dry bones far beyond the bounds of the Societies which they founded, incalculable in its results.
>
> When Wesley created the organisation which was to bind his followers together, he came to rely more and more on lay helpers for the day to day administration of that great body. The result of this was throughout the whole country there were found earnest and sincere men, many of them of the working classes, who were giving all their spare time, and some all of their time, to definite Christian work among their fellows. I used the word "incalculable" of the results of this movement: incalculable indeed was the result of the example of such men in that rough industrial world that was so swiftly growing up.
>
> In point of time I should perhaps have spoken of the religious revival of the 18th century before I sketched for you the development of co-operation in the industrial age, but I put it last so as to try

to impress it on your mind, and will make clear what I meant by insisting on the use of the word "incalculable" with reference to that Revival. No one, a hundred and fifty years ago, could have foreseen the rapid development of democracy, the shifting, as it were, of the political sense of gravity, in democratic States: far less could anyone have foretold the political developments within the different countries during the last quarter of a century. But in all these movements that have grown up among the working classes you will find their foundations are laid on a Christian basis. Amongst these the Friendly and Co-operative Societies and the Trade Union Movement are the most conspicuous and successful examples of self-help and self-government among the working classes. They embody and are naturally determined by the Christian social philosophy which prevailed throughout the greater part of the 19th century.

You will find amongst the creators of these organisations and amongst the workers in them, generation after generation, men who are themselves workers in the various Christian denominations to which they belong, men of markedly Christian lives, and their general aim, consciously or unconsciously, is to make life itself more worth living for themselves and for their fellows, to build up rather than to pull down. It has been a revolutionary spirit more in the religious than in the political sense. Here in my view lies the profound difference between our outlook and that which governs some of the current movements on the Continent, and so long as that outlook, temper, tradition, or whatever you like to call it, remains in England, so long will the Englishman fight to the end any attempt to subject him to a way of life which to him is death.

Stanley Baldwin, 1940, pp. 454–5.

A summary of the effects of the Reformation by Cunningham Geikie

It was the revolt of the human intellect and heart from mental and moral slavery. Christianity had brought such liberty at first; Protestantism was its resurrection …

It asserted triumphantly, once and for ever the absolute freedom of conscience in all our relations to our fellow men. Rome had demanded blind obedience to the Church, that is, in effect, to the individual priest, literally, on pain of hell. Protestantism, for "the Church", put God. It accepted no human Church or Church institution as free from error or the possibility of it, either in itself, its acts, or its utterances.

It held up the Scriptures as the supreme rule of faith and practice, and put them in the hands of all, that they might follow them for themselves. It allowed no man to stand between the soul and its Maker. It held that salvation depends on no human mediation, or priestly acts, but flows directly from the self-revelation of God in His Word. It saw that all the merits of the sacraments are dependent on no act of a priest, but on the direct communion of the soul with Christ.

It claimed the rights of private judgement in all demands on our belief, and thus made each man's conscience responsible only to God. While gratefully accepting all helps and ministrations to guide to a decision, that decision was reserved absolutely to the individual himself.

In the political sphere it imported the same grand principles. It demanded that no man should suffer for his religious opinion.[8] A principle long opposed, but now, at last, admitted to the full, in the rejection, by every English-speaking nation, of all religious disabilities. Force cannot be used to compel acceptance of opinions which conscience denies.

It secured protection to all in their fidelity to conscience. The rights of all were established to express freely their religious convictions, and to associate themselves with others in a public profession of these.

Thus all men were made free to form themselves into new religious societies, so long as the opinions advanced were not clearly opposed to the public welfare. This principle also is recognised in all English-speaking nations.

It not only sanctioned but imposes as a sacred duty the frankest investigation of all questions. Its unchanging motto was and is "Prove all things". It was henceforth impossible in Protestant countries to imprison a Galileo, or to keep an Index Expurgatorius and it became a religious duty to secure a sound education to the child of the poorest citizen. The very essence of Protestantism is to seek for more and more light.

8 John Foxe in his *Book of Martyrs*, particularly believed this, and Foxe and his famous martyrology did a great deal in this country to teach that man should not be put to death because he holds a different religious opinion from ourselves.

It taught that men become true members of Christ, not by any priestly acts, or by mere outward connection with "the Church" or obedience to it, as the vital connection, but by a living and active faith in Christ, evidenced by a holy life. And since this faith, which alone justifies the soul, is a personal act between it and God alone the soul is responsible for its faith to no one but Him.

It proclaimed that all true believers, over the whole earth, form, as such, the one true invisible Church, whose members are known surely to God alone, and will in the end be acknowledged by Him at the Great Day.

As to the results of these great principles, to which more might be added, they are seen on every hand.

Further they have freed the land from monks and monkery, which even Romanist countries have since put down as an intolerable evil. They have abolished the most fruitful source of immorality, the celibacy of the clergy, and have made layman and ecclesiastic alike subject to the civil courts. They have exploded the doctrine of purgatory—the richest line of priestly wealth and popular superstition. They have removed from between the soul and God the crowd of priests, saintly mediators, the Blessed Virgin, and the glorified dead, and pointed them to the only Mediator, our Lord Jesus Christ.

They have dispelled the belief that a sinful man, who calls himself a priest, can judicially absolve a man from his sins. They have swept away from amongst us the hateful system of compulsory secret confession—have purified our churches from miracle—working pictures and images; and turned to ridicule the thousand inventions and postures by which Rome kept hold on the souls of men. They have given us the spiritual communion with Christ in the ordinance, instead of the belief that a fragment of the bread can be changed by the priest into Christ Himself, and eaten as such. They have given us a pure and simple worship in our own language, instead of the endless bowings and kneelings, vestments, and incense, lights and thousand ceremonies of Rome. They have given us the Bible, with its divine wealth of heavenly and earthly wisdom, in our own tongue. And to crown all, by securing for us the fullest civil and religious liberty, they have made England, here and over the world, wherever her institutions have gone, the envy of every nation.

Cunningham Geike, *The English Reformation*, 1878

A summary of the effects of the Reformation from Wylie's History of Protestantism

In all the countries of the Reformation a great intellectual awakening was the immediate consequence of the introduction of Protestantism. Geneva and Zurich became centres of literary light and industrial activity; the Huguenots were the first soldiers, writers, merchants, and artisans of France. Holland became as renowned for letters and arts in the years that succeeded its great struggle, as it had been for arms when contending against Spain. But it was in England that the greatest intellectual outburst attendant on the Reformation culminated. Their mind opened out into an amplitude of faculty, a largeness of judgment, a strength and subtlety of reason, and a richness, boldness, and brilliancy of imagination, of which the world had seen no similar example, and which paled even the brightest era of classic times. By one quality were all the great thinkers and writers who illuminated the horizon of England in the Elizabethan age marked, namely, great creative power; and that eminently is the production of Protestantism. To it we owe our great thinkers and writers. Had not the Reformation gone before, Bacon would never have opened the path to true science; Shakespeare's mighty voice would have been dumb forever; Milton would never have written his epic; nor would Bunyan have told us his dream; Isaac Newton would never have discovered the law of gravitation; nor would Taylor, Baxter, Howe, and many more ever have discoursed; not one of these deathless names would have been known to us, nor would England or the world ever have possessed one of their immortal works.

J.A. Wylie, 1888–91

T.H.L. Parker rightly insists that the Reformation in England was:

The confession that Jesus Christ is the complete and only Mediator between God and men, and who therefore endeavoured so to shape the doctrine and practice of the Church that her earthly existence should correspond to the truth of His existence. In this definition we place the Reformation within the sphere of faith in Jesus Christ, of repentance for sin, of love for our neighbour, of looking above the bewildering turmoils of 16th century England, to the eternal and unchanging Kingdom of Heaven; within the sphere of the Church and of assembling together to worship God, and therefore of the ministry of reading and expounding the Bible, and for this reason once again of faith, hope, and love; within the sphere of being baptized and of receiving the Holy Communion, of singing of psalms and hymns and of praying in private and in public; within the sphere of obedience to God's demands and commands, and of a rightly ordered moral life in private and in society.

Parker, 1966, p. xv.

Chapter 11
The Influence of Puritanism on the Character of Peoples

This was a movement which grew first within the Church of England in the late 16th and 17th centuries to press for further Protestant reforms. When these reforms were not quickly implemented Puritans tended to divide into Independent, Presbyterians and later Baptist sects. Its heyday was in the days of Oliver Cromwell and the Commonwealth of England. It was bitterly persecuted in the days of Charles II, and found its freedom in the Act of Toleration 1689. Most Puritans embraced Calvinistic theology though a small minority were Arminian.

In this study we confine ourselves to the fruits of Puritanism.

Puritanism and individual liberty

During the years in which Puritanism was developing, many changes in the religious and political world had taken and were taking place. In all this changing scene in many respects the lives of ordinary people were not particularly considered. In his book *The Genius of Puritanism* Peter Lewis pointed out that Puritanism emphasised that the individual could never be regarded as a mere pawn of the times. Every man had an immortal soul. The Son of God himself had come to die for ordinary men and women just as much as for princes and prelates and those in high places.

> The Puritan emphasis on the place of conscience, its laws and liberties in the life of the individual, placed the subject over against the monarch but not under his feet, and from this new position "*Everyman*" gained a new and very different perspective of life.
>
> The Gospel certainly freed men and women from the bondage of sin and death. The doctrine of justification by faith alone delivered mankind from the oppressive teachings of the mediaeval Church, which taught that it was only through obedience to her and her demanding system that mankind had any hope of salvation.
>
> That liberty freed the human spirit and manifested itself in the glories of the first Elizabethan age.

> The erosion of these liberties by Charles I and the attempts of his bigoted Archbishop, William Laud, to once again manacle the free soul of Protestantism, drew down upon him the wrath of both an outraged piety and the newly awakened sense of the dignity and responsibility of the individual.
>
> It was this spirit that reached its high point, certainly at that time, (though it was to go on having repercussions in later British history and indeed still has to this present day) its fullest expression and greatest expansion under the enlightened rule of Oliver Cromwell.
>
> Lewis, 1979, p. 16.

William Haller in his *The Rise of Puritanism* notes the influence of the lesser sects within Puritanism, in promulgating the ideas of democracy and toleration, which eventually became characteristic of later Puritanism.

These sects in spite of their small beginnings had great significance for the future development of society at large.

> Relatively obscure in the early stages of the Puritan movement they became more important as it gained momentum, and they played a decisive role when it reached its peak in the period of the Civil Wars and the Commonwealth. As revolutionary Puritanism declined, they too declined as factors in public life and became merely aspects of Protestantism in modern society. They are important chiefly as symptoms of the democratisation of English society and culture which was being steadily advanced by Puritan preaching in general, by the translation and publication of the Bible, and by the spread of literacy. The end toward which the whole movement was tending was the reorganisation of society on the basis of a Bible-reading populace. Calvinism helped this movement forward by setting up a new criterion of aristocracy in opposition to the class distinctions of the existing system. But there was also a concept of equalitarianism implicit in Calvinism which transcended aristocracy and which the necessity the preachers were under of evangelising all the people brought steadily to the fore.
>
> The fact that salvation by the grace of God was available to everyone who really desired it went a long way towards the concept that all men must be treated alike because God's grace is available to all.
>
> Derived from Haller, 1957, p. 178.

It is true that these principles took some time to develop and that many of the mainline Puritans in the 17th century were violently opposed to liberty being given to those not of their persuasion, indeed taking the same attitudes as those who had previously denied them liberty.

We have to be aware however that these men rightly had a passion for the truth, and the value of it. So much so that they could see no virtue in allowing opinions that seemed to deviate from and threaten that truth.

Part of this involved the age-long controversy and dilemma of the relationship of the Church to the State.

The Puritans and a life conformed to the principles of Scripture

They regarded the Scripture as the library of the Holy Spirit graciously bequeathed to Christians. They viewed Scripture as God speaking to them as their Father, giving them the truth they could trust for all eternity. They saw it as Spirit—empowered to renew their minds and transform their lives.

The Puritans searched, heard, and sang the Word with delight and encouraged others to do the same.

Richard Baxter's great work *A Christian Directory* shows believers how to regard the Bible as a trustworthy guide for the whole of life.

Every case of conscience was subjected to Scripture directives.

John Flavel said:

> The Scriptures teach us the best way of living, the noblest way of suffering, and the most comfortable way of dying.

Henry Smith said,

> We should set the Word of God always before us like a rule, and believe nothing but that which it teaches, love nothing but that which it prescribeth, hate nothing but that which it forbiddeth, do nothing but that which it commandeth.
>
> See Beeke, 2006, p. xix

The Puritans did recognise that very often we have to make decisions in life for which there is no absolute specific direction and we have to use our Spirit-taught scripturally-instructed minds to make those decisions. William Gooch said:

> God's assistance and man's endeavour concur together; they may not be severed.

And Thomas Brooks interestingly said, though perhaps rather smugly:

> Where the Scripture is silent, there I love to be silent, and where the Scripture has no tongue there I have no ears.
>
> Quoted in Wakefield, *1957*, p. 14

Puritanism and private reading of Scripture

> We could say that there was nothing more important in the practice of Puritan piety than the private reading of Scripture. Before the Reformation, Richard Rollo's glossed English Psalter was the only book of the Bible that the laity might use without licence. Some Gospel harmonies were licensed as safer reading for the laity than the vernacular Gospels.
>
> Ibid. p. 15.

In the later Middle Ages this degenerated even further till it came to be believed that the source of piety lay in the hearing of the Mass. Also amongst Roman Catholic devotional works of that time such as Francis de Sales classic *An Introduction to a Devout Life*, though containing much scriptural material, nevertheless, when it comes to advice on private reading, it never even mentions the Bible.

The Puritans were reading the Bible at a time when the vernacular Bible in the hands of ordinary Christian people was a comparatively new thing. Everyone knew that it had been bought with the martyrs' blood. The doctrine of the illumination of the Holy Spirit throwing light upon the sacred page also greatly encouraged the reading of the Scriptures in private.

Puritans such as Green and Bailey expected the Bible to be read three times a day, "a chapter at a time". Bailey says, "Granted that so many Psalms instead of a chapter as our Church liturgy points for Morning or Evening Prayer, are read, the whole Bible can be gone through in the year, except six chapters, which thou mayest add to the task of the last day of the year." Ibid. pp. 17–18.

Puritanism and preaching

Almost needless to say the Puritans had a tremendously high view of the importance of preaching. Numerous quotations can be given.

Richard Sibbes said:

> Christ, when he ascended on high and led captivity captive (he would give no mean gift to them, when he was to ascend triumphantly to heaven) the greatest gift he could give was "some to be prophets, some apostles, some teachers (and preachers) for the building up of the body of Christ till we all meet, a perfect man in Christ."
>
> "I will send them pastors according to my own heart saith God" (Jeremiah 3:15). It is the gift of all gifts, the ordinance of preaching. God esteems it so, Christ esteems it so, and so should we esteem it.
>
> Quoted by Lewis, 1979, p. 36.

The Puritans believed a minister's preaching was his chief work and foremost responsibility.

William Perkins said:

> They are thoroughly deceived who think a minister can discharge sufficiently his duty though he preach not, if he keep good hospitality and make peace amongst his neighbours and perform other works of charity and a good life: but if he have not the gift and virtue of preaching he hath none.
>
> Ibid. p. 38

Puritan preaching was plain and easy to be understood, but not dull and certainly not predictable.

Puritan preaching was practical. The chief end of the Puritan preacher was the glorification of God in the restoration of his image in the souls and lives of men.

John Owen said that the purpose and principle of preaching was to promote, "*the growth of light, knowledge, godliness, strictness and fruitfulness of conversation*".

"Preachers," said Roger Ascham, "*ought to think like great men, but speak like common people.*"

Puritanism and the mind and heart

The Puritans paid attention to the mind, and the heart.

They viewed the mind as the place of faith. They had a saying which is very interesting, "In conversion, reason is elevated".

Another of their sayings was "Ignorance is the mother not of devotion but of heresy".

They believed that an anti-intellectual Gospel quickly becomes an empty, formless Gospel that does not get beyond "*felt needs*". A significant part of Puritan preaching was to inform the mind.

They saw that a mindless Christianity was a weak Christianity.

This is an important point because the Puritans grasped that a mindless Christianity creates a spineless Christianity. An anti-intellectual Gospel, a Gospel with no intellectual credibility, is easily dismissed and easily swept away. Where it becomes the case that there is little difference between what Christians and non-believers think and believe in their minds, there will soon be little difference in how they live.

True it is that Puritans refused to set the mind and the heart against each other but they taught that knowledge was the soil in which the Holy Spirit planted the seed of regeneration. They preached both to address the mind and the heart, and, as we shall see, the conscience.

Puritanism and the conscience

One Puritan wrote, "We must go with the stick of divine truth and beat every bush behind which a sinner hides, till like Adam who hid, he stands before God in his nakedness".

Everybody has a conscience … The conscience is the reflective part of the mind, the conscience, the moral compass, is placed in every man, and is one of those aspects and features of the fact that man is made in the image and likeness of God. Every man, woman, boy and girl born has a sense of the difference between right and wrong.

"Conscience is a domestic chaplain", wrote old John Trapp.

"God has set conscience as his representative in the heart of man". Nathaniel Rogers.

"Conscience is God's Sergeant whom he employs to arrest the sinner". William Gurnall.

"Conscience is either the greatest friend or the greatest enemy in the world". Richard Sibbes.

"Through the goodness of God the knowledge of many things which we ought to do or shun is still conserved in man's mind even after his Fall". William Ames.

How many there are like refugees fleeing from a guilty conscience. We hear sometimes of murderers who feel they cannot wash their victim's blood off their hands. It is a universal fact and reality that our sins will eventually find us out. (We may remember "The Tell-Tale Heart" in Edgar Allan Poe's *Tales of Mystery and Imagination*). A guilty conscience will not be silenced; there is no remedy for an accusing conscience but the blood of the Lamb, our Saviour Jesus Christ.

Puritanism and the Nonconformist conscience

The Nonconformist conscience has a long and illustrious history going back to Puritan times. In the 18th century, it denounced slavery and helped bring about its downfall; in the early part of the nineteenth century, it supported the Factory Acts and the Movement for Prison Reform; it stood against the abuse of alcohol, and it was said, "*hated the opium traffic with a perfect hatred*". It encouraged and advanced the principle of universal education, a restful Sabbath, fair pay for the underprivileged, and over the years it has been one of the chief promoters of public righteousness. It has stood against governmental interference with personal liberty. It sternly condemned the sins of self-indulgence, sexual irregularities and gambling. It has over the years consistently stood on the side of righteousness even when that side was far from popular.

The Puritans engaged the heart.

In preaching, the Puritans fed the mind and reasoned with the mind and confronted the conscience and, at the same time, they appealed to the heart. They preached to kindle in their hearers the spirit of thankfulness and the desire to know Christ better and to live wholly for him.

Puritanism handling the trials of life

The Puritans preached so as to show people how to handle the trials and afflictions of life.

Robert Leighton, whom we mentioned earlier, wrote:

> Affliction is the diamond dust that heaven polishes its jewels with.

We have William Bridge's *A Lifting up for the Downcast.*

We have Richard Sibbes's *The Bruised Reed.*

Like their Master they were physicians of the soul. They were far greater physicians of the soul than the modern day psychiatrists, or perhaps we should say the followers of Sigmund Freud and those like him.

They dealt with matters of lack of assurance, lack of a sense of the Lord's presence, unbelief and doubt, Satan's temptations, evil thoughts, etc.

They were well aware that men can fall into mental depression—the term they used for it was "*melancholy*", or "*melancholia*".

In this condition Christopher Love said of its symptoms and effects that "*The understanding may be darkened, the fancy troubled, reason perverted and the soul saddened*".

Thomas Brooks described it as follows:

> Melancholy is a dark and dusky humour which disturbs both the soul and the body, and the cure of it belongs to the physician rather than to the divine … It is a humour that unfits a man for all sorts of services, but especially those that concern his soul, the spiritual estate, his everlasting condition. The melancholic person tries the physician, grieves the minister, wounds relations and makes sport for the devil … Melancholy is a disease that works strange passions, strange imaginations and strange conclusions.

Richard Baxter has a famous sermon entitled: *The cure of Melancholy and Overmuch Sorrow by Faith and Physic.*

We might say that some of these Puritan ministers actually practised a crude form of medicine, where there were no doctors available for their parishioners. Richard Baxter was one in his parish at Kidderminster. There is the famous story of his swallowing what he described as a gold bullet; he had faith in the healing properties of gold. Whether he was right or wrong I do not know, but it seems to be an expensive cure. The Puritan born out of time was John Wesley of course, and he compiled his famous Primitive Physic, a book of remedies for the sick and infirm.

The Puritans knew how to strengthen people overcome by the battle of life. They were not psychologists in the modern sense of the word but they were great physicians of the soul. Here is an example of it from Richard Sibbes; book, *The Bruised Reed.* He reminds those who are going through periods of great affliction and difficulty of the realities of the way God deals with us. We may have in our minds a situation such as that of Jacob when his nine sons returned from Egypt, saying that the money they had taken to buy corn in Egypt had all been found in their sacks, and not only this but bearing the news that Simeon had been kept as a hostage and that, the man in authority there (Joseph) was demanding that Benjamin be taken down to prove they were not spies. Jacob's famous words on hearing the news, "*All these things are against me*".

How would we have answered Jacob in that situation? Well, we may imagine this answer of Richard Sibbes being given to a man in Jacobs's situation.

> Christ's work, both in the Church and in the hearts of Christians, often goes backward so that it may go forward better. As seed rots in the ground in the wintertime, but after comes up better, and the harder the winter the more flourishing the spring, so we learn to stand by falls, and get strength by weakness discovered—we take deeper root by shaking. And, as torches flame brighter by moving, thus it pleases Christ, out of his freedom, in this manner to maintain his government in us.
>
> Let us herein labour to exercise our faith, so that it may answer Christ's way of dealing with us. When we are foiled, let us believe we shall overcome; when we have fallen, let us believe we shall rise again. Jacob, after he received a blow which made him lame, yet would not give over wrestling (Genesis 32:25) till he had obtained the blessing. So let us never give up, but, in our thoughts, knit the beginning, progress and end together, and then we shall see ourselves in heaven out of the reach of all enemies.
>
> Sibbes, 1998, p. 95.

> The Puritans believed passionately in the providence of God. A well-known example of this no doubt often quoted, is the fact that Cromwell and Hampton had set their hearts on joining the Pilgrims in New England. They did not sail in the Mayflower but planned to do so on a later sailing. These were just the kind of men that the New World needed. However, they were unable to join the ship as they were detained by the authorities and what seemed to them at the time calamitous was the very thing which, "*In the fullness of time secured the liberties of England, and dissipated the cloud which hung over the Huguenots of France and the Albigensians of Switzerland, and changed the face of all England*".
>
> Dr Spring's, *Supremacy of God among the Nations.*
> Quoted by Hollis Read, [n.d.], p. 104.

Puritanism and the home

It is said that the English Puritans are to be credited with the concept of the family as we know it today, or perhaps we should say before the neo-Marxist, politically correct neo-orthodoxy of today got its hands upon it.

For the Puritans home was a moral and industrious place as well as a spiritual retreat from at best an amoral world.

> In considering our indebtedness to the Puritans, it should never be forgotten by those who value English home life that they gave it to us.

So wrote J.S. Flynn in his *The Influence of Puritanism on the political and religious thought of the English.*

He goes on to say, quoting J.R. Green in his *History of the English-Speaking People*, "*Home as we conceive it now was the creation of the Puritan*".

> If Puritanism occasioned the "loss of the passion, the caprice, the subtle and tender play of feeling, the breadth of sympathy, the quick pulse of delight of the Elizabethan age, on the other hand life gained in moral grandeur, in a sense of the dignity of manhood, in orderliness and equitable force. The larger geniality of the age that had passed away was replaced by an intense tenderness within the narrow circle of the whole. Gravity and seriousness reigned there, softened and warmed by family love, until the home of the honest, upright Englishman has become the sweetest and purest thing on earth:
>
> > A quiet centre in a troubled world,
> > A haven where the rough winds whistle never,
> > And the still sail in the sunbeams furled.

The picture of home is also expressed in the strains of the old song, "Home Sweet Home".

> Mid pleasures and palaces
> wheresoe'er I roam,
> be it ever so humble,
> there's no place like home.

There is much Puritan counsel about the choice of a wife and the preparation for marriage. Henry Smith: suggests five rules for a man choosing a wife. The lady's reputation, her looks (does she appear godly), speech or rather her silence. Apparel (i.e. sobriety of dress), and company.

Gooch thinks health and a common religious faith very important.

> The Puritans had something of the Jewish and biblical attitude to betrothal, and were strongly in favour of "contracts" before marriage was solemnised in Church. We are able to overhear Richard Green exhorting two of his young parishioners at such a ceremony on the duties for which they must prepare. "The husband is the head of the wife, but the purpose of this is that he may further her salvation and present her blameless before Christ; the wife is no passive partner, for she may win the unbelieving husband, and much more, assist in grace the faithful, while remembering that she is principally espoused unto Christ".
>
> The Puritan attitude to the married state was enlightened. Though the husband is the head of the wife, this does not mean that the woman is an inferior soul. Husband and wife should treat one another with loving dignity. Sentimental endearments are deplored, but true affection should be manifest. Above all there must be patience, and a readiness to forgive. False idealism is no help to marriage, for, as Bolton says, "Two angels are not met together in a matrimonial state, but a son and daughter of Adam".
>
> Procreation is not the only purpose of marriage, and the union must not be broken for want of children. But children are the great blessing of a marriage, and parents must watch over them by prayer, as well as in the prenatal period as afterwards. Bodily chastisement is an appropriate and Scriptural form of correction, provided it be adjusted to the psychology of the child, and applied in love and prayer and not to relieve parental feelings.
>
> Wakefield, 1957, pp. 56–57

Puritanism and the excellence of Jesus Christ

The Puritans considered any sermon in which Christ does not have the pre-eminence as not truly valid preaching. William Perkins said that the heart of all preaching was to, "*preach one Christ by Christ to the praise of Christ*".

Thomas Adams said, speaking of the Scriptures and Christ.

> Christ is the sum of the whole Bible, prophesied, typified, prefigured,

> exhibited, demonstrated, to be found in every leaf, almost in every line, the Scriptures being but as it were the swaddling bands of the child Jesus.
>
> See Beeke, 2012, pp. 961–2

Annie Ross Cousin is famous for putting into verse some of the writings of Samuel Rutherford; we will be familiar with the lines:

> O Christ he is the fountain,
> The deep, sweet well of love;
> The streams on earth I've tasted,
> More deep I'll drink above;
> There, to an ocean fullness,
> His mercy doth expand,
> And glory, glory dwelleth,
> In Immanuel's land.

Puritanism and prayer

The Puritans had no doubt that the public ordinances of the Christian faith were indispensable, and Richard Greenham, in an aside, assumes it is axiomatic that there is a greater blessing as he put it "*to be due by the Lord's own promise to public devotion than to private*".

At the same time the Puritans remind us that though prayer is performed in our families and in the congregation we must not think that this is enough; we are bound to a private life of prayer; this is our duty.

Richard Baxter reminds us that "*we seldom read of God's appearing by himself or his angels to any of his prophets or saints in throng, but frequently when they are alone*".

Robert Bolton is said by his biographer to have prayed six times a day, twice by himself in private, twice in public with his family, twice with his wife.

Morning and evening are the chief occasions for private prayer, following the times of sacrifice in the Jewish temple.

But, say the Puritan writers, beside this we must so cultivate communion with God as to be able to pray in season and out of season.

Downham, in his *Guide to Godliness*, said of these prayers offered in moments of anxiety or need:

> Unto which prayers there is not required that we should use our voice

> or gestures of the body which are used in set prayers, but sudden and short ejaculatory prayers and darting unto the Throne of Grace.

Perkins answers the question: Why should we pray?

> Why must we pray, since God has already decreed what will come to pass? The answer is that God has ordained not only ends but means, and prayer is his appointed means of carrying out his decree.

The Puritans following Luther and Calvin frequently commented on the Lord's Prayer at length.

There is an interesting piece on the Holy Spirit and prayer in *Puritan Devotion* by Gordon S. Wakefield on the statement in Scripture, "*The Spirit itself maketh intercession for us*".

John Owen deals with the problem of this dual intercession in expounding Zechariah 12:10:

> "I will pour upon the house of David and upon the inhabitants of Jerusalem the Spirit of grace and supplications". The Holy Spirit cannot make intercession for himself else would he be less than God; nor can he interpose in heaven on our behalf, for that is the priestly office of Christ. His intercession is—using the scholastic term of Owen—"efficient"; that is, he works in us, stirring us up to pray, and he makes us able to pray. Richard Sibbes teaches similarly: "The Gospel breeds love in us to God, and hath the Spirit together with it working a blessed frame of sanctification, whereby we are disposed to do every good duty". Thus it is by the strength and assistance of the Holy Spirit that we are enabled, albeit groaningly, to approach God through Christ. The Spirit brings us to Christ, and Christ to God. He is the Spirit of Christ, the legacy of the Lord now in glory, Christ's "shaliach" in the earth, to dispose us to all virtue and turn our hearts to Him who pleads before the throne. John Preston defines prayer as "an expression or offering of those holy and good dispositions to God, that arise from the spirit or the regenerative part, in the name of Jesus Christ". The Spirit alone makes possible those good and concentrated dispositions which are as a burning-glass held up to the sun, and bring light and heat to the soul from God.
>
> The Spirit who thus inspires our prayer is also the Spirit of adoption whereby we cry, "Abba Father". That simple cry of the child is true prayer as John Owen declares: "There is no more required to prayer either way but crying, "Abba, Father"—that is, the making our

> requests known unto him as our Father in Christ—with supplications and thanksgivings, according as our state and occasions do require. Dr Nuttall shows that for Puritans of all parties the basis of prayer in the Spirit is the conviction of the Fatherhood of God.
>
> The Puritan Cradock singles out four functions of the "power" of the Spirit: the first in dictating a world of prayer to us. We may make forms of prayer but only the Spirit can make spiritual petitions. Secondly in supplying us when we pray not. Thirdly in teaching us inwardly. Fourthly in working our works in and for us.
>
> The Puritans do not despise the human understanding.
>
> The Holy Spirit helps us to pray by crowning our natural aspirations. John Owen does not think the Spirit inspires our supplications by an immediate Divine revelation as he inspired the prophets of old, who did not fully comprehend his meaning, but rather by giving voice and action to—indeed making actual—our desires and requests. John Bunyan asserts that the understanding must be occupied in prayer as well as the Spirit. We must grasp with our minds, our needs, God's willingness to save us, the way to him, the largeness of the promises. We must also learn to wrestle with God, and to know what to pray for, and how to pray on each occasion. But this for Bunyan, as for St. Paul, is to be distinguished from the work of the Spirit in prayer. "I will pray with the Spirit and I will pray with the understanding also."
>
> Wakefield, 1957, pp. 80–81

Some Puritans such as Baxter held to the validity of set prayers, while others only favoured extempore praying.

Puritanism and how to live in two worlds

We might use the example of Richard Baxter's *The Saint's Everlasting Rest* to illustrate his point. This book was written while Baxter was travelling as a chaplain with Cromwell's army.

He wrote in his autobiography:

> I came to Major Swallows quarters at Sir John Cook's house at Melbourne, in the edge of Derbyshire beyond Ashby de la Zouch, in a cold and snowy season; and the cold, together with other things coincided to set my nose on bleeding. When I had let about a quart or two I opened four veins, but it did no good. I used divers other remedies for several days to little purpose; at last I gave myself a

> purge, which stopped it; this so much weakened me and altered my complexion that my acquaintance who came to visit me scarce knew me. Coming after so long weakness and frequent loss of blood before, it made the physicians conclude me hopeless after it was stopped, supposing I would never escape a dropsy.

It was in this condition that he wrote;

> I began to contemplate more seriously on the everlasting rest, which I apprehended myself to be just on the borders of. But that my thoughts might not too much scatter in my meditation, I began to write something on that subject, intending to make it the subject of a sermon or two; but being continued long in weakness where I had no books or no better employment, I followed it on, till it was enlarged to the book which has since been published.

It was however a book of something like 800 pages and it became a classic in Puritan homes. It has been an inspiration to thousands since, showing the power that the hope of heaven affords to direct and control and energise our life here on earth.

Bunyan's *Pilgrim's Progress*, of course, is another outworking of the same truth.

> The Puritans believed that we should have heaven in our eye throughout our earthly pilgrimage. The "hope of glory" should be our guide and shape our lives here on earth. The Puritans taught us to live in the light of eternity and this necessitated radical self-denial. They taught, as one put it, that preparing to die is the first step in learning to live.
>
> See Beeke, 2006, p. xxiii

Puritanism and maturity

Maturity is a compound of wisdom, goodwill, resilience and creativity. The Puritan exemplified maturity, we do not. The Puritans by contrast, as a body, were giants. They were great souls serving a great God. In them clear-headed passion and warm-hearted compassion combined: visionary and practical, idealistic and realistic too, goal-orientated and methodical. They were great believers, great hopers, great doers, and great sufferers. But their sufferings, on both sides of the ocean (in Old England from the authorities and in New England from the elements), seasoned and ripened them till they gained stature that was nothing short of heroic. Ease and luxury, such as our affluence brings us today, do not make for maturity; hardship and struggle however do. The Puritans battled against the Evangelical climactic wilderness in which God set them and produced the ability of character, undaunted and unsinkable, rising above discouragement and fears for which the true precedents and models I may liken to Moses, Nehemiah, and Peter after Pentecost and the apostle Paul.

Spiritual warfare made the Puritans what they were. They accepted conflict as their calling, seeing themselves as their Lord's soldiers—pilgrims just as in Bunyan's allegory, and did not expect to be able to advance a single step without opposition of one sort or another.

Wrote John Geree, in his tract *The Character of an Old English Puritan or Nonconformist.* "In his home life he encountered a warfare, wherein Christ was his captain, his arms, prayers and tears. The Cross his banner, and his word (motto) 'Vincit qui patitur' (he who suffers conquerors)." J.I. Packer, *Among God's Giants*,p. 24

Puritanism left behind it an ideal that has ever since been a priceless heritage of our nation—although foolishly neglected these days—that the object of life is service not pleasure. Puritanism, in laying stress upon obedience to law and the decencies of a well-ordered life, strengthens that respect for law and order which has done so much for our national greatness.

JI Packer said "*The Puritan exemplified maturity, we do not …*"

We might close by saying that the Act of Toleration which received the royal assent in May 24, 1689 marked the triumph of Puritanism over the power of absolute monarchy in England. It has left a framework of thought that guards against the rise of tyranny and provides the framework for resisting the development of excessive governmental powers. In the Puritan view religion and politics cannot be separated. The true Puritan has the utmost concern for the well-being of the state. The Puritan believes that civil and religious liberties go hand in hand.

We might say that at the end of the 17th century the Church of the Puritan slumbered until roused again by the voice of John Wesley and George Whitefield, Wesley being the grandson of one of the ministers ejected from the National Church by the Act of Uniformity 1662, Dr Annesley. That great revival of the 18th century was regarded by many as the return of Puritanism. "*This is the old Puritanism revived*", said one.

And so Puritanism will always be an element within the Church of

Jesus Christ and a very important element indeed. It can be seen within the Church of England in the 19th century, and, as we have noted above, it very much characterised the Clapham Sect at the beginning of the century, and at the end of the century was represented in men like J.C. Ryle.

And it lived in the 20th century in the work of the Sovereign Grace Union, The Banner of Truth Trust, the writings of Poole-Connor, and men such as Dr Martyn Lloyd-Jones, who achieved so much in bringing it again to the fore. It is a fact that there are more books on the market by Puritan authors today than have been available for a very long time.

And we might say even in the general population where there is any backbone, any depth, any sense of the value of liberty, any sense of duty and responsibility, any true devotion to our Lord Jesus Christ, we will trace the influence and characteristics of our Puritan forebears.

Chapter 12
Christianity in the 18th Century

Christianity indestructible

As we turn to the 18th century we can remind ourselves that just as there are high spiritual and moral points in history there are also low points of unbelief and moral collapse.

The opening years of the 18th century have been described as one of the "*glacial epochs*" of Church history.

There are many contemporary descriptions of this low state which have come down to us, for example:

The Weekly Miscellany of 1732 stated:

> … That zeal for godliness looks as odd upon a man as the dress of his great-grandfather.

Rivington, the publisher of religious books, complained in 1736 of the fact that:

> Many of the young men in his parish had left off attendance at all public services and professed Deism and there had been a visible decline in the sale of good books.

1738, Archbishop Secker of Oxford stated:

> … That an open and professed disregard for religion is become, through a variety of causes, a distinguishing characteristic of the present age.

This same disregard for religion led to the same open disregard for morality. In 1736, every sixth house in London was a grog shop and the purveyors of cheap gin hung signs outside their shops advertising, "*Drunk for a penny, dead drunk for tuppence, clean straw for nothing*".

As well as acute drunkenness, licentiousness and brutality, gang warfare raged in London. Not only amongst the lower ranks of society did immorality prevail, but amongst leading and influential figures also; one French observer commented on the fact that in England not more than four or five of the members of Parliament were regular attenders at church.

Illegitimacy was rife, and unwanted children were ruthlessly destroyed.

The condition of the churches both Established and Free was in the main dire.

> The English Nonconformists at the beginning of the [eighteenth] century were losing their courage and their earnestness. The clergy ejected in 1662 had disappeared and the fervours of Puritanism had disappeared with them. Dr. Doddridge and his contemporaries wrote desponding pamphlets about "The Decay of the Dissenting Interest." Most of the Independents and the Baptists retained their Evangelical creed, but a keen east wind of rationalism was chilling the very life of both ministers and people. Latitudinarianism and religious indifference were spreading through the English Church, and the Evangelical Nonconformists suffered from the infection. The Presbyterians were rapidly drifting into Unitarianism.
>
> Dale, 1880, pp. 12–13.

It was into this situation that God sent revival.

Chapter 13
The 18th-century Revival and its Multitudinous Benefits

We may trace the origins of this revival to the activities of certain individuals in Wales, namely to Griffith Jones, often called the Morning Star of the Revival in Wales, who was greatly used of God in the latter part of the 17th century and early 18th century in the region in and around Carmarthenshire. His itinerant and outdoor ministry was an anticipation of that which was to later characterise the ministries of Whitefield and Wesley. Other figures that could be named would be Daniel Rowland and his ministry in Llangeitho in the early 1730s. The name of Howell Harris should also be mentioned who first met with Whitefield in Cardiff in 1738. Amongst the first fruits of the spiritual and moral awakening of this time was the establishing of The Foundling Hospital by Thomas Coram in London in 1740.[9]

At the same time God was using the ministry of Jonathan Edwards in New England. Vishal Mangalwadi describes the American awakening of the 1730s and its British counterpart as watershed movements in shaping America and Great Britain. Its teaching people to revere God's Word and its principles ensured the success of America's independence and Britain's democracy. In contrast, the secular enlightenment in France led to a revolution that catastrophically degenerated into totalitarianism. (This was a well-known observation made famous by Elie Halévy the French historian which we shall comment on in a moment.) Here we can emphasise the point made by Mangalwadi in *The Book that Made your World*, where he makes the observation that every country in South and Central America and the Caribbean which followed the French Revolution fell into dictatorship. Secular revolutions merely replaced one sinful authority with another.

In contrast, at the heart of the Great Awakening was a revival of personal piety. Its social consequences were far-reaching and united 80% of all Americans in a common world and life view, which

---

9 The protracted crusade on behalf of the foundling and exploited children was, we repeat, one of the marks of the gradually awakening Social Conscience: and that awakening was a product of the new religious emphasis on the sanctity of all human life. J. Wesley Bready, *England Before and After Wesley*, p. 145.

ensured that America remained one nation even though Americans were divided among many denominations. Thanks to the earlier contributions by men such as Roger Williams, the Awakening made it possible for America to accept the non-established denominations of European dissenters. A cultural precedent was set that has made religious toleration a defining characteristic of American life.

The Awakening also helped to cultivate "grassroots intellectualism". Its emphasis on studying the Bible inspired people to enhance the quality and quantity of American educational opportunities. Jonathan Edwards became president of Princeton University. George Whitefield, the second most important leader of the Great Awakening, founded the school that became the University of Pennsylvania.

Its inaugural faculty members were Presbyterian ministers whose interest in education was rooted in their concern for souls. It reflected the peculiarly Protestant notion that education should be available for all because the Bible teaches that God wants everyone to know the truth.

The Great Awakening's sense of responsibility for human souls extended to Native Americans and slaves. George Whitefield was the first European to preach to black people. As a result of his efforts, American slaves began to cherish literacy; they wanted to read the Bible and were encouraged to do so. While the First Great Awakening did not address slavery, it did become a force that democratised America and led to the American Revolution. That inspired many more quests for political liberty, eventually ending colonialism. Some evangelicals began denouncing slavery. The British revival led to the ending of the slave trade. In the United States, the abolition of slavery followed the Second Awakening, which began under the antislavery preachers such as Charles Finney, Lyman Beecher, his sons and his daughter Harriet who wrote *Uncle Tom's Cabin.*

The Great Awakening took our Lord's promise of "rest for your souls" to the masses. That promise released many from anxiety at the core of their being on the authority of God's Word. The leaders of the revival assured believers that God had accepted them as his own children. This helped ordinary people find meaning in their lives … This generated the peculiar volunteerism that defined American compassion, until the socialist mind-set began dismantling it in favour of entitlement attitudes. Yet, it was the power of American volunteerism, fired by the

Bible's vision of the kingdom of God, which enabled a ragtag army to win history's most successful revolution.

Historian Gregory Nobles is one of the many who have documented how the Great Awakening forced communities to take a more active role in local political and religious affairs, creating the community vibrancy that fostered the spirit driving the American War of Independence.

After studying the sermons of that era, historian William McLoughlin concluded that "the roots of the Revolution as a political movement were so deeply embedded in the soil of the first Great Awakening forty years earlier that it can be truly said that the Revolution was the natural outgrowth of that profound and widespread religious movement."

The American Revolution was fuelled also by the covenant theology which began with Calvin in Geneva and was developed by Coeccius and others. It came to America with the Puritans and Presbyterians. Daniel Elazar is one of many who have documented that "the covenants of the Bible are the founding covenants of Western civilisation".

Vishal Mangalwadi also has these comments on the criticisms of Jonathan Edwards that are often levelled against him in regard to his famous sermon "*Sinners in the hands of an angry God*".

> In this sermon Edwards compared the human condition to that of a spider dangling by his web over a hot fire. He pointed out that an individual could lose his hold on life at any moment and his soul be plunged into the fires of eternal damnation. People who reject Edwards' teachings on the soul or of God's hatred for sin dislike this sermon. They dislike the thought that God holds human beings accountable to an absolute standard of right conduct.
>
> The principles of responsibility and accountability are the flipside of dignity and freedom. For a person to be free to choose, he or she must accept responsibility and be judged for the choices he or she makes. Some hold that a serial rapist and murderer should not be punished, for example, because his behaviour was conditioned by the way his father treated him. This reduces a human person to the level of a fish that can make no free choices, doing only what it has learned. The atheistic USSR, China, and Kampuchea demonstrate that when you exclude the spiritual dimension and abolish the fear of God, as Watson and Skinner did, you replace them with fearsome

> totalitarianism. Sermons such as Edwards' helped create the West's freedom because Edwards' hearers knew that, like our Lord Jesus Christ, Edwards was inviting sinners to the eternal bosom of a loving and forgiving Father.
>
> Mangalwadi, 2011, pp. 379–382.

The principal instruments used in the revival here in England are well known

These were John and Charles Wesley together with George Whitefield; though of course there were many others whom God used in these tremendous times.

The effects of this revival which were indeed a return to the great doctrines of the Reformation, and beyond that to the great doctrines of the Bible itself, resulted in a genuine spiritual rejuvenation of the nation.

As we have earlier noted, Canon Overton once famously described its effects in the following terms:

> That which enabled a man to abandon the cherished habits of a lifetime, and to go forth ready to spend and be spent in his Master's service, which nerved him to overcome the natural fear of death and indeed to welcome the last enemy as his best friend who would introduce him to the better land he had long been living for, which made the selfish man self-denying and the discontented happy, the worldling spiritually-minded, the drunkard sober, the sensual chaste, the liar truthful, the thief honest, the proud humble, the godless godly and the thriftless thrifty.
>
> J.H. Overton, *The Evangelical Revival in the 18th century*

Not only were the fruits of the revival seen in the transformation of the lives of countless individuals, but the whole Church and nation were fired with a new zeal for godliness. Robert Southey compared the godly influence of Wesley in England with his rationalistic counterpart in France, Voltaire. He said while one (Wesley) set mighty principles at work in England the other (Voltaire) scattered the seeds of immorality and unbelief in France, brought down the whole fabric of government, overturned her altars, subverted her throne, and carried guilt, devastation and misery into every part of the country. (See Robert Southey's *Life of Wesley*)

As we noticed above the French historian Elie Halévy forcibly argued that Methodism saved Britain from the bloody revolution that took place in France. Halévy made a study and analysis of the political, judicial, economic, legislative, and popular life in England at this period and discovered chaos and anarchy in every direction. His question then was—"how could it come about that from such uncompromising conditions the later Victorian era became such a period of exceptional stability and prosperity?"

His answer was that the solution lay in the effects of the Evangelical Revival and the moral and spiritual quickening of the English people that flowed from it.

Halévy remarked:

> If the materialistic interpretation of history is to be trusted, if economic facts explain the course taken by the human race in its progress, then England of the 19th century was surely, above all other countries, destined to revolution, both political and religious. But it was not to be so. In no other country of Europe have social changes been accomplished with such a marked and gradual continuity. The source of such continuity and comparative stability is, as we have seen, not to be found in the economic organization of the country. We have seen, also, that it cannot be found in the political institutions of England, which were essentially unstable and wanting in order. To find it we must pass on to another category of social phenomena—to beliefs, emotions and opinions, as well as to the institutions and sects which these beliefs, emotions and opinions take a form suitable for scientific enquiry.

Halévy concludes that the spirit of revolt and discontentment, instead of turning to revolution turned to the preaching of John Wesley and George Whitefield and that movement commonly called Methodism.

We may note in passing that the modern notion of today's secularists and humanists that society can be maintained, held together, and make progress without any reference to spirituality, morality and absolutes, is manifestly unworkable, and blindly omits and denies the very best and essential elements in human life.

The 18th century Revival and the Industrial Revolution

It must not be forgotten that the Evangelical Revival corresponded with the time that the Industrial Revolution was beginning to get underway.

Here we might quote from some direct effects of the Revival on the conditions which prevailed in the region of Coalbrookdale, Shropshire, often said to have been at the very heart of the then burgeoning Industrial Revolution.

Barry Trinder, writing in his *The Industrial Revolution in Shropshire*, comments that this period saw the development of a new type of society, one shaped as much by the Evangelical Revival as by industrialisation.

The dislocation of the existing social order and the migration into the district from many of the surrounding areas and indeed further afield of individuals and families looking for work and a better life brought with it a breakdown of moral restraints. The area became renowned for drunkenness, riots, strikes, and immorality. In the pits and iron works it was difficult for employers to secure the regular attendance of the employees. There was a great deal of unrest at the level of pay; there were frequent strikes and periodic outbreaks of fighting amongst the workforce.

John Fletcher in his Journal wrote in 1783:

> The continued increase of the poor rates is occasioned by the corrupted morals of the lower classes of the people who are seduced into idleness and neglect of their families in the public house to be met with at every turn.
>
> Ibid. p. 362

Joshua Gilpin described the efforts made by John Fletcher ministering under such conditions as follows:

> It was a common thing in his parish for young persons of both sexes to meet at stated times for the purpose of what was called recreation and this recreation usually continued from evening till morning, consisting chiefly of dancing, revelling, drunkenness and obscenity. These licentious assemblies he considered a disgrace to the Christian name, and determined to exert his ministerial authority for their total suppression. He has frequently burst in upon these disorderly companies with a holy indignation, making war upon Satan in places peculiarly appropriated to his service. Nor was his labour altogether in vain among the children of dissipation and folly. After standing the first shock of their rudeness and brutality, his exhortations have been generally received with silent submission and have sometimes

> produced partial if not an entire reformation in many who were accustomed to frequent these assemblies.
>
> Ibid p. 363

Animal cruelty sports, particularly cockfighting and bull baiting were regarded by many observers as typifying the violence of the coalfield. Indeed, all types of violence were to be found amidst the social dislocation and harsh working conditions in the pits and iron works of the region. "This district", wrote a Wesleyan minister of Oakengates in 1835, "is the most notorious for vice of every kind, and especially for the grossest violation of the Sabbath and the cruel practice of bull baiting".

The Methodist Revival and later the Primitive Methodist Revival exerted a most marked and considerable influence in bringing to an end these disorders, and occasioned one of the iron companies' agents Gilbert Gilpin to note to the employers "… *that the Methodists were the best workmen, without whom the works could not operate*".

This last comment and the events surrounding this birthplace of the Industrial Revolution strongly suggest that the Industrial Revolution could never have properly taken hold or achieve what it did but for the calming and dignified influence of the Christian Gospel.

Turning again to the wider benefits brought about by the 18th century revival we may quote the words of the historian John Richard Green who wrote of it, having produced, *Philanthropy which reformed our prisons, infused clemency and wisdom into our penal system, abolished the slave trade, and gave the first impulse to popular education.*

A Short History of the English People

In the 20th century H. Richard Niebuhr commented:

> The Evangelical pieties of the Methodists means primarily an inward change of heart. But such change is not a private affair. True faith involves works and charity, just as love of God, "the one perfect good," involves the love of neighbor. Methodism is as intensely social as it is intensely inward. Salvation does not mean a private preparation for heaven; it means a life of moral purity and social concern.
>
> Wesley was by no means blind to the tragic maladjustments which the Industrial Revolution brought in his lifetime. In traditional Protestant fashion, he located the source of this maladjustment not in the machine, nor industrialism itself, but in "ungodliness" and

vice. But his his *Journal* records his burning concern with the bleak poverty and the course living of the crowds who came to hear him. He himself was unflaggingly busy in all sorts of social salvage and social reform enterprises. He visited English prisons many times, preaching to the inmates and commenting bitterly in his letters on the misery of prison conditions. He set up a simple loan society among his Methodists to help keep his poor followers from the clutches of the pawnbrokers and out of the debtor's prisons. He fought hard liquor as much for economic as for moral reasons. He edited a *Christian Library*, fifty volumes of extracts from Christian literature, for popular use. He established a free medical dispensary and wrote a book of simple home remedies for the sick called *Primitive Physic* which ran to twenty-three editions. He established a home for widows and a home for poor children.

... Wesley preaches to these folk essentially the principle of vocation and Calvinistic stewardship. What one acquires by way of earthly goods is to be acquired diligently and honestly without hurt to others. "Save all you can" does not mean to invest or hoard; it means simplicity of living: waste nothing, spend nothing on cheap or degrading pastimes. And "give all you can" means the sacrificial mutual sharing among the poor, not the handouts of the rich from their superfluity. The practice of this ethic gives a religious impetus to the Methodists to combat the depressing economic and cultural forces arrayed against them, to become self-respecting and reliable workers, to buy books instead of gin, to rise economically, and to educate their children.

Beach and Niebuhr, 1955, p. 361–3

The 18th century Revival and the origin of the Sunday School Movement

The Sunday School Movement was begun by Robert Raikes in Gloucester in 1780.

At this time, children were employed often from the ages of seven or eight, either as farm labourers or included increasingly in the burgeoning factories of the Industrial Revolution.

Children however were free on Sundays and often roamed the streets, creating mayhem. Robert Raikes began his first Sunday School in a rented kitchen and invited both boys and girls from some of the poorest homes to attend. They were required to come with clean hands and faces, combed hair, and with some measure of clean clothing.

Often he himself had to provide the shoes and the clothing. Robert Raikes' primary purpose was to teach the children the Bible, but he quickly discovered that most of them could not read nor write. Before he could teach them the Bible he first had to teach them how to read. They had to attend from 10 until 12 o'clock on Sunday mornings, returned at 1 o'clock, and continued their lessons till 5:30. The afternoon period included attendance at the service in the church. When dismissed they were told to go home without making a noise and not to play in the streets.

His work was opposed by some who regarded that he was violating the Sabbath day by such activities. However, he was supported by some of the outstanding Church leaders of the day including John Wesley and his brother Charles, John Newton, William Cowper, John Howard, Hannah More and others. He soon gathered a body of helpers and the work progressed and was very successful. He even received encouragement from King George III and Queen Charlotte and was invited to an audience with them in order to describe his work.

We have already seen that Martin Luther set up a number of Sunday Schools in Germany in his day. It is said that "*he established religious schools on the Lord's day, devoted to the study of biblical catechism, singing the praises of God and the great duty of prayer*".

In 1688 the Rev. Joseph Alleine, the author of the book *An Alarm to the Unconverted*, started a Sunday School at his church in Taunton. In 1769, Hannah Ball, who had been converted under the preaching of John Wesley, set up a Sunday School in High Wycombe. Thomas King, a Dissenter, started up another school in Dursley, Gloucestershire, and there were certainly many other individual Sunday Schools in existence up and down the land in this period.

The Oxford historian, John Richard Green, in his *A Short History of the English People*, in the section dealing with the 18th century says:

> The result of the religious revival was the steady attempt, which has never ceased from that date to this, to remedy the guilt, the ignorance, the physical suffering, the social degradation of the poor. It was not until the Wesleyan movement commenced its work that this philanthropic impulse began. The Sunday Schools established by Mr. Raikes of Gloucester at the close of the century were the beginnings of popular education.
>
> It is true to say though, that when Robert Raikes opened his first Sunday School in July 1780 the modern concept of universal

> education was really born. Although those we have mentioned above were evangelicals and had a real concern for the souls of youngsters, they were also used of God in a practical way to improve the lives of many by giving them the gift of education.
>
> Christopher Clark article on Robert Raikes, Crich Baptist Church, Derbyshire, Internet

Hannah More and Sunday Schools

Hannah More lived not far from Raikes in Cheddar, Somerset. She was born in Bristol in 1745. She went to school when she was 12 years old and later taught at the same school. At an early age she found that she had a gift for writing and spent a long time writing plays, poems and other literary works. In 1774 she went to London and there met with John Newton, William Wilberforce and other members of the Clapham Sect. These were a group consisting mainly of wealthy Anglicans, an evangelically minded group of men who were devoted to making the evangelical message known in carefully timed and presented works for the upper classes. At the same time, they were involved in various social activities, including giving support to William Wilberforce and his campaign to abolish the slave trade. The same were also committed to a great variety of societies and pressure groups working for social improvement, and were closely connected with the foundation of the Church Missionary Society (1799), The British and Foreign Bible Society (1804) and fought a successful parliamentary battle in 1813 to legalise the sending of missionaries to India.

The members of the Clapham Sect supported Hannah More in her work. During the following ten years she opened twelve more schools mainly in the villages around her home in Somerset. Most of the finance to start the schools was given by members of the Clapham Sect.

She wrote a book entitled *Hints on how to run a Sunday School* in which she wrote that programmes had to be planned and suited to the level of the students, that there needed to be variety, and that classes had to be as entertaining as possible with singing. She argued that it was possible to get the best out of children if their affections were engaged by kindness. At the same time, she wrote "*I believe that children are not innocent beings, but rather beings of corrupt nature and evil dispositions*".

She gave her children prizes for coming along, a penny if they came four consecutive Sundays, and once a year distributed books according to merit. In addition to work with children, she also started meetings at the schools on weeknight evenings to work with young people and adults where, alongside the teaching of reading, they were taught knitting and sewing.

During the next fifty years many Sunday Schools were started, some of these like the famous one in Stockport, reputed to be the largest Sunday School in the world. This Sunday School was not exclusively connected with a particular denomination, but boasted that it had in its membership in 1833, 5,244 children. This school like that of Robert Raikes in Gloucester used the Bible as the schoolbook, and the children were taken to various church services during the day. It had its own large building opened in 1805 and it was supported by subscription from local businesses and individuals and had an annual income of £1,000. It was run by its own committee and later had the patronage of Queen Victoria.

William Fox Draper, member of Prescott Street Particular Baptist Chapel, London, in 1785, along with some others, established "*The Society for the Establishment and Support of the Sunday School*". This was later to be called *The Sunday School Union*. (Notes taken from a lecture given by Christopher Clark at Crich Baptist Church 2016, Internet).

Records given by the Social Affairs Unit, London, record that in 1888 about three out of every four children in England and Wales attended Sunday School. Also the following observations are given marking the connection between Sunday School attendance and falls in crime rates.

British rates of recorded crime fell markedly in the latter part of the 19th century. The overall incidence of serious offences recorded by the police in the 1890s was only about 60% of what it had been in the 1850s, and, given that the efficiency of the reporting and recording of crime was improving at the time, the real fall in the crime rate is probably far greater than that indicated by official statistics. Thus in 1900 Britain was not only a less violent and dishonest country than today, also less violent and dishonest than it had been in the earlier part of the 19th century.

It is worth noting in passing that "*progressive*" opinion in the 19th century was unwilling to accept that crime rates were falling in capitalist free-market Britain, just as their successors of today have tried to deny that crime has risen inexorably since the introduction of various forms of socialistic or "*liberal*" social engineering.

Even in 1944 George Orwell and Geoffrey Gorer were amazed at the way in which British society had been transformed from a rowdy, dangerous place to a state of remarkable orderliness.

Orwell remarked:

> An imaginary foreign observer would certainly be struck by the gentleness, by the orderly behaviour of English crowds, the lack of pushing and quarrelling … And except for certain well-defined areas in half a dozen big towns, there is very little crime of violence … The prevailing gentleness of manners is a recent thing, however. Well within living memory it was impossible for a smartly dressed person to walk down Radcliffe Highway without being assaulted, and an eminent jurist, asked to name a typically English crime, could answer: "Kicking your wife to death …". It is not much more than a hundred years since the distinguishing mark of English life was its brutality. The common people, to judge by the press, spent their time in an almost unending round of fighting, brawling, drunkenness and bull baiting … What had these people in common with the gentle mannered, undemonstrative, law-abiding English of today.

Likewise, Geoffrey Gorer, in his study *Exploring English Character* commented:

> In public life today, the English are certainly among the most peaceful, gentle, courteous and orderly populations that the civilised world has ever seen. But from the psychological point of view this is still the same problem; the control of aggression which has gone to such remarkable lengths that you hardly ever see a fight in a bar (a not uncommon spectacle in most of the rest of Europe or the USA), when football crowds are as orderly as church meetings … This orderliness and gentleness, this absence of overt aggression calls for an explanation.
>
> Quoted in Anderson (ed.), p. 6

The same publication goes on to say one of the key agencies in spreading and transmitting what Gorer described as "*strict conscience and self-control*" was the Sunday School whose enrolments rose in numbers throughout the late 19th and early 20th centuries. "*There seems to be a clear inverse relationship between the rise and fall of the*

Sunday School and the fall and rise of deviant behaviour. In 1957, 76% of those over 30 years of age had attended Sunday School at some time in their lives, but for those under 30 the corresponding figure was only 61%."

The 18th century Revival and the Formation of Numerous Beneficial Societies

This period also gave birth to numerous beneficial societies such as the Religious Tract Society of 1799, the Naval and Military Bible Society 1779, the British and Foreign Bible Society 1804, the Baptist Missionary Society 1792, the London Missionary Society 1795, the Church Missionary Society 1799, the Society for the Distribution of Religious Tracts amongst the Poor 1782, to name but a few.

Chapter 14
The Enormous Influence of Christianity in the Nineteenth Century

During the 18th century there had grown up a spirit of religious apathy and scepticism among some in the intellectual circles of the age. This spirit we might note was an offshoot of the Renaissance period, which at the same time produced Christian humanism and its beneficial effects, but also produced a form of secular humanism which has exercised its blight upon society to the present age. The rationalism of the 18th century was certainly antagonistic towards Christianity and its exponents such as Voltaire in France and Hume here in Britain openly attacked and poured ridicule upon Christianity and the churches.

In spite of this however, as has been said, "*Christianity in the nineteenth century entered upon the century of its greatest influence*". (Latourettte, vol. 3, p. 457.)

Missionary Advance

By the close of the 18th century Christianity was already represented in all the five continents. Never before had any religion been planted over such a large proportion of the earth's surface. In Europe it was the professed faith of the large majority of the population. Roman Catholicism existed along the southern coast of India, Ceylon (Sri Lanka), Burma (Myanmar) and Siam (Thailand). The same prevailed in French Indo-China (Vietnam, Cambodia, and Laos) and into Tibet, Korea, the Philippine Islands and even Japan contain a few hidden remnants of Roman Catholic communities. In Africa, Egypt and Abyssinia (Ethiopia) there still survived some ancient churches in spite of the influx of Islam. The Dutch settlements of the Cape of Good Hope and the Portuguese possessions on the east coast of Africa contained believers. The Azores, the Madeiras, the Cape Verde Islands to the west of Africa, and Reunion and Mauritius on the east contained Christians. In the Western Hemisphere the majority of the population were professed Christians. In the West Indies, in Dutch Guiana (Suriname), and in Greenland Protestants were strong, and in Alaska a variant of Russian Orthodoxy survived, brought over by way of Siberia.

However, Protestant missionaries in the 19th Century were instrumental in carrying the Gospel of Jesus Christ to areas not evangelised for centuries and amongst tribes and peoples heretofore never reached by the Gospel. Never before had Christianity given birth and impulse to so many new missionary societies and movements. This revival showed itself primarily among Protestants.

One aspect of this was the pressure which Christian evangelicals put upon governments in regard to British foreign policy. This was that British influence should never be responsible for hindering the global progress of the Gospel.

The founding of numerous philanthropic societies, including the work of the great social reformers

The list of philanthropic societies founded in this period is endless. Some of these movements have already been mentioned on pages 230–233 of this present work. We may add to this list

The Female Bible and Domestic Mission which appointed Bible-Women to serve the poor and to help the latter to help themselves. This movement eventually supported Bible Women not only in the British Isles but also on the continent, in Egypt, and in Palestine.

In London at this time, studying medicine in preparation for service as missionary in China, Thomas John Barnardo, son of a wealthy merchant, became interested in the abandoned children who lived in the streets and alleys of the Metropolis. Giving up his plans for China, he ran a mission for these abandoned unfortunates. The rule of his mission was, "No destitute child ever refused admission". Among those he rescued he found useful occupations for them, helping some of them to find better lives in the colonies.

In the second quarter of the 19th century David Naismith established city missions in Glasgow, Dublin, London and Paris, as well as in several cities in North America. These missions from their first inception ministered to the spiritual and physical needs of the very poor.

At the same time the Mildmay Mission in London was established. Its deaconesses ministered amongst the poor districts of that city. The same mission eventually set up the famous Mildmay Hospital.

Also in the Metropolis the Wesleyans established the London Methodist Mission which carried out similar work in its many branches throughout the city.

In the 1880s the Mission to Deep Sea Fishermen was established. This was a mission focusing on North Sea fishermen. It fought drink, provided hospital ships, held services, and distributed Christian literature.

The building of churches

At the beginning of the century the Church of England made gigantic efforts to build churches in the burgeoning industrial towns and recruited and trained clergy to meet the demands of such populations. It is said that between 1801 and 1858 £11,000,000 were contributed towards the erection of 3,150 church buildings for the Established Church.

In 1827 the Church Pastoral Aid Society was inaugurated.

In Scotland the Free Church of Scotland engaged in phenomenal activity towards the setting up of new churches. The Church of Scotland at this time also embarked on a large-scale building scheme. A similar story of growth and expansion could be told of the churches in the Scandinavian countries. Several revivals took place in these areas. Though on the one hand secularism was beginning to make its appearance felt, on the other hand it could be said that the Protestant churches were more vigorous than at any other time in their history. (Latourette, p. 151).

In Germany at this time Protestantism gave rise to many societies and institutions for the relief of human suffering. One of these was the "*Inner Mission*" that had its origins in the work of Theodore Fliedner who, for more than 25 years was pastor in Kaiserswerth, made it a centre and example for European philanthropy. In 1826 he founded the Prisoner's Society of Germany. He and his wife inaugurated a home for discharged women convicts. From the mission developed schools for infants and cripples, rescue homes, care for the poor, the sick, and the mentally subnormal, services for discharged prisoners and families of prisoners, lodging houses, clubs for apprentices, and campaigns against beggary, drunkenness, and prostitution. Florence Nightingale said that it was one of his reports which convinced her that God wanted her to pursue a career in nursing. It was in fact to Kaiserswerth that she went for her initial training in nursing. It is not going too far to say from this Christian influence via Florence Nightingale the concept of modern nursing as a profession arose.

Also in Germany at this time Daniel von der Heydt, through the reading of Scripture, began a plan for the organised care of children which was adopted in several German cities.

In Scotland Thomas Chalmers (1780–1847) working in his Glasgow parish established an improved system to encourage the principle of self-help.

It is well-known that George Müller (1805–98) at this time through prayer and without directly soliciting for funds, built orphanages which cared for over 10,000 children.

Following on from the activities of the Clapham Sect, Anthony Ashley Cooper, 7th Earl of Shaftesbury, often known as Lord Shaftesbury (1801–85), though destined for high office as a parliamentarian, nevertheless renounced selfish ambition to use his position and influence to bring about legislation for the bringing of better conditions for labourers in mills and factories, limiting the working day to ten hours, barring boys under thirteen and women from working in the mines. He also introduced better protection for chimney sweeps, and an act which brought about an improvement in housing conditions. He himself built a model village on his estate.

Evangelical Christians at this time were a powerful influence within Parliament

More than a hundred Evangelical MPs sat in the House of Commons in the 50 years between 1782 and 1832. Following their participation in the successful campaign for the abolition of slavery, they made regular interventions in public life, leaving no single contemporary need or institution untouched. It was partly under their influence that Parliament became at times the vehicle for many national crusades with the result that the political process itself was imbued with profound moral and religious overtones. (Kenneth Brown writing in *Evangelical Faith and Public Zeal*, p. 138).

At this time Henry Thornton said "*I voted today so that if my Master had come again at that moment I might have been able to give an account of my stewardship.*"

It was said at this time that the greatest achievements of the evangelicals within Parliament was "*To have established politics as an honourable profession for honest men rather than as a playground for party hacks.*" Quoted in Ian Bradley, *The Call to Seriousness. The Evangelical Impact on the Victorians*, p. 166.

Evangelical Archbishop of Canterbury

At this time John Bird Sumner, Bishop of Chester (1828–48) and Archbishop of Canterbury (1848–1862), taught his generation of evangelicals something of the mysteries of the Wealth of Nations and the problem of an ever rising population. He is credited with translating the arguments of Adam Smith and Thomas Malthus into terms which evangelicals could understand and act upon. The result was that evangelicals looked to a set of stable moral laws, ordained by divine providence and generating rewards and punishments by which human behaviour might be shaped consistently. The inferences Sumner drew included relying on existing state structures for the management of the problems posed by poverty, together with the sanctions of the market which came upon the immoral and the unthinking as they wasted their money and produced more children. Scarcity was a gift, a challenge, divinely ordained. Inequalities challenged human ingenuity, evoked industry, promoted civilisation and discouraged idleness. Sumner had turned the bleak pessimism of Malthus into a celebration of divine wisdom which evangelicals could understand and from which they could draw confidence to act. (Brian Dickley, *Evangelical Faith and Public Zeal*, p. 43)

From the time of the 1833 Poor Law Report, Sumner became more willing to contemplate charitable intervention to resist or at least ameliorate the worst effects of the economy, and even of the Poor Laws, upon the poor. He called in the later 1830s and 1840s for intelligent but not indiscriminate charity, which could lead the way for new legislation, but continued to emphasise the need for recognition of "*the divine root from which benevolent conduct springs*". Christian charity was born, not of rules of economic theory or the regulations of the Poor Laws, but of an experience of God's grace and love to a forgiven sinner. Public communal charity was certainly appropriate, indeed still necessary. Sumner participated in any number of charitable activities, both national and local, and it is important to emphasise his increasing willingness to act in practical, philanthropic ways. However, for him the primary task of the Church itself remained the provision of increased facilities for worship and spiritual instruction. Christian conversion was the most reliable means of securing a lasting improvement in the social as well as spiritual condition of the individual.

See Wolffe (ed.), 1995, p. 43.

More on the societies

Turning again to the efforts of individuals and societies we might mention the Christian faith of Samuel Plimsoll (1824–98) who brought about legislation for the safety of mariners, having the Plimsoll line marked on the side of vessels to prevent overloading.

Agnes Weston also did a great deal of work for the well-being of sailors. Sailors all over the world knew of Aggie Weston's Medal, an award for sobriety.

Miss Sandes did similar work for soldiers, and Mary Sumner turned her attentions to the well-being of families.

Again in Germany at this time Pastor Oberlin (1740–1826) out of a deep piety brought about tremendous social reforms, in the formation of schools, building roads and bridges, encouraging better agricultural techniques, and establishing savings and loan associations amongst his many activities. Inspired by Pastor Oberlin's work in Germany Lord Shaftesbury commenced his work in England. Daniel Le Grand implemented similar reforms into the legislation of France. Another Frenchman, Stephen Grellet, a member of the French nobility, who later would become a missionary of the Society of Friends, did much to improve prisons here in England and on the continent. It was his work that inspired Elizabeth Fry into a lifetime of labour for the amelioration of prisoners. Two other devout Quakers at this time, George and Robert Cadbury, who had created a large cocoa and chocolate business, moved their works into the country, and built a model village for their employees. The same did extensive charitable and missionary work throughout the city of Birmingham and beyond.

In 1824 Arthur Broome founded the Royal Society for the Prevention of Cruelty to Animals.

Mrs Josephine Butler, the wife of a clergyman, was led by the death of her daughter to devote herself to the care of wayward girls and the fight against licenced prostitution and the white slave traffic. Josephine Butler wrote in 1882 the book *The Hour Before Dawn*, in which she showed that it was the duty of men so to live as to allow women to live in purity.

Many set up similar movements such as the Rev. Baptist Noel

who established the *Midnight Meeting Movement* of the early 1860s addressing meetings for young gentlemen attending music halls and dance halls, pointing out that the blame for much of the "*social evil*" lay with them.

Several other similar societies on the same lines were established in the 1870s and 1880s such as The Social Purity Alliance, The White Cross Army, and the Church of England's Purity Society.

The Temperance Movement

Christianity at the same time was largely responsible for the widespread agitation for a more moderate use of alcoholic beverages. One pioneer of this movement was an Irishman named Theobald Matthew. The movement however really got underway in England through the work of Joseph Livesey, born in 1794 at Walton, near Preston, Lancashire. It was in an adult school that he began the movement. He opened a small printing press in 1832 and became a prolific writer and publisher of temperance literature and the champion of all kinds of social reform. He took part in the campaign for the abolition of the Corn Laws, and started a small weekly paper called *The Struggle*, the pioneer of social reform papers. He toured Lancashire and Cheshire bearing a white silk banner, distributing temperance tracts and holding meetings as he went. One night he organised a meeting in Stockport. Arriving in Stockport he found to his dismay that the organisers had not secured a hall for the meeting. At 6:30 however through his untiring efforts he managed to secure the use of the Primitive Methodist Chapel. He toured the streets on a cart, beating a drum advertising the meeting and managed to secure a large crowd.

The Temperance Movement was massive in Victorian England, giving rise to various organisations such as the Band of Hope, the United Kingdom Alliance, the National Temperance League, the Church of England Total Abstinence Society, the British Women's Temperance Association, the Temperance Union of Christian Workers, the Blue Ribbon Army, the Independent Order of Rechabites, and the Sons of Temperance. (The latter two of American origin.)

Further attempts to stem consumption of alcohol gave rise to the Coffee House Movement and the Cocoa Room Movements. Dr Barnardo was responsible for two of the earliest coffee palaces, the Edinburgh Castle (1873) and the Dublin Castle (1876).

Robert Lockhart was the chairman of the British Workmen's

Public House Company in Liverpool, and he was responsible for the opening of a Cocoa Room near the new North Docks for the use of the men employed there. It was a place where cocoa, tea and coffee with cheese snacks, hotpot (scouse) and sausages could be obtained. It was intended as an alternative to the public house and it proved very popular, so that others were started and soon "*Lockhart's Cocoa Rooms*", as they were called were found in the poorer parts of London and other provincial cities. The St Giles Christian Mission issued a half-crown book of tickets to ex-prisoners for use at Lockhart's.

Another characteristic feature of Victorian evangelical influence was that of the Ragged School Movement

During the 18th century there had been concern for the poor children and their education, and again this had been one of the fruits of the 18th-century revival. Charity Schools were set up for this purpose in many parishes, and the Sunday Schools established by Robert Raikes and many others after him were by this time a regular part of the Church's work. In the early part of the 19th century particularly catering for the needs of poor children, The British and Foreign Schools Society was formed in 1808, followed by the National Schools Society in 1811. In spite of this however there were still many children living at an even lower level of society, on the very edge of destitution, for which there was no educational provision whatsoever.

John Pounds of Portsmouth is often regarded as the originator of Ragged Schools for children of this type, but it does seem that others had similar ideas in different parts of the country. For example, in 1810 some ten years before John Pounds set up his school, Thomas Cranfield of Camberwell was teaching children who were regarded as unsuitable for the Sunday Schools in the area. John Pounds' school however was significant in that it developed methods which were followed later in subsequent Ragged Schools up and down the country. He was aware that the child must be fed and clothed if it were to get any advantage from his teaching, and that the teaching must involve some element of future training for employment. It was seeing a painting of John Pounds, the cobbler, surrounded by his ragged and unkempt children, which inspired Dr Guthrie to introduce such schools in Edinburgh and Sheriff Watson in Aberdeen.

The Ragged School Union was formed in 1844, "*to give permanence, regularity and vigour to the existing Ragged Schools and to promote the formation of new ones*". The chairman of this newly formed union was Lord Shaftesbury and on its committee was the Rev. Baptist Noel, who had close connections with the *London City Mission*, and George Hitchcock later to be associated with the *YMCA*. The *Ragged School Union* calculated that in the 1860s something like 25,000 to 26,000 children came under its care in one way or another. These schools at the beginning were held in such places as barns, cow sheds, stables, railway arches or disused warehouses. Such renowned individuals as General Gordon and Dr Barnardo were amongst those who during periods of their life taught in Ragged Schools. Baroness Mayer de Rothschild provided dinners for fifty children daily at the *New Tot Hill Street Ragged School* in Westminster.

Children's homes

Mention has already been made of children's homes and orphanages, and the work of Dr Barnardo. However, he was not alone in this area of responsibility. *The National Children's Home* was begun by the Rev. Thomas Bowman Stevenson, a Wesleyan minister at the Waterloo Road Chapel in the New Cut, Lambeth. *The Waifs and Strays Society* now called the *Church of England Children's Society* was begun by two brothers, Edward and Robert de Montjoy Rudolf, who were teachers in the St Ann's Sunday School, South Lambeth, 1881. The great Baptist preacher Charles Haddon Spurgeon commenced the *Stockwell Orphanage*, since known as *Spurgeon's Homes*, as a result of a prayer meeting of the Metropolitan Tabernacle in 1867. The homes established by George Müller in Bristol have already been mentioned. Others such as Archibald Browne's orphanage 1872, and the Brixton orphanage 1876 could be added to the list. William Quarrier commenced the *Orphan Homes of Scotland*. Leonard K Shaw commenced the *Manchester and Salford Boys and Girls Welfare Society* in 1870.

Many other societies were formed too numerous to mention such as the *National Society for the Prevention of Cruelty to Children, the Children's Country Holiday Fund, the Royal National Institute for the Blind, the Boys Brigade, The Needle Woman's Institute, Missions to Cab Drivers, The Charity Organisation Society, The Children's Aid Society, The Children's League of Pity, The Children's Special Service Mission, The Church Army, The Salvation Army, The Church Penitentiary Association, The Society for the Welfare of City Work Girls, The Medical Mission Convalescent Homes, The Society for the Employment of*

Cripples, The Invalid Children's Aid Society, The Shaftesbury Society, The Society for the Care of the Deaf, Flower and Letter Missions, Homes for Working Boys, Railway Missions, The Royal Society for Discharged Prisoners, The Home for Asiatic Sailors, The Deaf and Dumb Society, Mission to the Jews, The National Vigilance Association, Navy Missions, The British Sailor's Society, The Mission to Seamen, Sailors Rest Homes, The Young Women's Help Society.

Information gathered from Wolffe (ed.), 1995.

Christian literature, periodicals and magazines

We can also add to this list the influence of many periodicals and magazines which supported and encouraged this work available at that particular time. These again are far too numerous to give a full list, but for example *The Magazine of the London City Mission*, *The Missing Link Magazine* of Mrs Ranyard's Mission, *The Sword and Trowel*, the wider circulating magazines though not always thoroughly evangelical but certainly supporting Christian truth and Christian activity such as *The Quiver*, *The Leisure Hour*, *Good Words*, *The War Cry*, *The Christian*, *The Sunday at Home*, *The Sunday Magazine*, *The Revival*, together with the children's papers such as, *The Boy's Own Paper*, *The Girl's Own Paper*, *Little Dots*, …

Add to these the vast list of story books aimed at children to instil Christian truth and Christian virtues, Christy's *Old Organ*, by Mrs O.F. Walton, also her *Peep Behind the Scenes*, and numerous others.

Space fails us to number countless other areas of mission undertaken at this time such as the work of the *London City Mission* which allocated special missionaries to groups such as policemen, railwaymen, navvies, postmen and gypsies. Their function was evangelistic rather than social work, though they did, through their reports and their contacts with social workers, make the needs of these people more widely known. This led others to concentrate upon their social welfare, and to provide various services for them.

To this we may add the efforts of individual churches and chapels.

One notable example can suffice i.e. that of the famous Metropolitan Tabernacle, London.

Name of mission etc.	**teachers and workers**	**scholars**
Almshouses Sunday School	12	153
Dunn's Institute	–	–
Boddy's Bridge	3	90
Portobello Road, Notting Hill	9	190
Battersea Park Road	–	–
Lavina Road, King's Cross	12	120
Little George Street, Bermondsey	12	120
Bedfont, near Hounslow	–	–
North Cheam	4	30
Waltham Abbey	–	–
Townsend Street, Old Kent Road	35	250
Centenary Memorial	38	408
Richmond Street, Walworth, Sunday and Ragged Schools	76	1080
Haddon Hall, Bermondsey	50	959
Surrey Gardens Memorial Hall	20	300
Stockwell Orphanage	40	440
Lansdowne Place	45	300
Rock Mission, Camberwell	5	60
Jireh Mission, Garden Row	–	–
Bermondsey Ragged School	13	250
Boundary Lane, Camberwell	18	275
Edbury Street S.W.	–	–
Great Hunter Street	15	170
North Street, Kensington	15	170
Snow's Fields, Bermondsey	13	160
Palmer's Green	–	–
Wanstead	–	–
Surrey Square, Old Kent Road	22	380
Townley Street, Walworth	9	200

Vinegar Ground, Old Street	11	167
Ormside Street, Old Kent Road	5	80
Scovill Road, Borough	12	255
Metropolitan Tabernacle Sunday School	103	1450

Ten Bible classes:—one for men only, one for women only, one for men and women, the remainder for young men and young women.

Metropolitan Tabernacle Christian Brothers' Benefit Society.

Metropolitan Tabernacle Evangelists' Association and Country Mission (with Training Classes for the workers).

Metropolitan Tabernacle Flower Mission.

Metropolitan Tabernacle Gospel Temperance Society.

Metropolitan Tabernacle Ladies' Benevolent Society.

Metropolitan Tabernacle Ladies' Maternal Society.

Metropolitan Tabernacle Lone Tract Society (for the household distribution of Mr Spurgeon's Sermons in the neighbourhood of the Tabernacle).

Spurgeon's Sermons' Tract Society. (For the circulation of Mr Spurgeon's Sermons in country districts).

Metropolitan Tabernacle Poor Ministers' Clothing Society.

City Missionaries, Bible Women, Mothers' Meetings, Orphanage, and Colportage Working Societies, and numerous other agencies.

Where no figures are inserted in the table above, it is to be understood that the Mission had a Sunday School connected with it.

R. Shindler, *From the Usher's Desk to the Tabernacle Pulpit, C.H. Spurgeon, his Life and Work*, p. 269

Kathleen Heasman concludes her work on *Evangelicals in Action*, which is a survey of evangelical practical influence in the 19th century, as follows:

> Lord Shaftesbury was right when he maintained in 1880 that most of the great philanthropic movement of the century sprang from the Evangelicals. The Evangelicals, in their massive amount of philanthropy, emphasised old needs, pointed to new ones and, according to their lights, tackled an enormous amount of destitution, distress and degradation amongst the poorer groups of the community. They set the precedent for many of the techniques which are followed today and their spirit of personal service still prevails. Criticism of their work was plentiful and often justified, but this does

> not detract from the fact that the Evangelicals supplied help at a time when it was greatly needed and not available to any significant extent from other sources.
>
> Heasman, 1962, p. 294.

Commenting on the 19th century Kenneth Scott Latourette remarks:

> Protestantism, particularly that of the British Isles, gave rise to many groups in society, and stimulated many a man and woman to propagate the faith, to relieve distress, and to change social customs and institutions.
>
> Although exact measurements are impossible, it is probable that never before had Christianity displayed in Western Europe such abounding vitality and been so potent in modifying and moulding the cultures in which it was set.

Chapter 15
Christianity in the 20th Century

THE 20TH CENTURY BEGAN IN MANY RESPECTS WITH A SURGE OF optimism amongst the churches. Church and chapel attendance was still comparatively high and Christian influence in the country significant. Christians were members of Parliament, local councillors, Trades Union officials, Mayors and Aldermen. Many of the great manufacturing companies, textile companies, shipping companies, retail chains, and all manner of small businesses were Christian-owned and run on Christian principles. The Ten Commandments were still the basis of English law, and Christian morality and outlook were still the norm.

Many of the Free Church groups exerted mammoth efforts to raise what they called "Twentieth Century Funds". A new era called for new efforts and Wesleyans, Baptists and Congregationalists raised respectively, one million guineas, £250,000, and 500,000 guineas. The Primitive Methodists raised a Jubilee Fund between 1893 and 1900 bringing in a total of £50,048. The Baptist women established a "Million Shillings Fund". The grand total of all these efforts amounted to £1,967,000. (We are talking of over £100 million in modern equivalence). In 1908, Baptists and Congregationalists went on to raise a further £250,000 in "Sustentation Funds" to supplement the stipends of their worst paid ministers. The *Twentieth Century Funds* still stand as one of the greatest religious fundraising efforts in English history.

In the early months of 1901 the Free Church Council of England and Wales organised a large-scale Simultaneous Mission, as they called it. "*What results do you expect?*" asked a leaflet about the mission issued by three London churches. "*We dare not expect small results*", was the answer. "*That would not be God's way. He is waiting to give us large things; Christians will be revived, led into larger truth, raised into holier experience. Backsliders will be brought back. The cold and indifferent will be warmed into interest; sinners will be saved*".

Taken from Charles Booth's *Life and Labour of the People in England*, Third Series, p. 239. Quoted by David Bebbington *Protestant Nonconformity in the Twentieth Century*, p. 184.

These meetings were held throughout London, the opening meeting being held in the London Guildhall chaired by Joseph Parker of the City Temple, who was then in the last year of his life. This meeting was held only six days after the death of Queen Victoria, and this added a certain solemnity and seriousness to the meetings. For ten days, eminent preachers gave stirring Gospel addresses in many of the largest churches throughout the capital, others were sent out to the large cities in the provinces and there were also visits arranged in country districts to fulfil the plan of the nationwide coverage.

What has to be observed in this period is that there was still an evangelical ethos in those representative Free Churches. Admittedly this evangelical ethos was considerably weaker than it had been fifty years before. Many of these denominations had suffered a theological downgrade. However, it was still considered to be the norm that men and women needed to be saved. "*Ye must be born again*", was still the general tenor of the messages preached. The Bible was still regarded with high authority. The cross still held a central place in the preaching. David Bebbington, quoted above, states that:

> A Programme of Conversionism, Crucicentrism, Biblicism, and Activism marked Evangelical Nonconformity. A current of popular evangelicalism still flowed through the chapels. (Ibid, p. 185)

The 1910 Edinburgh Missionary Conference

This conference, sometimes referred to as the World Missionary Conference, was held on the 14th to 23rd of June 1910.

It has been seen as the culmination of 19th century Protestant Christian missions and at the same time the formal beginning of the modern ecumenical movement.

It was chaired by Lord Balfour, of the Church of Scotland, and a former Unionist cabinet minister. A total of 1,215 representatives were present with delegates coming from Britain, Europe and North America. The famous motto of the conference was "*The Evangelisation of the World in this Generation*".

Eight themes or subjects formed the main addresses.

1. Carrying the Gospel to all the Non-Christian world.
2. The Church in the Mission-field.
3. Education in relation to the Christianisation of National Life.
4. Missionary Message in relation to the Non-Christian world.
5. The Preparation of Missionaries.

6. The Home Base of Missions.
7. Missions and Governments.
8. Co-operation and the Promotion of Unity.

There was a high degree of expectation at this meeting that these aims and objectives could be achieved in the first half of the 20th century.

In spite of the buoyant expectancy of the opening years of the century, under the surface however a decay was already setting in. Even before the First World War began, churches were registering falling numbers. This decline was registered both in the Church of England and in the Free Churches.

The Nonconformists made various efforts to stem this decline by providing leisure facilities within the church programme such as football, cricket, cycling, tennis and billiards. These provisions, though harmless enough in themselves, nevertheless coincided with a certain lowering of confidence in the power of the Gospel itself to affect the lives of men and women or hold congregations. Some reacted against these things, such as the group which called itself the Wesley Bible Union, these breaking away from the main body of Methodists. There was also a decline in the general piety of the churches. Prayer meetings were less well attended and within Methodism class meetings were well-nigh abandoned or changed into discussion groups or Wesley Guilds, which ran a programme of informative lectures on both social, literary, and practical subjects as well as devotional subjects.

On a more serious level there came about the subtle change in relation to the social and benevolent activities of the church. Whereas up to this point such activities, as we have seen in this study so far, had been seen and understood as the fruits and blessings of the Gospel spilling over into society at large. Now as the 20th century went on, they began to be seen as the Gospel itself. It was commented by those of perception at that time that the churches *were now preaching a social gospel, without a saving Christ.* G.W. McAlpine, the founder of the great McAlpine building enterprise based then in Accrington, Lancashire, rightly declared that it was wrong to assert that the first duty of the Church was social activity, rather its first duty was, on the contrary, to preach the Gospel.

It is true that there were individuals who kept firmly to the evangelical faith such as F.B. Meyer in Leicester, who established a church which both provided recreational facilities and was involved in a great deal of social work and managed to maintain a strong emphasis on the preaching of the Gospel, yet this was not the general rule. (It might be added here that F.B. Meyer also took a very strong view against the rising tide of biblical criticism following very much in the steps of C.H. Spurgeon). In many, many cases the recreational aspect, or the social aspect, gradually took the place of distinctive Gospel preaching, and lowered the spiritual tone and damaged the spiritual health of many churches that pursued this pattern, often leading to the spiritual death and eventual closure of such churches.

Alongside these tendencies the 20th century also saw attacks made on the basic fundamental core of evangelical belief.

The inroads of the Higher Critical Movement had already infiltrated many of the theological colleges towards the latter part of the 19th century. These views were now becoming popularised by writers such as Wood in his *The Bible, What it is and What it is Not*. Patterson was another such popular writer. F.W. Farrar, Dean of Canterbury, whose books on *The Life of Christ* and the *Life of St Paul*, had gained wide readership and acceptance, and to this day can be read with profit, brought out a studied and popular undermining of the utter integrity of Scripture, in his *The Bible, its Meaning and Supremacy*.

The story of this baneful influence upon the churches of the 20th century is well illustrated by the account of the influence of Arthur Peake, the principal of the newly opened Hartley Primitive Methodist College in Manchester. Peake produced a commentary on the Bible in 1919, upon which E.J. Poole-Connor in his *Evangelicalism in England* makes the following remarks.

In dealing with the subject of authority and religion, the commentary states: *that after the Reformation, Protestants fell back on the Bible as the ultimate standard of religious truth, and that around this idea there clustered a formidable set of affirmations regarding its inerrancy, and its perfect consistency with itself.* "*The rise of historical and linguistic criticism*" he asserts "*has finally destroyed this claim*". How final and thorough, in the eyes of the compilers of the commentary, was its destruction, the following quotations will show.

> "In reading the Old Testament, we are not dealing with history at all, in the modern sense of the term; it lacks nearly all the notes of modern history. As we have no means of getting at the facts except through the record, does not the new view of the Bible leave us in the

> state of uncertainty from which there is no escape? The answer must be frankly, yes, as regards many of the details".
>
> "Exodus at best enshrines some kernel of fact that would have been lost, but for its protective husk of unconsciously imaginative form."
>
> "Even the most plausible details (in the Book of Numbers) can only pass as history in the absence of anything more trustworthy."
>
> "What proportion if any, of the narrative is fact, it is impossible to say."
>
> "Joshua appears to be a medley of contradictory narratives, most of which are unhistorical. It has to be admitted that the writers knew nothing of history in the modern sense of the term; myth, legend, tradition, were all accepted without question; a simple historical fact (Jericho) has been altered out of all recognition. The author stated that what he thought ought to have occurred (Cities of Refuge) did, as a fact, actually occur."

These quotations are but a small sample of many others which occur in this commentary.

Further to these attacks on Scripture there now rose a proliferation of attacks on the very core of evangelical belief.

Kenneth Brown in his *A Social History of the Nonconformist Ministry in England and Wales 1800–1930*, pointed out that in the first decade of the 20th century not even candidates for the ministry could necessarily testify to a conversion experience. The growth and influence of the Romantic Movement was causing the Christian life to be understood as a gradual growth like a bud to its flower.

Notable among these influences was Reginald John Campbell, the minister of the City Temple in London, at that time something of a cathedral of Nonconformity. Whilst a student at Oxford he had come under the influence of Charles Gore and the *Lux Mundi School* of High Anglicans, though we might add Gore was later on critical of Campbell's brand of New Theology.

A summary of Campbell's beliefs and life is given in Martin Welling's *Evangelicals Embattled*:

> The main theme of Campbell's theology was the doctrine of divine immanence, which he soon developed into an assertion of an essential identity between the human and the divine. A theological address on this subject to a minister's meeting in 1906 was noticed by the press and in January 1907 Campbell was interviewed by a

> Special Correspondent of the Daily Mail. He told the reporter that "We believe that there is … No real distinction between humanity and Deity … We reject wholly the common interpretation of the Atonement … We believe that Jesus is and was divine, but so are we. His mission was to make us realise our divinity and our oneness with God". Orthodox Nonconformists like Robertson Nicholl and P.T. Forsyth led the attack on Campbell, who responded by producing a summary of his beliefs under the title *The New Theology*, published in March 1907. The controversy continued, developing into a debate on Christology in the early 1910s, until Campbell withdrew his book, resigned from the City Temple and entered the Church of England as an orthodox High Churchman in 1916.
>
> Wellings, 2003, p. 235

Theological liberalism slowly began to contaminate the main-line Free Churches as it had previously done in the Church of England. Methodists in the 1920s began to notice the virtual disappearance of the subject of the cross from their pulpits. The Wesleyans had appointed a theological chair to George Jackson in 1913 and it was well known that he was a moderate advocate of biblical criticism. From a group of Congregationalists came the publication of a book entitled *A Restatement of Christian Thought*, issued in 1933. It was modernistic in tone and was to lead eventually to the creation of the *Modern Free Churchmen's Union* in imitation of the *Modern Churchmen's Union* in the Church of England. Amongst its circle was T. Rhonda Williams, the chairman of the Congregational Union in 1929. He showed himself willing to repudiate the evangelical tradition altogether. Methodist Union in 1933 produced for the occasion a doctrinal statement, leaving the door wide open to liberal influences. In 1920 Russell Maltby, warden of the *Wesley Deaconess Institute* produced a book which rejected the traditional evangelical doctrine of penal substitution.

Into this confusing melee came Rudolf Bultmann, making a spectacular effort to conform Christianity to the modern scientific world-view (so called). His existential theology insisted on the reality of the transcendent but spoke of the supernatural as myth. The biblical account of the supernatural, he contended, simply is an attempt to promote our self-understanding and need of spiritual decision, not to give us objective truth about God or to inform us how ultimate reality is constituted. Bultmann also minimised the importance of the historical aspects of our Lord's life as unimportant for faith and stressed the centrality of the apostolic preaching of Jesus Christ. Bultmann indeed showed extreme scepticism about the historical reliability of the Gospels. (Patterson, 1983, p. 145)

After Bultmann came Paul Tillich (1886–1965) who taught that modern theology must begin from the questions which men ask. It must not present a fully worked out metaphysical picture of reality with a "*take it or leave it*" attitude. Instead it must explore the fundamental questions or areas of concern which worry modern man and show how the Christian Gospel sheds light upon them. This was popularly described as a theology from below as opposed to a theology from above.

Secondly, Tillich argued that 20th-century man is concerned about what would traditionally be called religious questions, but that the way in which Christianity is usually expressed is not helpful to him. He argued that the idea of God as a person separate from the world, a language which implied some "*other*" world in which God was to be located distinct from the world of nature and history, was no longer tenable.

These ideas were further expressed and popularised by John A.T. Robinson in his infamous work *Honest to God.*

Robinson, following Tillich argued that all men have experiences of "*depth*", these are moments when they feel they are penetrating below the superficial level on which life is often lived. Robinson decided to base his reconstructed picture of God upon Tillich's presentation of God as ultimate reality, the Ground of man's own being and not a separate Being over against man. This experience of "*depth*", Robinson maintained, could not be limited to conventionally religious people. Critics of Robinson rightly point out that if this is the way to God it raises questions about the uniqueness of our Lord Jesus Christ, the practice of prayer and the normal understanding of Christian morality. Robinson described our Lord Jesus as "*the man for others*" (a term borrowed from Bonhoeffer) and one who because he was totally open to the "*Ground of Being*" could be described as "*transparent to God*" or "*a window into God*". In a further publication entitled *The Human Face of God* he argued that Jesus Christ differed from other men only in the degree to which he was open to God. On Robinson's grounds, prayer could have been mainly meditation, but he preferred to link it with practical social engagement rather than with petition or withdrawal from the world. Morality became situation ethics, that is, not a predetermined code but responding to each situation in love.

All these deviations from biblical Christianity fed into and further stimulated the growing amorality of the 20th century. With all these issues Christianity had to contend in that century. A study and awareness of this false teaching throws considerable light on why society is disintegrating and the churches are empty at this present time.

Because this is only a survey we must leave out a great deal on this theme, but point out that in the twentieth century the Church had to deal with all these challenges and deviations to the faith once given to the saints.

However, under this heading before we leave it, mention must be made of a rather enigmatic figure, that of Karl Barth (1886–1968). Barth was trained in the earlier liberal Protestant tradition. He was a pastor of the Swiss Reformed Church and this led him to conclude that the liberal theology which he had been taught, had little to offer men and women in real-life situations. Barth was challenging the sunny confidence that man, at any rate Western man, was steadily advancing in civilisation and culture. By the end of the First World War Barth was ready to write a book which, as is well known, was said *to have descended as a bomb dropping on the playground of theologians.* It was a commentary on the Epistle to the Romans and it challenged the easy-going optimistic liberal Christianity that had been so popular up to the time of the First World War. Barth was a significant theologian of the 20th century, though his views on the inspiration of Scripture and other matters fell short of the traditional belief in the infallibility of Scripture and orthodox Christianity. Others followed in the same vein such as Emile Brunner, Reinhold Niebuhr, D.R. Davies, all holding similar inadequate views of the inspiration of Scripture, but at the same time conscious that Christianity had been led astray by many of the liberal notions that had crept into it, such as:

A false estimation of human nature.
The practical banishment of the otherworldly element in the Christian ethic.
The denial of the uniqueness of Christianity.
The secularisation of life and religion.

In regard to D.R. Davies, in 1939 he produced a work entitled *On to*

Orthodoxy. The book was published again in 1941, and it does highlight the shallowness, failure and inadequacy of the popular theological liberalising movement of that time. He made these pertinent remarks:

> The evils of the pre-Christian world still abound in Christendom; that is not to disprove the faith of prophetic religion. On the contrary, it is its profound and tragic corroboration. What it does disprove, of course, is the falsity of the Liberal denunciation of Christianity of its absolute, supernatural, non-historic essence. No philosophy of life and history could be less adequate to the historic situation than that of Humanism and its aborted miscarriage, theological Liberalism and its utter hollowness. Such an exposure—proof—becomes thrice certain when we consider the specific social evils inherent in successive civilisations. Many of them persist from age to age, not only in substance, but even in form. In face of this fact, what becomes of the illusions of modern man about his pride, his omnipotence, his independence, his ability to be the architect of his own fate? (p. 94)
>
> I know beyond any further possibility of doubt that Humanism is a false faith and that Christian liberalism is an aberration and an abortion. Not all the King's horses nor all the king's men can put that particular Humpty Dumpty together again. For me, Humanism and Modernism were shattered beyond hope of repair. I have submitted evidence which, I claim, puts beyond doubt the fact that human nature is evil in its fibre and structure. I was driven back to the classic, basic Christian doctrine of original sin. I was compelled to acknowledge the Fall of Man and that opened the door for the return to orthodoxy. But before I saw that open door, I passed through the valley of despair. (p. 103)
>
> From what I have said it will now be plain that I regard the preaching of the Gospel of forgiveness of sin as the distinctive, unique and certainly most important task of the Church. Whatever she does in the way of socials is no substitute; however, many cheap meals she provides for the unemployed; however many billion table tennis clubs she gives to young people; however, many psychological clinics she opens—all these are worse than useless without preaching. Though she gives her body to be burned and preach not sin, and man's powerlessness, and his need of the grace of God, it shall profit her nothing."
>
> Davies, 1941, p. 190

It also has to be remembered that the twentieth century Church had to contend with the impact of two world wars.

These, we might say to some extent, again exposed the threadbare nature of liberal theology, and to a large degree undermined the "*faith*" of those who had heard no other teaching. The failure of the Roman Church and the mainline Protestant churches in Germany to stand up to the atrocities carried out on the Jews and others by the Nazi regime, exposed massive weakness within these churches. The so-called *German Christian* churches entirely capitulated to the Nazi regime and adopted National Socialism as part of their creed. The Vatican signed a *Concordat* with the Nazi regime in July 1933. Other smaller groups adopted the course of pietism, and shut themselves away from all that was going on and said nothing. It is true that many individual Christians did make a stand of sorts and an organisation of Protestant churches, who identified themselves as the Confessing Church, did issue the Barmen Declaration in 1934.

Amongst those who in the name of Christ resisted the Nazi regime at this time we can list the names of Dietrich Bonhoeffer (hanged by the Gestapo, 9 April 1945), Hans von Dohnanyi (also put to death in April 1945), Bernhard Letterhaus (a Catholic put to death 14 November 1944), Franz Leuningen (1 March 1945), Helmuth von Moltke (23 January 1945), Otto Muller, (12 October 1944), Frederick Justus Perels (22 April 1945), Elizabeth von Thaden (8 September 1944), Hermann Wehrle (14 September 1944).

I give this selection of individuals and the dates of their martyrdoms to illustrate that there were such people, and that so vehement was Hitler's contempt of Christianity, that he saw to it that any future potential leaders should be put to death, as he saw his regime crumbling.

A similar kind of story could be told of the bravery and courage of many believers behind the Iron Curtain and in China under Communism who display, and many who continue to display, the power of true faith to stand in the face of the most severe and oppressive conditions.

Chapter 16
Conclusion

It is not going too far to say that the better elements of European history are a manifestation of the superhuman power and reality of the Christian faith and the New Testament message. It is an incontrovertible fact that the Christian faith has made an incalculably valuable contribution to the life of millions even where it has only superficially touched them, or where it has only been presented in a very diluted form.

The outward manifestations of this are still clearly seen in the massive cathedrals dominating the skylines of many European cities. These things still resonate in our best literature and music. Milton's *Paradise Lost* and *Paradise Regained*, not to mention the Authorised Version of the Bible, are outstanding masterpieces of literature. We might mention Rembrandt's engravings of the biblical stories, Bach's *St Matthew's Passion* or Handel's *Messiah* to give but a few further examples.

We have touched on the fact of our democratic state and the fact that so many of our public and private charitable institutions have been founded in the name of Jesus Christ. We have mentioned schools, colleges and universities, reminding ourselves that the most illustrious institutions of higher learning were the foundations of Christian communities and churches and were primarily designed for the promotion of Christian knowledge. We might mention that up to the end of the 19th century almost every European individual was baptised and instructed by the Christian Church, and furthermore, at least in a superficial sense, the contents of the Bible's message were known and believed by almost everybody and shaped their judgement of what is true and false, good and evil, desirable and undesirable.

True there were sceptics; there are always some doubters and some heretics. But most of these were unwilling to manifest themselves as such: such was public opinion. Certainly there was probably in all ages a measure of indifferent and lukewarm, nominal Christianity; but even these stood in an unbroken tradition of doctrine of faith, and even their consciences were formed by the Commandments of the Bible, whether they acted according to their conscience or not.

The masses, and the large majority of educated men and women, always thought in the categories of biblical Christian tradition, however diverted or misshaped and distorted the Gospel may have been in their minds.

It is therefore self-evident that in such a world of nations, civilisation was deeply imbued, determined and guided by the Christian faith, its concepts, its norms, its virtues. All this is an undeniable fact.

Sad it is that this knowledge and this reality is being denied to the rising generations, not by neglect, but by a determined policy of a faceless elite, so-called, of individuals who in essence have a Communistic and Marxist theory of life.

This theory in essence is a belief in the perfectibility of human society, its methods include the rewriting of history, the rubbishing of the past, the denigration of Christianity, the discouragement of people thinking for themselves, often achieved by excessive work, or trivial entertainment. Such ideologies are also characterised by excessive legislation and state control of all aspects of life, and the silencing, dismissing and the demeaning of anyone who deviates from what the State has declared to be normal or acceptable. To achieve this end, of course, the old moral norms based on the Ten Commandments and the Christian ethic have to be dismissed.

Back in 1952 the then Archbishop of York, Cyril Garbett, expressed his concern that the dominant form of neo-Marxist philosophy, bitterly opposed to Christianity, was manifesting itself not only in Russia and in Germany, but also in France, and many of the central European and Balkan nations where Christianity is treated with either hatred or contempt. Sad to say this state of affairs is increasingly the case in our own country at this very moment.

The aim of this book has been to challenge the enormous prejudice and ignorance prevalent in today's society in respect to the massive part played by Christianity for the well-being of society. It is true that we do not live in a perfect world; it is indeed a fundamental truth of Christianity that we live in a fallen world. Christ has come into the world to save sinners, and to lift man up from degradation and condemnation, to forgiveness, justification and reconciliation with God. He has come to defeat sin and death in the lives of men and women, to enable them to live purposeful, and holy lives, and to set them on the road to heaven.

As we have seen, Christianity has brought to the world a true understanding of the nature of God and of mankind. It answers the ultimate question, what is the purpose of life? It reminds mankind that he is made in the image and likeness of God, all of which gives him dignity and a noble standing. It reminds him that his purpose "*is to glorify God and enjoy him forever*". It treats him as a responsible individual who at last shall give account, and as we have seen "*the principles of responsibility and accountability are the flipside of dignity and freedom*".

The coming of Christ into the world 2,000 years ago not only has been the means of man's personal salvation, but as we have seen in this study, also prevented the world many times from tearing itself apart. It has brought into being gracious, softening, and humanising influences that have over the years permeated society. Many times in the history of the world it has provided the route out of totalitarianism, despotism, oppression and injustice.

Paul Johnson in his *History of Christianity* draws to his conclusion by remarking, "*Mankind without Christianity conjures up a dismal prospect*". The twentieth century saw the birth of two sinister political ideologies, utterly and manifestly seen to be totally opposed to Christianity, namely Communism and National Socialism. Their fruits are well known. Today we live in what is identified as a secular society, its baneful fruits are also becoming increasingly well known. It is true also that there have been periods in the history of Christianity where ,in its name, injustice and war has been carried out. But though these things may be admitted, they pale into insignificance, before the evidence of the destruction, horror and downright cruelty, man-centred philosophies and political systems have produced. We may say in regard to our own so-called secular society that we are witnessing the first, perhaps distant, views of a de-Christianised society, and what we catch a glimpse of bears all the characteristics of slavery and oppression. Years ago Francis Bacon said: "*They that deny God destroy man's nobility: for certainly man is of kin to the beasts by his body; and, if he be not kin to God by his spirit, he is a base and ignoble creature*".

In the same way Scripture says that man without God is without hope in the world. Belief in a sovereign God, who is good and righteous in all his ways, has inspired the noblest efforts of men in the realm of politics, social reform, music, art, literature, and philanthropy. Christ Jesus the Saviour of sinners, the Redeemer by his blood, is also our great example, and as we have seen in this work he has infused into the world the spirit of kindness and humanity, that makes human life in such a fallen world tolerable, and even beneficial. As John Newton, the converted vagabond and slave dealer, put it,

> He makes the wounded spirit whole,
> And calms the troubled breast:
> 'Tis manna to the hungry soul,
> And to the weary rest.
>
> Dear name! The rock on which I build,
> My shield and hiding place,
> My never-failing Treasury filled
> With boundless stores of grace.

It is always helpful for our understanding to get to the root meaning of words. The word *religion* is no exception, and we are thinking here of the Christian religion.

> It comes from the verb "to care for" or "to give heed to". Both explanations add up to much the same thing. The person giving heed to the divine is the person who acknowledges an obligation (a binding) to that which is beyond his own personal existence. He or she acknowledges a law other than his or her own wishes, a truth other than their own experience, standards other than current opinion.
>
> The secular man or woman on the other hand, being the person who does not care about the transcendent, is not bound to care for anything beyond their immediate interests. They may, perhaps, decide to care for others out of a sense of social solidarity (the ethical individual). But equally, they may be those who "couldn't care less". This is why, in the sphere of conduct, the religious individual is concerned more with preserving firm standards of morality than with the personal happiness of individuals. To obey the will of God for them is more important than to find immediate personal development; such a one believes that enduring happiness lies in the way of obedience to the Lord whose service is perfect freedom.
>
> Hamilton, 1968, p. 164

Hopelessness and selfishness seem to be the hallmarks of modern secular society J.I. Packer commented along these lines,

> Hopelessness is hell—literally. As God made us to fulfil a function and attain an end (for man's chief end is "to glorify God, and to

> enjoy him forever"), so he made us creatures for whom hope is life, and whose lives become living deaths when we have nothing good to look forward to. As the deep hopelessness of post-Christian Western culture tightens its chilly grip on us, we are made to feel this increasingly, and so can better appreciate the infinite value for life today of that exuberant, unstoppable, intoxicating, energising hope and joy with Jesus in the Father's presence forever which is so pervasive a mark of New Testament Christianity.
>
> Whereas those without Christ, without God and without hope, live already in the dusk of the spirit that is destined to grow darker and colder. Christians are in the sunshine, endlessly rejoicing in "Christ Jesus our hope". The inescapable alternatives are false hope (Marxism? Spiritism? Happiness through having things? Endless good health?—false hopes, every one), or else no hope (total pessimism, inviting suicide), or else Christian hope, the electrifying knowledge of "Christ in you, the hope of glory."
>
> Packer, 2009, p. 159

And finally a quote from the much esteemed Church historian, Kenneth Scott Latourette;

Kenneth Scott Latourette wrote at the end of his massive seven volume *History of the Expansion of Christianity*, speaking of the influence of Jesus Christ the Son of God.

> No life ever lived on this planet has been so influential in the affairs of men. From it has grown the most nearly universal fellowship, the Christian Church, that man has known. That Churches are to be found amongst almost all tribes and peoples, on all the continents, and on the large majority of the islands of the sea, even some of the loneliest and remote …
>
> From that brief life and its apparent frustration has flowed a more powerful force for the triumphal waging of man's long battle than any other ever known by the human race. Through it millions have had their inner conflicts resolved in progressive victory over their baser impulses. By it millions have been sustained in the greatest tragedies of life and have come through radiant. Through it hundreds of millions have been lifted from illiteracy and ignorance and have been placed upon the road of growing intellectual freedom and of control over their physical environment. It has done more to allay the physical ills of disease and famine than any other impulse known

to man. It has emancipated millions from the shackles of slavery and millions of others from thraldom of vice. It has protected tens of millions from exploitation by their fellows. It has been the most fruitful source of movements to lessen the horrors of war and to put the relations of men and nations on the basis of justice and peace.

Seldom if ever has the trial been clear cut and complete. The greatest saints are aware that they have not fully attained. The Church is divided by jealousies and strife. In its great forward surges, the faith has been closely associated with movements in economics, statecraft, and international, interracial, and interclass contention which are contrary to its aspirations. Again and again, even within the Church itself, the elements appear dominant which bound Jesus Christ to his cross and he seems crucified afresh. Some of the hereditary evils of the race attain their most colossal dimensions among the peoples and cultures in which the faith which stemmed from Jesus Christ has been longest represented. Always the faith seems dying, yet it lives. Culture after culture with which the faith has been intimately associated has passed into history, seemingly to carry it also into oblivion. Yet the faith spreads ever more widely and moulds more and more peoples.

It is the very core of the Christian's faith that the God and Father of our Lord Jesus Christ will not be defeated. The Christian holds the resurrection of Jesus Christ also to be a fact. The life of Christ, so he confidently maintains, did not end on the cross. Nor was it continued merely through the growing influence of Jesus Christ, amazing though that has been. The Christian is bold to declare that through the resurrection, Jesus Christ entered into a fresh stage of life, glorifying, endless, and inconceivably rich in love and power. He holds that in the resurrection God was working, bringing out of the evil of man's rejection of Christ a good far greater than could have been possible without that defeat. The Christian affirms that through Jesus Christ God makes possible for all who will receive him a similar endless life of growing and glorified fellowship with himself. He declares that through his Spirit, "the Spirit which proceedeth from the Father and the Son", God is even now in history. At times the Christian is staggered by the all too obvious and clamant evil in his own heart and in the world around him, but in what he believes to be his moments of clearest insight he is certain that God and his Christ will triumph. He knows that, if not within the long span which men call history, itself but a moment against the background of sidereal time then beyond history, God's purpose for man will be fully realised. Not always have God's thoughts been man's thoughts, nor God's ways man's ways. Yet God's Word, so the Christian when he is most Christian knows, shall not return unto him void but shall accomplish that which he pleases and prosper in the thing whereunto he sent it.

The Christian is certain that Christ is central in human history. His confident faith is that in those who give themselves to God as they see him in Christ there is working the power of endless life, and that from them God will build, to be consummated beyond time, the heavenly city, the ideal community, in which will be realised fully the possibilities of the children of God. This eternal life in this ideal community are, in the last analysis, not the fruit of man's striving, but the gift of a love which man does not deserve, and are from the quite unmerited grace of God.

Latourette, 1941, Vol. 7, pp. 503–505

Appendix 1
Christianity and the Magna Carta

When the barons forced King John to sign the Magna Carta (great charter) in 1215 at Runnymede outside London, they obtained a number of rights they did not have before this historic occasion. Specifically, the charter granted the following:

1. Justice could no longer be sold or denied to free men who were under the authority of barons.
2. No taxes could be levied without representation.
3. No one could be imprisoned without trial.
4. Property could not be taken from the owner without just and fair compensation.

These achievements were monumental and history-making. The era of the King being above the law had effectively come to an end in England. Commonly this document is rightly hailed as ushering in British liberty and justice. Some 500 years later it also served as a courageous precedent to the American patriots to establish liberty and justice in America. The early advocates of American independence often referred to the Magna Carta in support of their arguments.

The Magna Carta lifted civilisation to a higher plateau, not only in England but eventually in other parts of the Western world, and it had a lot to do with its Christian origins. The preamble began, "John, by the grace of God," … And stated that the charter was formulated out of "reverence for God and the salvation of our souls and those of all our ancestors and heirs, for the honour of God and the exaltation of the Holy Church and the reform of the realm, on the advice of our reverend (Church) Fathers".

One of the "reverend fathers" involved in the birth of the Magna Carta was Stephen Langton, Archbishop of Canterbury (credited with the dividing of the Bible into chapters). Langton's involvement in the Magna Carta together with the help of his Christian colleagues, did not, however, have the approval of Pope Innocent III, who actually suspended him for two years. The Pope's opposition, of course, does not nullify the argument that the Magna Carta bears the marks of Christian influence.

Finally, another Christian influences is worth noting. In the year 325, at the Council of Nicaea, Christian bishops wrote and adopted a formal code of fundamental belief to which all Christians were expected to adhere. This was really the first time in history that a formal, written document of religious beliefs had ever been issued. The pagan Greeks and Romans had no formal religious creed or confessions of faith. Although the Magna Carta was a political document, it was also a type of creed in that it showed what its formulators i.e. Christian leaders (evident in the preamble), believed in regard to liberty and justice. Thus, the architects of the Magna Carta followed the precedent set by the Christian bishops at the Council of Nicaea.

Stephen Langton died on 9 July 1228 and was buried in Canterbury Cathedral. Langton was a renowned theologian, his commentaries finding a place in all mediaeval libraries.

Two other Langtons were prelates of note.

Thomas Langton, Bishop of Winchester, was later chosen to be the Archbishop of Canterbury, but died in 1501, before his consecration.

Walter Langton (d. 1321) was Bishop of Lichfield.

Appendix 2
Christianity and Economics in The Middle Ages

Through the influence of Monasticism Christianity contributed to the dignity of labour, and added greatly to agriculture and the development of new and more efficient and effective methods of food production.

Under the rule of St Benedict work was obligatory.

Kenneth Scott Latourette tells us that in industry and trade the impact of Christianity was uneven at this time.

In principle the taking of interest was strictly condemned (usury) and absolution could only be obtained by full restitution of the sums so acquired. It was John Calvin who was to later argue that there was a legitimate sense in which interest could be charged, and that this would indeed stimulate industry, and be of benefit to society at large.

The Church also supported the view that private property was permissible.

At the same time, it was held that God was the supreme owner of the world, and the cattle on a thousand hills belong to him. All things were for the benefit of all mankind and therefore greed and excessive acquisitiveness were to be condemned.

Much of the trade and commerce of that period was carried on through Guilds. The Guilds had a Christian ethos and therefore were supposed to be guided by Christian standards.

The idea of a just price was generally acknowledged, that is, the merchant or artisan should ask for his goods only what was fair. In theory a just price was applied to wages as well as to the sale of the products of labour.

Through the influence of the Gospel there was a growing value placed upon the individual as possessing an eternal soul for whose salvation the Son of God had laid down his life.

Meister Eckhart, the early German mystic, said that authorities usually taught that all persons are of equal rank by nature, but went further and said that the meaning of the Incarnation is that God became man not that he might just lift a few, but the entire human race and conform them to his likeness and enable them to enjoy his fellowship.

St Bridget is known to have rebuked the king of Sweden for his callous exploitation of the poor, and also for his homosexuality.

Before this, King Olaf Haralson of Norway was responsible for the conversion of his country. In doing so, he forbade the exposure of infants, and decreed that at the opening of the National Assembly a slave should not be sacrificed, as had been the previous custom, but freed. Many of these stories could be added to show the general movement of society at this time away from paganism and into the principles of Christianity.

One could not sing the Magnificat with its affirmation that God had put down the mighty from their seats and exalted the humble and meek, filled the hungry with good things, and sent the rich empty away, without questioning the established structure of society.

The Christian teaching was that slaves had souls and equally with their masters could be heirs of eternal salvation.

The freeing of slaves at this time became frequent. This was done often shortly before their death and was intended to make them or move them to seek salvation.

In 1102 the Church Council in London forbade the slave trade.

In 1179 the Third Lateran Council, theoretically acting for the whole of the Catholic Church, declared that no Christian should be subjected to slavery.

Appendix 3
Christianity and Science

UNDOUBTEDLY BIBLICAL CHRISTIANITY IS THE MOTHER OF MODERN science because it insists that the God who created the universe has revealed himself in the Bible to be the kind of God he is. Consequently, there is a sufficient basis for science to study the universe. This must be emphasised as much current popular opinion would hold that science grew thanks to the classical tradition and in spite of the biblical tradition. Much is made of the retarding influence of the medieval Church on the development of science. The role played by medieval biblical exegesis in offering resistance to the new scientific spirit on the movements of the earth and the planets has been emphasised again and again. In the first place we might say just as it would be wrong to blame Aristotle for all the prejudiced, dogmatic and even silly interpretations of his philosophy put forward by his medieval scholastic followers, so it would be wrong to lay to the account of the biblical authors the short sighted interpretations of those who used the Scriptures to oppose legitimate scientific opinions and discoveries.

Herbert Butterfield, Regius Professor of History at Cambridge, wrote in his *The Origins of Modern Science* that modern scientific investigation is firmly rooted in the Reformation. Scientific thinkers amongst the French Huguenots, the Dutch and English Protestants and the later Puritans believed that they should come to the book of God's works with the same reverence as they came to the book of God's words.

They believed that as God had made all things in order, so the natural laws of creation are orderly, and therefore the subject of scientific investigation.

Just as God at the beginning of the Bible in Genesis caused Adam to name the animals and creatures, so all living things can be classified and studied in an orderly fashion.

As in the Bible we see moral cause and effect, so the natural laws of creation can be studied as to their cause and effects.

As God has promised the stability of natural laws in his Word, therefore, the natural laws are stable and can be the subjects of rational study.

Finally, God the Creator is revealed in Scripture as good, so the creation is for the benefit of mankind and we should learn therefore all we can about the laws of nature and use this knowledge for the good of man in his earthly condition.

C.S. Lewis summed this up well when he said,

> "Men became scientific because they expected Law in nature, and they expected Law in nature because they believed in a Legislator."
>
> Quoted by Prior, 1975, p. 77

Appendix 4
Christianity: Reformation Thinking in Relation to the State and the Individual

Under the influence of Luther, the view prevailed which saw in the state something superior to the individual will, an institution which served to direct all the efforts of the people. At the same time the Reformation gave the decisive impetus to the development of the constitutional state into a cultural community.

It was the Reformation that first set a rigid limit to the absolute power of the state. Luther also established freedom of conscience, whose defence he made an individual obligation, as a rational principle for the state. The means that the state utilises, and must utilise, is its power, and its power must have limits. By the coercive power, the use of which it is entitled, it can subjugate the body, but it cannot reach the soul; if the state attempts this, it will only produce hypocrites.

The basic principle of Luther was taken up by his followers. It was observed at the very first opportunity that offered itself, the visitation in the Electorate of Saxony in 1527–8. On this occasion the Elector of Saxony explicitly renounced the forcible coercion of any subjects to his faith; it was not his intention, so the instructions read, to bind anyone as to what he should hold or believe. Therefore, the Elector allowed those who dissented the freedom to leave the country. This occurrence in a small German territory had general historical significance. It was a departure from the tradition of more than a thousand years, the first fundamental limitation of its own powers by the state and the first formal recognition of individual right in matters of faith.

At this time, nor at any time whatsoever, did the protestant states brand a Catholic a "heretic" for his faith, let alone punish him. He could even stay in the country, if he kept quiet. The law on heresy which the evangelical states still held necessary, pertained only to those who questioned the doctrine of the Trinity and the divinity of Christ, i.e., not to those who deviated from the specific evangelical doctrine, but to those who denied the basic and universal Christian doctrine, whose truth seemed so certain that to touch it must count as indubitable blasphemy. Even in this instance the Protestant law on heresy goes into effect, in contrast to the Catholic, only when someone speaks publicly against these doctrines.

One will, therefore, have to concede to the Reformation respect which only a prejudiced or superficial reading of history could deny, for being the first of all in modern times to have made a way for freedom of conscience in the state.

Luther proclaimed the duty to work for the sake of production, and by proclaiming simultaneously the spirit of humble simplicity, he gave a tremendous boost to the economic production of goods. But at the same time, following his concept of community, Luther emphasised not only the individual's duty of consideration and helpfulness toward his neighbour but also the duty of the community as a whole to take care of those unable to work and to protect the weak from the strong.

Adapted from Knoll, 1959

Appendix 5
Christianity's Influence on Everyday Life

It is well known that the Evangelical revival brought about a moral transformation of Britain and, as we tend to forget, many other countries also. Canon Overton wrote of its effects as follows:

> It was the faith which enabled a man to abandon the cherished habits of a lifetime and to go forth ready to spend and be spent in his Master's service; which nerved a man to overcome the natural fear of death, and, indeed, to welcome the last enemy as his best friend who would introduce him to the better land he had long been living for; which made the selfish man self-denying, the discontented happy, the worldling spiritually minded, the drunkard sober, the sensual chaste, the liar truthful, the thief honest, the proud humble, the thriftless thrifty and the godless godly.
>
> Overton, 1900, p. 131

In 1787 George III issued a proclamation for the "Encouragement of Piety and Virtue, and for the Preventing and Punishing of Vice, Profaneness, and Immorality". This stimulated the setting up of various societies such as: The Society for the Preservation of Public Morals, The Society for the Suppression of Public Lewdness, The Society for the External Observance of the Lord's Day, etc. Many other societies were formed including The British and Foreign Bible Society formed in 1807, the forerunner of our Trinitarian Bible Society, 1832.

In the early and mid-Victorian era, the Bible held massive sway in our nation. On the Sunday of the 1851 census the records show that half the population were in church. On the same day over two million of the nation's children were in Sunday School and the figures for Sunday School attendance continued to rise throughout the century. From the 1850s the crime rate was also falling every year in spite of an increase in population.

Serious crime fell by 60% between 1850 and 1890. In 1888 three out of every four children attended Sunday School. Illegitimacy fell by the end of the 19th century to 4%, divorce was almost unknown, and single parent families in the modern sense virtually unheard of. Drunkenness was a decreasing problem due to the influence of the Temperance Movement.

The virtues of self-control, self-help, self-discipline, hard work, independence, thrift, propriety, the concept of cleanliness is next to godliness, temperance, honesty, promptness, regularity, etc., were held in the highest regard.

Margaret Thatcher, reminiscing in 1983, summed this up when she spoke of the values (she ought to have said virtues) which made this country great.

> We were taught to work jolly hard. We were taught to prove yourself; we were taught self-reliance; we were taught to live within our income. You were taught that cleanliness is next to godliness. We were taught self-respect. You were taught always to give a hand to your neighbour. You were taught tremendous pride in our country.
>
> www.azquotes.com/quote/1344380. (Accessed 17 November 2020)

Appendix 6
Christianity and the 18th Century revival's impact on nonconformist England in the 19th century

In 1899 the then President of the National Free Church Council, the Rev. Charles Kelly, a foremost Wesleyan Methodist, stated that, "*for the Free Churches the 19th century has been a great century. It has been rich in splendid opportunities …*" It is difficult for us now to calculate the enormous impact Nonconformity had on English life both in the countryside and the great expanding cities and suburbs of the Midlands and the North. The Primitive Methodists, the most working-class of the denominations could confidently state in 1901: "*It is a source of much satisfaction that all people everywhere are participating in the social and intellectual advance of the times.*"

In 1900, out of 186 Liberal MPs returned to Parliament, 129 were Nonconformist. The leading figures of the political world in the early years of the 20th century were H.H. Asquith, David Lloyd George, R.B Haldane and Keir Hardie, all Nonconformist.

The *British Weekly* reported that there were some forty Nonconformist mayors in England and Wales.

The century had seen the influence of General Booth with the Salvation Army, Dr Barnardo establishing children's homes, and George Cadbury, who pioneered the "garden suburb" and town planning. The YMCA had almost entirely been the creation of Nonconformists. The National Society for the Prevention of Cruelty to Children had been founded by Benjamin Waugh, a Congregationalist minister.

In the area of research into the new urban civilisation which had developed out of the Industrial Revolution, men such as Seebohm Rowntree and Charles Booth were again leading Nonconformists. In the area of literature, journalism, publishing, and academic life not only in the new universities which had sprung up in the manufacturing towns such as Birmingham, Liverpool and Manchester, but even at Oxford and Cambridge, Nonconformists were playing an increasingly influential part. The compiler of the first *Oxford English Dictionary*,

James Murray, was a Nonconformist as were some of the leading historians of the day, men such as Firth, Stoughton and Gardner. Wealth earned by leading industrialists and merchants, such as John Ryland, Charles Booth, Frederick Horniman, Sir Richard Tangye, W.H. Lever, Sir Henry Tate and Samuel Courtauld, was invested into public service, and the building up of major centres of scholarly research, academic excellence and the collecting of all art treasures that were purposely made accessible to the general public.

John Curwin, a Congregationalist minister, developed tonic sol-fa (from Sarah Ann Glover's earlier system) in order to teach Sunday School children to sing. This encouraged the spread of choirs and the enjoyment of music generally. In the area of law, England had the first Nonconformist-born Lord Chancellor in Farrer Herschell; and in the civil service Rowland Hill, who implemented the Penny Post, was also a Nonconformist. In the area of scientific research once again some of the foremost names were Nonconformists. For example Joseph Lister, Michael Faraday, Philip Gosse, and Henry Seebohm. A Wesleyan Methodist minister, W.H. Dallinger, was four times President of the Royal Microscopic Society and also was elected to the Royal Society in 1880.

As we shall see many of the leading innovators in industrial development were also pioneered by Nonconformists, such as the Crossleys in Halifax, the Tangyes in Birmingham, the Levers in Port Sunlight, Titus Salt in Bradford, Corys in Cardiff, the Reckitts in Hull, the Cadburys also in Birmingham, and men like Sir John Brunner who established the Brunner Mond Company in North Cheshire and Merseyside which was later to become the Imperial Chemical Industries.

In the realm of Christian overseas missions, David Livingstone had become a national hero. Even in the Army, the Baptist Sir Henry Havelock, who had led the relief of Lucknow in 1857, had become a household name and national hero.

In poetry and literature Robert and Elizabeth Barrett Browning had become exceedingly popular and well known.

Nonconformist ministers were leading figures in many of the provincial towns. Men such as R.W. Dale of Birmingham, J.B. Paton in Nottingham, Alexander Maclaren in Manchester, F.B. Meyer in Leicester. Preachers such as C.H. Spurgeon, Joseph Parker, and Hugh Price Hughes in London were known throughout the nation, and it was said that visitors to London would be just as inclined to want to see the Metropolitan Tabernacle, or the City Temple as they might wish to catch a sight of Buckingham Palace or visit Madame Tussaud's.

All the leading denominations increased their membership during the last third of the 19th century. Baptists had increased by 51% and stood at 243,534. Wesleyan Methodists had grown by 27%, to 404,890. Primitive Methodists had grown by 23%, to 183,505. Accurate figures for 1870, the year of the comparison, are not available for Congregationalists, but by 1901 they numbered 258,434 in England. It is not unreasonable to assume that their membership had increased by about the same percentage as the Wesleyans. Again we are looking at membership and even though the Wesleyan and Primitive Methodists and the Congregationalists used infant baptism, membership among the latter was based on the profession of religious belief. Methodists only became full members after a period of probation and through admission to the Class Meeting. The 1909 official *History of Methodism* felt that membership totals should be multiplied by four to take account of children, "probationers" and "hearers" who did not hold a class ticket.

In 1901 it was observed that there were 8,140,767 seats in Nonconformist chapels in England and Wales. There were in addition 384,175 Sunday School teachers, with 3,276,895 Sunday School children, 10,097 fully employed ministers and 52,341 local or lay preachers.

Victorian Nonconformists spent an incredible amount of money in their work and this extended back for a large part of the century. In the 1870s, for example, Primitive Methodists, perhaps the poorest of the four largest denominations, spent £1,057,511 on 897 new chapels. On 19 January 1875 the Congregationalists opened their Memorial Hall, the first denominational headquarters in London. It was built on the site of the old Fleet Prison which had once held Protestant martyrs. It cost £3,628,300. Andrew Mearns, who compiled these records, asserted as a "low calculation" that by 1885 Congregational churches were raising just over £1,000,000 a year. That is £129,465,909 value in 2019 because of the vast inflation which has taken place since that time. We see what enormous sacrifices such people were making to maintain the Christian presence.

In the last decade of the century Baptist, Wesleyan and Primitive Methodists spent just under £11,000,000 on home missions, ministerial education, repayment of loans, the past, building, and foreign missions. All this does not take into account the mammoth efforts put forth by all leading denominations at the turn of the century to raise '20th Century Funds'. A new era called for new efforts and Wesleyans, Baptists and Congregationalists all had funds to raise, respectively one million guineas, £250,000 and 500,000 guineas. Primitive Methodists had raised a Jubilee Fund between 1893 and 1900 of £50,048 and Baptist women had a 'Million Shillings Fund'. This made a grand total among the four for the new century of £1,967,000 (*we are talking of £243,587,293 in modern value*). In 1908 Baptists and Congregationalists went on to raise a further £250,000 in "Sustentation Funds" to supplement the stipends of their worst paid ministers. There was some criticism of the 20th-Century Funds but they still stand as one of the greatest religious fund raising efforts in English history.

(Adapted from Munson, 1991, pp. 6–13.)

List of the Leading Nonconformist Industrialists and Manufacturers of the 19th Century

- Samuel Morley, Nottingham, and London, the largest hosiery manufacturer in the country. Congregationalist. Known as the Philanthropic Merchant. Member of Thomas Binney's King's Weigh House Chapel.
- Sir W. Hesketh Lever. Built Port Sunlight, Largest soap manufacturer in the world. Congregationalist. The Lever Art Gallery.
- Richard Tangye, Engineer and Engine builder, Birmingham. Quaker. Founder of Birmingham Art Gallery and the Birmingham School of Art.
- Frederick Horniman. Tea Merchant, London. Quaker.
- J.S. Fry Bristol. Chocolate Manufacture. Quaker.
- Joseph Rowntree. York. Chocolate Manufacture. Quaker.
- George Cadbury. Birmingham. Chocolate Manufacture. Quaker.
- Sir Titus Salt. Alpaca spinners. Bradford, Saltaire. Congregationalist. The first Nonconformist manufacturer to set up a model village for his workers in Saltaire on the banks of the River Aire north of Bradford.
- Richard Walls. London. Pork Sausage Manufacturers. Supporter of the YMCA. Family set up the Thomas Wall Charitable Trust.
- Frank Coopers. Oxford. Marmalade Manufacturer.
- Callards. London. Sweet Manufacturer.

- Bryant and May. Match Makers. Liverpool.
- Pickfords. Furniture Removers. This company was purchased by Joseph Baxendale but still retained the company name Pickfords. Baxendale's excellent character and public service are described in Samuel Smile's book, *Thrift*.
- Jeremiah Chubb. Lock Maker. Wolverhampton.
- Cassells. Publishers.
- Allen and Unwin. Publisher.
- James Clarke. Publisher.
- Hodder and Stoughton. Publishers.
- Morgan and Scott. Paternoster Row, London. Publishers.
- Lloyds. Bankers. Samson Lloyd and John Taylor. Birmingham. Quakers.
- Barclays. Bankers. Quakers.
- Chamberlains. Screw Manufacturers. Birmingham. Family forebears of Joseph Chamberlain, Prime Minister. Unitarian.
- Courtaulds. Silk Spinners and Textile Manufacturers. Unitarian.
- Ashworths. Cotton Spinners and Linen Weavers. Rochdale. Congregationalists.
- Elkanah Armitage. Manchester. Sailcloth, Ginghams and Checks. Nassau Mills, Patricroft. Congregationalist.
- John Rylands, James Rylands. Cotton Weavers, Wire Manufacturers, Warrington. Congregationalists/Baptists. Family founded the John Rylands Library, Manchester.
- J.S. Higham. Accrington, Lancashire. Cotton Spinners and Cloth Manufacturers. Congregationalist.
- Beechams Pharmaceuticals. St Helens, Lancashire.
- Thomas Cook. Tour operator, born Derbyshire, based Leicester. Strict Baptist. Supporter of the Temperance Movement.
- John Crossley. Woollen Weaver. Halifax, Yorkshire. Built The Square Chapel, Halifax, and also an orphanage and alms houses. Congregationalist. Mrs Craik's *John Halifax Gentleman*, the main character in the novel, is said to have been based on the character of John Crossley.
- William Hartley. Jam Manufacturer. Liverpool. Built Hartley College, Manchester. Primitive Methodist.
- John Cory. Ship Owner and Coal Exporter. Cardiff. Built Coryville.
- Sir Christopher Furness. Ship Owner and M.P. Methodist.
- Jeremiah Coleman. Mustard Manufacturer. Norwich. Baptist.

Married into a United Methodist Free Church family, and later became a Congregationalist.

- Sir James Reckitt. Blueing Manufacturer. Hull. Also built a model village.
- Sir Henry Lunn. Continental Tour Operator. Methodist.
- Thomas and Mark Firth. Steel Makers. Sheffield. Built Firth College, later to become Sheffield University. Methodist New Connection.
- H.V. Macintosh. Toffee Manufacturer. Halifax. Methodist New Connection.
- John and his son Jesse Boot. Chemists. Concerned that the poor should have affordable medicine. Methodist.
- Joseph Rank. Flour Millers. The Rank Foundation Charity. Methodist.

Appendix 7
Christianity and Education: John Wesley and Education for All

John Wesley, well known as the great preacher of the 18th Century Revival, was one of the most educated and widely read men of his day. He was first taught by his mother, Susanna, and later sent to Charterhouse School in Surrey, where he was noted "for his diligence and progress in learning". From Charterhouse he went on to Oxford University and studied at Christ Church College.

John Wesley lived at a time when schools for ordinary people were few and far between. He did not think it was right that he and his brothers and sisters, (there were nineteen of them in all) had the benefit of a very good education while others had none at all. Wesley believed that everyone should have the opportunity to learn. He was a man who did not just think certain things might be a good idea, but he did all that he could to make such things happen. Someone said of him that he was the only person of importance in England in the 18th century who was really and practically interested in the education of all children. The historian J.R. Green said that the revival led by Wesley and Whitefield, gave the first impulse to education for all in Britain.

John Wesley was a very busy man with many responsibilities. He was first and foremost a preacher of the Gospel, and he travelled literally thousands of miles preaching the Gospel throughout the British Isles. He realised time was short for all the things that he had to do and one thing he never did was waste time. He saw every moment as a sacred gift from God. He realised that Christ died to save him from his sins, and therefore he wanted to dedicate the whole of his life to spreading the good news of the Gospel. He said that in life you should …

> Do all the good that you can,
> In all the ways that you can,
> In all the places you can,
> To all the people you can,
> As long as ever you can.

One of the things he crammed into his busy life was the setting up of several schools. In London he set up the Foundery School which was a school for orphans. He also set up a similar school in Newcastle upon Tyne. In Bristol he began the Kingswood Schools which were for teaching coalminers to read and write, and later in Bristol he set up a Christian boarding school.

He also did everything that he could to encourage others to establish schools. Some of these people's names are almost forgotten now, such as Hannah Ball and Sophia Cooke. But one name is well remembered, that of Robert Raikes who in 1780 began the first modern Sunday School in the City of Gloucester.

Wesley firmly believed that if a young person put God first in their lives they would learn much faster. The Proverb says, "The fear of the Lord is the beginning of wisdom," and Wesley clearly believed that this is the case.

Knowledge is very important, but of course the first and most important thing is to know Jesus Christ as our Lord and Saviour, whom to know is life eternal.

Appendix 8
Christianity under Attack—The French Revolution, Atheism and the Denigration of Marriage

During the French Revolution, in 1793 …,

> The world, for the first time, heard an assembly of men, born and educated in civilization, and assuming the right to govern one of the finest of the European nations, uplift their united voice to deny the most solemn truth which man's soul receives, and renounce unanimously the belief and worship of a Deity.
>
> Scott, Vol. 1, ch. 17, p. 239.

> France is the only nation in the world concerning which the authentic record survives, that as a nation she lifted up her hand in open rebellion against the Author of the Universe. Plenty of blasphemers, plenty of infidels there have been, and still continue to be, in England, Germany, Spain, and elsewhere; but France stands apart in the world's history as the single state which, by the decree of her Legislative Assembly, pronounced that there was no God, and of which the entire population of the capital and a vast majority elsewhere, women as well as men, danced and sang with joy in accepting the announcement.
>
> *Blackwood's Magazine*, Nov. 1870.

> Intimately connected with these laws affecting religion, was that which reduced the union of marriage, the most sacred engagement which human beings can form, and the permanence of which leads most strongly to the consolidation of society, to the state of a mere civil contract of a transitory character, which any two persons might engage in, and cast loose at pleasure … If fiends had set themselves to work to discover a mode of most effectually destroying whatever is venerable, graceful, or permanent in domestic life, and of obtaining at the same time an assurance that the mischief which it was their object to create should be perpetuated from one generation to another, they could not have invented a more effectual plan than the degradation of marriage … Sophie Arnoult, an actress famous for

the witty things she said, described the Republican marriage as the Sacrament of adultery.

Scott, Vol. 1, ch. 17, p. 240.

Appendix 9
Christianity in Victorian England

In the English villages and small towns of the 1870s and 80s practically all the inhabitants above infancy attended either church or chapel every Sunday, many of them twice or even three times. The children also went twice to Sunday School. Apart from cases of necessity, the only exceptions to this universal worship would be, here and there, a few known village ne'er-do-wells. In addition, the chapels held prayer meetings during the week, and the church offered a regular weeknight service—both well attended.

The observance of Sunday was the norm for all. No games of any kind were ever played on it; no field sports indulged in, no entertainments given, publicly or privately. Novels were not read on that day; the Bible or serious literature were appropriate reading for Sunday. Thus sermons had large sales, and so did "magazines for Sunday reading". The habit of setting apart one rest day in the week for Christian worship and serious thinking deepened the character of the nation. And some high peaks of literature—the Bible, *Paradise Lost*, *Pilgrim's Progress*, for instance—became extremely familiar to a wide class of people who today would never read anything on that level.

The progress and prosperity of Victorian England certainly had a Christian basis. As one leading historian has said (R.C.K. Ensor): "No one will ever understand Victorian England who does not appreciate that it was one of the most religious countries that the world has known. Moreover, its particular type of Christianity laid direct emphasis upon conduct … If one asks how 19th century British merchants earned the reputation of being the most honest in the world (a very real factor in the 19th century primacy of British trade) the answer is that they were deeply imbued with Christian principles and for them the Last Judgement was as real as the week's balance sheet … They put duty before pleasure—that means they worked hard, they shrank from spending money on amusements and seldom wasted any; a large part of those savings passed by gift or bequest to the churches and chapels which were springing up in their thousands and to the great charitable organisations of the day. The rest went back into industry and created more work and made more money. Thrift, like honesty, was manifestly the best policy." We ourselves today, to some degree, still live on the legacy they left behind.

Appendix 10
Christianty and Education—Dean Inge

In training young Britons into good citizens of this country who will, we hope, turn into true and loyal citizens, we shall presumably find them most responsive to the language, literature and history of their own country. This would be a commonplace, and not worth answering, in any other country; in England it is, unfortunately, far from being generally accepted. Nothing sets in a stronger light the inertia and thoughtlessness, not to say stupidity, of the British character, in all matters outside the domain of material and moral interests, than our neglect of the magnificent spiritual heritage which we possess in our own history and literature. Wordsworth, in one of his noble sonnets says:

> We must be free or die, who speak the tongue
> That Shakespeare spake; the faith and morals hold
> That Milton held. In everything we are sprung
> Of Earth's best blood, have titles manifold.

It is a high boast, but it is true. But what have we done to fire the imagination of our boys and girls with the vision of our great and ancient nation? What have we taught them of Shakespeare and Milton, of Elizabeth and Cromwell, of Nelson and Wellington? Have we even tried to make them understand that they are called to be the temporary custodians of very glorious traditions, and trustees of a spiritual wealth compared with which the finest gold is but dross? Do we even teach them, in any rational manner, the fine old language which has been slowly perfected for centuries, and which is now being used up and debased by the rubbishy newspapers which form almost the sole reading of the majority?

There is a real danger of a generation now growing up which is cut off from the living past. Christianity has been a valuable educator in this way, especially when it includes intelligent knowledge of the Bible. But the secular education of the majority is now so severed from the streams of tradition and sentiment which unites us with the older civilisations, that the very language of the churches is becoming unintelligible to them, and the influence of organised religion touches only a dwindling minority. And yet the past lives in us all; lives inevitably in its dangers, which the accumulated experience of civilisation, valued so slightly by us on its spiritual side, can help us to surmount. A nation, like an individual, must "wish his days to be bound each to each by natural piety". It soon must strive to keep its memory green, to remember the days of old and the years that are past. The Jews have always had their sacred books, a magnificent embodiment of the spirit of their race; and who can say how much their incomparable tenacity and ineradicable hopefulness has done to the education thus imparted to every Jewish child?

Britain's future is precious only to those to whom her past is dear.

I am not suggesting that the history and literature of other nations should be neglected, or that foreign languages should form no part of education. But the main object is to turn out good citizens of this country who will continue to develop further our worthy national tradition. To do this, we must appeal constantly to the imagination, which Wordsworth has boldly called "reason in her most exalted mood". For the intellectual life, like divine philosophy, is not dull and crabbed, as fools suppose, but musical as is Apollo's lute.

What is education but to awaken the soul; and to set before it whatsoever things are true, lovely, and of good report; and to remove the obstacles which stunt and cripple the mind and heart?

Adapted from *The Church in the World* William Ralph Inge (1860–1954) Dean of St Paul's 1911–1934

Appendix 11
Christianity's Power to Elevate Whole Societies

Many detailed examples of Christianity's elevating effect upon whole societies can be given. One of these would be John Wesley Bready's *England before and After Wesley*.

The following example however illustrates the effects of John Calvin's ministry in Geneva in the 1530s.

In August of 1535 the Council of Two Hundred, governing Geneva, voted to reject Catholicism and align the city with the Protestant Reformation.

They had very little idea what this meant. Up to that point the city had been notorious for its riots, gambling, indecent dancing, drunkenness, adultery, and other vices. People would literally run around the streets naked, singing indecent songs and blaspheming God. The people expected this state of affairs to continue, even after they became Protestants. The Council did not know what to do to restrain the vice and remedy the situation. Nothing worked. Public discipline and morals continued to decline.

Calvin came to Geneva in August of 1536, a year after the change. He was practically ignored. He was not even paid the first year. As everybody knows, his first attempts to preach proved so unpopular he was dismissed by the Council in early 1538 and went to Strasbourg. Calvin was happy in Strasbourg and had no desire to return. But the situation got so bad in Geneva that public opinion turned to him again in desperation. He told his friend William Farel, "I should prefer 100 other deaths than this cross on which I should have to die 1000 times a day."

Driven by a sense of duty, Calvin returned to Geneva on 13 September 1541. He had no weapon but the Word of God. From the very first his emphasis was on Bible teaching, and he returned to it now, picking up his exposition of Scripture at precisely the place he had left it three and a half years earlier. He preached from the Word every day, and under the power of his preaching the city changed. As the people of Geneva acquired knowledge of God's Word and allowed it to influence their behaviour, the city became almost a New Jerusalem, and the Gospel spread from there to the rest of Europe and to Great Britain, and the New World.

Moreover, this change made other changes possible. One student of this historical period writes:

> Cleanliness was practically unknown in towns of his generation and epidemics were numerous. Calvin moved the Council to make permanent regulations for establishing sanitary conditions and supervision of markets. Beggars were prohibited from the streets, but a hospital and poor house were provided and well conducted. Calvin laboured zealously for the education of all classes and established the famous Academy, whose influence reached all parts of Europe and even to the British Isles. He urged the Council to introduce the cloth and silk industry and thus laid the foundation for the temporal wealth of Geneva. This industry ... proved especially successful in Geneva because Calvin, through the Gospel, created within the individual the love of work, honesty, thrift and cooperation. He taught that capital was not an evil thing, but the blessed result of honest labour and that it could be used for the welfare of mankind. Countries under the influence of Protestantism/Calvinism were invariably connected with growing industry and wealth ...
>
> It is no mere coincidence that religious and political liberty arose in those countries where Protestantism penetrated the most deeply, namely Switzerland, Holland, Germany, Scotland, England, Wales and colonial America.
>
> Kik, 1963, p. 83. Quoted by Boice, 1994, pp. 141–2.

Appendix 12
Francis Schaeffer's Insights into Aspects of Modern Culture

It is possible to study the irrational leap towards non-rational values in existentialism, by looking at three French, German and Swiss philosophers, Jean Paul Sartre, Martin Heidegger and Carl Jaspers. The early Wittgenstein, too, is central. But here I will limit myself to just one more aspect before discussing the student rebellion in more detail.

That aspect is best seen in Aldous Huxley. You cannot understand the student generation without understanding him. Huxley is the father of the modern cult of drug taking. Huxley did not suggest drugs as an escape. Rather, he said, because reason is not going to take us anywhere, one could give healthy people drugs and help them to have some kind of experience which one could hope would be optimistic.

Huxley never gave up on this. In the last chapter of *The Humanist Frame*, which was edited by his brother Julian, it is clear that Aldous held this position to the end. He also made his wife promise that when he was dying she would give him LSD so he would die in the midst of a trip. This is the drug world. I have spoken with hundreds of people on drugs, but I have never met a really serious drug taker who did not understand that he was following Huxley's concept of the upper storey leap, the upper storey hope.

Modern theology has not helped us. From Karl Barth on, it is an upper storey phenomenon. Faith is totally an upstairs leap. The difficulty with modern theology is that it is no different from taking drugs; it is one trip or another. It makes no difference—both are trips, separated from all reason.

What we are left with is God-words. Students coming out of all kinds of backgrounds are saying, "I'm sick of God-words." And I must respond, "So am I."

These theologians have cut themselves off from any concept of propositional, verbalised revelation in the Bible. They are left upstairs with only connotation words and no content. For them any concept of a personal God is dead, and any content about God is dead. They are cut off from any categories of absolute right and wrong and thus they are left with total situational ethics. That is all. As you listen to him, the modern theologian is only saying what the surrounding consensus is saying but in theological terms. There is no help here.

Malcolm Muggeridge has written much that is worthwhile, but to me the most striking thing that he ever wrote was the article in the *New Statesman*, 11 March 1966, that showed he had changed his direction from the New Guardian Leftism to the new Malcolm Muggeridge. He called it "The Great Liberal Death-Wish". He simply admitted that he had realised that the goal towards which he had been optimistically moving was not going to be realised. The liberalism in which he had placed his hopes cut away all the groundwork and left no categories with which to judge. Muggeridge still feels this strongly: liberalism has committed suicide because it has cut away its foundation. So the faculty screams with glee when students storm the administrative offices but squeals with anguish once the same students turn against the faculty. They have cut away their own foundations, and they have no categories with which to say what is right and what is wrong, and they have no way to stop the flood they have loosed.

Law is King

This is a complete contrast with that upon which government was built in the United States. We had freedom and form, form and freedom. Almost all human discussion can turn upon this frame—form and freedom: in the arts, in government, in society. Of course, we have had in the United States in the past a far from perfect situation and much for which we must say we are sorry. Yet the Northern European Reformation culture has had a form and a freedom that no culture in the world has ever had before—unless it was a few small Greek city states for a few years, and there is a question in my mind concerning that. But the Northern European countries built on the Reformation had form and freedom, and there are specific Anglo-Saxon varieties of this: Samuel Rutherford, for example, the great leader of the second Reformation in Scotland and his book, *Lex Rex*. Law is King.

How could law—rather than arbitrary judgements of individuals or an elite—be king? Simply because God had spoken; there was a base upon which to build law. Law is not to be seen as floating on a sociological set of statistics but on a solid foundation. This notion came largely into the United States Constitution through John Locke. John Locke secularised this base, though even he cheated sometimes and quoted from the Gospels. The American constitution rests on *Lex Rex*, toned down through Locke, through such men as Jefferson, and directly through the great Witherspoon.

There is a huge painting by Paul Robert, a Swiss artist from a great family of artists, who painted in the Supreme Court Building in Switzerland just before 1900. Through Hugh Alexander he had become a Christian, and then in his painting began to express his Christianity in his art. When he was asked to paint this tremendous mural on the stairway leading up to the Supreme Court offices, he expressed in painting what Samuel Rutherford expressed in magnificent words. The title of the painting is *Justice Instructing the Judges*. In the foreground are all sorts of litigation—the wife against the husband, the architect against the builder. Above them stands the Swiss judges with their little white dickeys. How are these people with their little white dickeys going to judge the litigation? A whole sociological theory is open to question here. Robert's answer is this: Justice, not blindfolded with her sword vertical, as is common, but is unblindfolded with her sword pointing downward to a book on which is written "The Word of God". Here is *Lex Rex*, because justice is not merely statistical averages. Here is something to build on.

Compare this with Wittgenstein's and Bergman's understanding of the problem of silence. In Robert's scheme we are no longer like the fish in the room; no longer do we face cosmic alienation; no longer is there a lack of categories to explain why some things are right and some things are wrong; no reason in such a case why we cannot build without alienation. For there is revelation from outside man—propositional, verbalised revelation. It is not the Christians who have to leap. It is humanistic man who must leap. Into a mysticism with nothing there.

It is a matter of presuppositions. Many people catch the presuppositions like some children catch measles. They have no idea where they come from. But that is not the way the thinker chooses his presuppositions. His presuppositions are selected on the basis of which presuppositions fit what is; that is, what presuppositions give solid answers concerning what is. It is only the Christian presuppositions which explain what is—in regard to the universe and in regard to man.

Schaeffer, 1970, pp. 26–31.

Appendix 13
Christianity and European Culture

What follows below is an extract from a speech given by TS Eliot to a German audience in the immediate aftermath of the Second World War.

> The dominant force in creating a common culture between peoples each of which has its distinct culture, is religion. Please do not, at this point, make a mistake in anticipating my meaning. This is not a religious talk, and I am not setting out to convert anybody. I am simply stating a fact. I am not so much concerned with the communion of Christian believers today; I am talking about the common tradition of Christianity which has made Europe what it is, and about the common cultural elements which this common Christianity has brought with it. If Asia were converted to Christianity to-morrow, it would not thereby become a part of Europe. It is in Christianity that our arts have developed; it is in Christianity that the laws of Europe have—until recently—been rooted. It is against a background of Christianity that all our thought has significance. An individual European may not believe that the Christian Faith is true, and yet what he says, and makes, and does, will all spring out of his heritage of Christian culture and depend upon that culture for its meaning. Only Christian culture could have produced a Voltaire or a Nietzsche. I do not believe that the culture of Europe could survive the complete disappearance of the Christian Faith. And I am convinced of that, not merely because I am a Christian myself, but as a student of social biology. If Christianity goes, the whole of our culture goes. Then you must start painfully again, and you cannot put on a new culture ready-made. You must wait for the grass to grow to feed the sheep to give the wool out of which your new coat will be made. You must pass through many centuries of barbarism. We should not live to see the new culture, nor would our great-great-great-grandchildren: and if we did, not one of us would be happy in it.
>
> To our Christian heritage we owe many things besides religious faith. Through it we trace the evolution of our arts, through it we

> have our conception of Roman Law which has done so much to shape the Western World, through it we have our conceptions of private and public morality. And through it we have our common standards of literature, in the literatures of Greece and Rome. The Western world has its unity in this heritage, in Christianity and in the ancient civilisations of Greece, Rome and Israel, from which, owing to two thousand years of Christianity, we trace our descent. I shall not elaborate this point. What I wish to say is, that this unity in the common elements of culture, throughout many centuries, is the true bond between us. No political and economic organisation, however much goodwill it commands, can supply what this culture unity gives. If we dissipate or throw away our common patrimony of culture, then all the organisation and planning of the most ingenious minds will not help us, or bring us closer together.
>
> The unity of culture, in contrast to the unity of political organisation, does not require us all to have only one loyalty: it means that there will be a variety of loyalties. It is wrong that the only duty of the individual should be held to be towards the State; it is fantastic to hold that the supreme duty of every individual should be towards a Super-State. I will give one instance of what I mean by a variety of loyalties. No university ought to be merely a national institution, even if it is supported by the nation. The universities of Europe should have their common ideals, they should have their obligations towards each other. They should be independent of the governments of the countries in which they are situated. They should not be institutions for the training of an efficient bureaucracy, or for equipping scientists to get the better of foreign scientists; they should stand for the preservation of learning, for the pursuit of truth, and in so far as men are capable of it, the attainment of wisdom.

He ended his speech by saying:

> In a world which has seen such material devastation as ours, these spiritual possessions are also in imminent peril.
>
> Eliot, 1948, pp. 122–124.

Appendix 14
General Summary of the Influence of Christianity on Western Civilisation

> "The kingdom of heaven is like to a grain of mustard seed, which a man took, and sowed in his field; which indeed is the least of all seeds; but when it is grown, it is the greatest among herbs, and becometh of a tree, so that the birds of the air come and lodge in the branches thereof." Matthew 13:31–32.

Many people in the course of their lives have made and brought about very significant transformational changes in the various departments of human life, whether it be in medicine, or education or government, scientific discovery and development, or social reform or whatever it may be, and their names are forever enshrined in the annals of human history.

But none of these approaches come even near to our Lord Jesus Christ, the greatest man who ever lived, and who has changed for the good virtually every aspect of human life.

One wrote:

> "The greatest tragedy of the Christmas season each year is not so much its commercialisation (gross and distasteful as that is), but its trivialisation. How tragic it is that people have forgotten Him to whom they owe so very much."
>
> Kennedy and Newcombe, 2001, p. 13.

Another part of this tragedy is that though we live in an age that boasts of eliminating all prejudice, yet it actively encourages prejudice against Christianity. We could say that we live in an age in which only one prejudice is tolerated—that is anti-Christian bigotry.

Be that as it may; our Lord says in Revelation chapter 21:5:

> "Behold, I make all things new."

If we look up that word *behold*, in the original it is the Greek word *idou* which means "*note well*", "*look closely*", "*examine carefully*".

If we look at the influence of our Lord Jesus Christ in the life of the world carefully and closely we see plainly that he has transformed for the better everything that he has touched.

One example of this of course is that of the way we record time. All history is divided into BC (before Christ) and AD (*Anno Domini*, In the year of our Lord).

It's ironic that even the bitterest atheist is compelled to acknowledge this whenever he uses the date. Even atheistic Soviet Russia when it came into being was forced to acknowledge that it came into existence in 1917, in the year of our Lord.

The beginnings of Christianity were small but it has touched the whole of the world, and it is estimated that there are in the region of 2 billion professing believers alive at this moment.

Napoleon, who was well accustomed to political power, said that he would be amazed if a Roman emperor could rule from the grave, and yet that is what Jesus Christ has been doing all these years. We would disagree with him that our Lord is ruling from the grave because we know he is not dead but alive, but we understand what Napoleon was trying to say.

Despite its humble origins, Christianity has made more changes on earth for good than any other movement or force in history. The following list has been compiled showing the widespread nature of these changes.

Hospitals as true places for caring for the sick essentially began through the influence of Christianity. There were doctors and physicians before but hospitals in the generally accepted sense are the fruit of the Gospel.

Universities, which began during the early Middle Ages, began on a Christian foundation. We may think of the great universities of Oxford or Paris, founded as centres for the study of theology.

Literacy and the education of the masses.

Free enterprise in the economic sense. The idea of property and ownership.

Representative government.

Civil liberties.

The abolition of slavery both in antiquity and in more modern times.

Modern science, Francis Bacon, and earlier Roger Bacon.

The discovery of the New World by Christopher Columbus and the later voyages of discovery and colonisation. Read Richard Hakluyt's *Divers Voyages Touching the Discoverie of America* (1582, modern editions available).

Respect in the treatment of women and acknowledgement of their role.

Benevolence and charity; for example, the good Samaritan ethic.

Higher standards of justice.

The improvement in the conditions of the common man.

The condemnation of adultery, homosexuality, et cetera. This undoubtedly has helped to preserve the human race, and spared many from heartache.

High regard for human life.

Greater development of art and music. The inspiration of some of the greatest works of art and music.

The codifying and setting to writing many of the world's languages.

Not forgetting the countless changed lives transformed from liabilities into assets of society because of the Gospel.

And vitally, more importantly of course, the eternal salvation of countless men and women, boys and girls.

We might add that the last mentioned in this list is the primary goal of Christianity. All the other benefits are in a sense the by-products of what Christianity produces in daily life.

> "When Jesus Christ took upon himself the form of man, he imbued mankind with a dignity and inherent value that had never been dreamt of before. Whatever Jesus touched or whatever he did transformed that aspect of human life. Many people will read about the innumerable small incidents in the life of Christ while never dreaming that those casually mentioned "little" things were to transform the history of mankind."
>
> Kennedy and Newcombe, 2001, p. 16.

Christopher Wordsworth, the cousin of William Wordsworth, with wordsworthian eloquence, gives us these lines.

> "The Bible is the fountain of all true patriotism and loyalty in states. It is the source of all true wisdom, sound policy, and equity in Senates, Council Chambers, and Courts of Justice. It is the spring of all true discipline and obedience, and of all valour and chivalry, in armies and fleets, in the battlefield and on the wide sea. It is the origin of all probity and integrity in commerce and in trade, in marts and in shops, banks and exchanges, in the public resorts of men and the secret silence of the heart. It is the pure, unsullied fountain of all love and peace, happiness, quietness and joy, in families and households.

> Wherever it is duly obeyed it makes the desert of the world to rejoice and blossom as the rose."
>
> Christopher Wordsworth, *Inspiration*, p. 113.
> Quoted by Ryle, 2003, p. 21.

Or to quote David Thomas:

> "The coming of Christ was the creation of the sun in man's moral heaven, the opening of the fountain in man's moral desert. All that is wholesome in government, pure in morals, benevolent in institutions, wholesome in the spirit and manners of the world, owes its existence to this fact. Insignificant as this planet is compared with other orbs, the fact that Christ has trod its soil has given it a lustre that pales the brightness of them all."
>
> Quoted in Joseph S. Excell, *The Biblical Illustrator*, John, vol 3, p. 102.

Bibliography

Anthony E. Alcock (2002), *A short history of Europe: from the Greeks and Romans to the present day*, 2nd Rev. and updated ed. (Basingstoke: Houndmills; New York: Palgrave Macmillan).

Digby Anderson (ed.) (1992), *The Loss of Virtue: moral confusion and social disorder in Britain and America* (London: The Social Affairs Unit)

Anon (2018) 'Doom book', *Wikipedia* [Online]. Available at https://en.wikipedia.org/w/index.php?title=Doom_book&oldid=841747541 (Accessed 6 August 2019).

Arnold, M. (1867) *Obermann once more* [Online]. Available at https://www.bartleby.com/254/127.html (Accessed 28 July 2019).

John Baillie (1950), *The Belief in Progress* (Oxford University Press, 1950)

Roland Bainton (1963), *Here I Stand—A Life Of Martin Luther* (Mentor Books, 1963)

Stanley Baldwin (1928), *British Life and Thought* (Hodder and Stoughton, 1928)

Waldo Beach and H. Richard Niebuhr (eds) (1955), *Christian Ethics* (New York: The Ronald Press Co., 1955)

Charles Beard (1883), *Hibbert Lectures*

D.W. Bebbington (1989), *Evangelicalism in Modern Britain* (Abingdon: Routledge)

Joel R. Beeke (2006), *Meet the Puritans* (Reformation Heritage Books)

Joel R. Beeke and Mark Jones (2012), *A Puritan Theology* (Reformation Heritage Books)

Joseph Benson (1817), *The Life of John William de la Flechere* (London,)

Benson Bobrick (2003), *The Making of the English Bible* (Phoenix)

James Montgomery Boice (2006), *Genesis* (Baker Book House)

James Montgomery Boice (1994), *Standing on the Rock* (Grand Rapids, MI: Baker Book House)

F.W. Boreham (1933), *A Bunch of Everlastings* (Epworth Press)

C. Loring Brace (1897) *Gesta Christi: or, A history of humane progress under Christianity*, New York: A. C. Armstrong & Son [Online]. Available at http://archive.org/details/gestachristiorhioobrac (Accessed 30 July 2019).

H. Bracton (n.d.), *Bracton Online—English*, Thorne., vol. 2 [Online]. Available at http://amesfoundation.law.harvard.edu/Bracton/Unframed/English/v2/33.htm (Accessed 7 August 2019).

Melvin Bragg (2006), *Twelve Books that Changed the World* (Hodder and Stoughton)
Brunner, E. (1948) *Christianity and Civilisation. First Part: Foundations*, (London, John Nisbet & Co., vol. 1).
Arthur Bryant (1967), *Protestant Island* (Collins)
Herbert Butterfield (1957), *The Origins of Modern Science* (G. Bell and Sons Ltd)
D.S. Cairns (1937), *The Riddle of the World* (SCM Press)
John Calvin, ed. McNeill, J. T. and Battles, F. L. (1960) *Institutes of the Christian religion*, London, The Westminster Press.
Allan Cameron (2016) *Great Men and Movements of the Christian Church* (classic reprint), Forgotten Books [Online]. Available at https://www.forgottenbooks.com.
J. Carcopino (1943), *Daily Life in Ancient Rome*, Rowell, H. T. (ed), (London, George Routledge and Sons Ltd).
Anne W. Carroll (1976), *Christ the King, Lord of History* (Tan Books)
Anne W. Carroll (1994), *Christ the King, Lord of History: A Catholic World History from Ancient to Modern Times* (Tan Books).
Winston S. Churchhill (1946), *War Speeches 1940–1945* (Cassell and Co.)
E. Churton (1840), *The Early English Church* (London: James Burns)
E. Churton (1878), *The Early English church*, London: Pickering [Online]. Available at archive.org (Accessed 24 August 2019).
Christopher Clark, Lecture given at Crich Baptist Church 2016 (Internet, 2016)
A. Compton-Rickett (2018), *A History of English Literature*, Franklin Classics Trade Press [Online]. Available at books.google.co.uk (reprint of Thomas Nelson and Sons, 1946)
C. A. Coulson (1958), *Science and Christian Belief* (Fontana Books)
Anthony Cross and Alan Sell (eds.) (2003), *Protestant Nonconformity in the 20th Century* (Paternoster)
R.W. Dale (1880), *The Evangelical Revival* (Hodder and Stoughton)
D.R. Davies (1941), *On to Orthodoxy* (Hodder and Stoughton)
Norman Davies (1997), *Europe: a history*, Reprinted with corrections., Oxford, Oxford University Press.
T.S. Eliot (1948), *Notes Towards a Definition of Culture* (Faber and Faber)
Eusebius (1861), *History of the Martyrs in Palestine* (trans. W. Cureton), London, Williams and Norgate.

Joseph S. Excell, *The Biblical Illustrator: John* (James Nisbet & Co.)
A. M. Fairbairn (1894), *Religion in History and in Modern Life*, New York, Anson D. F. Randolph & Co. Inc.
A.M. Fairbairn (1912), *The Cambridge Modern History* (Cambridge University Press)
F. W. Farrar (1875), *The Witness of History to Christ*, 3rd edn, MacMillan and Co.
F. W. Farrar (1881), *Seekers after God*, London, MacMillan and Co.
C. L. Feltoe (1918), *St. Dionysius of Alexandria: Letters and Treatises*, London, SPCK.
Guglielmo Ferrero (1921), *The Ruin of Ancient Civilisation and the Triumph of Christianity* (G. P. Putnam's and Sons)
J.S. Flynn (1920), *The Influence of Puritanism* (John Murray)
David Fountain (1984), *John Wycliffe: The Dawn of the Reformation* (Mayflower Christian Books)
Alfred Ernest Garvie, Percy William Bunting and John Brown Paton (1910), *Christ and Civilisation* (National Council of Evangelical Free Churches)
Cunningham Geike (1878), *The English Reformation* (Cassell and Company)
Robin Gill (ed.) (1995), *Readings in Modern Theology* (SPCK)
J. E. A. Gosselin (1853), *The Power of the Pope during the Middle Ages* (trans. M. Kelly), London, C. Dolman, vol. 1 [Online]. Available at archive.org.
G. Grant (1991) *Third time around: a history of pro-life movement from the first century to the present*, 1st ed., Brentwood, Tenn, Wolgemuth & Hyatt, Publishers.
John Richard Green (1920), *A Short History of the English People* (MacMillan & Co.)
Samuel G. Green (1904), *A Handbook of Church History AD 30–1483*, London, The Religious Tract Society [Online]. Available at archive. org (Accessed 6 August 2019).
F. Gregorovius (1895), *History of the City of Rome in the Middle Ages* (trans. A. Hamilton) (London, George Bell & Sons, vol. 3).
Elie Halévy (1971), *The Birth of Methodism in England* (University of Chicago Press)
William Haller (1957), *The Rise of Puritanism* (Harper Torch Books)
Kenneth Hamilton (1968), *What's New in Religion?* (Paternoster Press)

J.A. Hammerton (ed.) (1925), *Harmsworth's Universal Encyclopaedia* (The Educational Book Co. Ltd.)

Georgia Harkness (1931), *John Calvin the Man and his Ethics* (Henry Holt and Co.)

H. B. Harris (1891), *The Newly Recovered Apology Of Aristides Its Doctrine And Ethics*, London, Hodder & Stoughton [Online]. Available at archive.org.

Kathleen Heasman (1962), *Evangelicals in Action* (London: Geoffrey Bless)

Matthew Henry (1985), *Matthew Henry's commentary* (Macdonald Publishing Company)

H. Hensley Henson (1941), *Last Words in Westminster Abbey* (Hodder and Stoughton)

Christopher Hill (1992), *The English Bible in the 17th Century Revolution* (Penguin Press)

Gertrude Himmelfarb (1994), *The De-moralization of society* (New York: Vintage Books)

R. Hooykaas (2008), *Religion and the rise of modern science* (Vancouver, Regent College Publishing).

A. Mitchell Hunter (1950), *The Teaching of Calvin: A Modern Interpretation* (James Clark and Co.)

John Henry Huxley (1945), *Religion without Revelation* (Watts)

Dean William Ralph Inge (1927), *The Church in the World* (Longman and Green)

C. H. Irwin (1928), *The Universal Bible Commentary* (London: The Religious Tract Society).

Paul Johnson (1979), *History of Christianity* (New York: Touchstone). Available at https://antilogicalism.com/wp-content/uploads/2018/03/history-of-christianity.pdf (Accessed 28 July 2019).

G. Hartwell Jones (1903), *The Dawn of European Civilization* (London, Kegan Paul, Trench, Trübner & Co., Ltd).

D. J. Kennedy and J. Newcombe (2001), *What if Jesus had never been born?: the positive impact of Christianity in history*, Nashville, T. Nelson Publishers [Online]. Available at archive.org (Accessed 25 July 2019).

Marcellus Kik (1963), *Church and State: The Story of Two Kingdoms* (Thomas Nelson and Son)

Karl Knoll (1959),*The Cultural Significance of the Reformation* (Living Age Books)

Kenneth Scott Latourette (1941), *History of the Expansion of Christianity* (New York: Harper & Brothers)

William Edward Hartpole Lecky (1890), *History of European Morals From Augustus to Charlemagne*, ninth ed., London, Longmans, Green, and Co., vol. 1 [Online]. Available at https://www.gutenberg.org/ebooks/39273.

Peter Lewis (1979), *The Genius of Puritanism* (Carey Publications)

H. P. Liddon (1904) *Sermons on the Old Testament* (London: Longmans, Green & Co).

D. Martin Lloyd-Jones (1978), *God's Ultimate Purpose* (Edinburgh: Banner of Truth)

Donald Macleod (2010), *A Faith to Live by: Understanding Christian Doctrine* (Christian Focus)

Magnus MacLean (1902), *The Literature of the Celts: Its History and Romance*, Blackie and Son Ltd. [Online]. Available at books.google.co.uk.

John Magonet (1997), *The subversive Bible*, London, SCM Press.

Vishal Mangalwadi (2011), *The Book that Made Your World* (Thomas Nelson)

W.R. Matthews (1936), *The Christian Faith* (Eyre and Spottiswood, London)

John L. McKenzie (1974), *A Theology of the Old Testament*, Doubleday.

John McQuarrie (2003), *Stubborn Theological Questions* (SCM Press)

Arthur Mee (1941) *Our Finest Hour* (Hodder and Stoughton)

H. Henry Meeter (1990), *The Basic Ideas of Calvinism* (revised ed. Baker Book House)

Henry M. Morris (2009), *The Genesis record: a scientific and devotional commentary on the book of beginnings*, Grand Rapids, MI., Baker Books [Online]. Available at http://public.eblib.com/choice/publicfullrecord.aspx?p=4448480 (Accessed 23 September 2019).

William Muir (1911), *Our Grand Old Bible* (Morgan and Scott)

James Munson (1991), *The Nonconformists* (SPCK)

R.H. Murray in J.A. Hammerton (ed.) (1927), *Universal History of the World*, vol. VI (London: The Educational Book Co.), p. 3346.

James Orr (1908), *The Christian View of God and the World*, 9th edn, New York, Charles Scribner's Sons.

J.H. Overton (1900), *The Evangelical Revival in the 18th Century* (Longmans, Green and Co.)

J.I. Packer (1991), *Among God's Giants: Puritan Vision of the Christian Life* (Kingsway)
J.I. Packer (2009), *The J.I. Packer Collection* (Regent College Publishing)
T.H.L Parker (1966), *Reformation in England* (SCM Press)
Bob E. Patterson (1983), *Carl F.H. Henry* (Word Books)
A. W. Pink (1993), *The Sovereignty of God*, Edinburgh, Banner of Truth Trust.
E.J. Poole-Connor (1966), *Evangelicalism in England* (Henry E. Walter Ltd.)
Robert L. Raymond (2004), *John Calvin his Life and Influence* (Fearn: Christian Focus)
Hollis Read ([n.d.]), *The Hand of God in History* (James Blackwood)
F.W. Prior (1975), *The Gospel in a Pagan Society* (Hodder and Stoughton)
E. V. Rieu (1952), *The Four Gospels*, Penguin Books.
A. Robertson (1901), *Regnum Dei—Bampton Lectures 1901* (Methuen and Co.)
E.H. Robertson (1962), *Christians against Hitler* (SCM Press)
J. T. Rosenthal (ed.) (1990), *Medieval Women and the Sources of Medieval History* (Athens, GA, University of Georgia Press).
E.G. Rupp and Benjamin Drewery (1970), *Martin Luther* (Documents of Modern History series) (Palgrave, Macmillan)
J.C. Ryle (1891), *What we owe to the Reformation* (Protestant Truth Society)
J.C. Ryle (2003), *Is the Bible Inspired?* (Edinburgh, The Banner of Truth)
Jonathan Sacks (2012), *The great partnership: God, science and the search for meaning* (Paperback ed., London: Hodder & Stoughton)
Gabriel Sivan (1973), *The Bible and Civilisation* (Jerusalem: Keter Publishing House)
Francis A. Schaeffer (2005), *How should we then live? the rise and decline of western thought and culture* (L'Abri 50th anniversary ed., Wheaton, IL: Crossway Books).
Francis A. Schaeffer (1972), *Genesis in space & time: the flow of Biblical history* (Glendale, CA: Regal Books).
Francis A. Schaeffer (1970), *The Church at the End of the 20th Century* (The Norfok Press)
Alvin J. Schmidt (2004), *How Christianity Changed the World* (Grand Rapids, MI, Zondervan).
Sir Walter Scott (1827), *Life of Napoleon Buonerparte Emperor of the*

French. With a preliminary view of the French Revolution (New York: J. & J. Harper)

Roger Scruton (2006), *England an Elegy (*Bloomsbury)

R. Shindler (1897), *From the Usher's Desk to The Tabernacle Pulpit* (London: Passmore and Alabaster)

Richard Sibbes (1998), *The Bruised Reed* (Banner of Truth)

C.E. Simcox (1957), *Living the Ten Commandments* (London: Dacre Press)

Gabrielivan (1973), *The Bible and Civilisation* (Quadrangle)

E. Smedley (1845), Hugh James Rose, and Henry John Rose (eds.), *Encyclopaedia Metropolitana* (London, F. and J. Rivington), vol. xi.

Wilbur M. Smith, *Therefore, Stand*, A Shepherd illustrated classic (Keats Pub., 1981) [Online]. Available at https://books.google.co.uk/books?id=yrMLAAAACAAJ.

H. D. M. Spence-Jones (1906), *The Golden Age of the Church* (London: SPCK) [Online]. Available at archive.org.

Rodney Stark (1966), *The Triumph of Christianity* (Harper One).

Principal Alexander Stewart (1904), *Handbook of Christian Evidences* (London: Adam and Charles Black)

Richard S. Storrs (1884), *The Divine Origin of Christianity indicated by its historical effects* (New York: Anson D. F. Randolph & Company) [Online]. Available at archive.org.

Tertullian ([n.d.]), 'Apologetic', in Schaff, Philip (ed) *Ante-Nicene Fathers*, Grand Rapids, MI: Christian Classics Ethereal Library, vol. 3 [Online]. Available at https://www.ccel.org/ccel/schaff/anf03.html.

H. Trevor Roper (1965), *The Rise of Christian Europe* (London: Thames and Hudson)

Barrie Trinder (1973), *The Industrial Revolution in Shropshire* (Phillimore & Co Ltd.)

D. E. Trueblood (1948), *Foundations of Civilization* (London, Eyre & Spottiswoode).

Alec R. Vidler (1965), *20th Century Defenders of the Faith* (SCM Press)

Gordon S. Wakefield (1957), *Puritan Devotion: Its Place in the Development of Christian Piety* (Epworth Press)

B.B. Warfield (1981), *Calvin and Calvinism* (Baker Book House)

Hugh Watt (1927), *Representative Churchmen of Twenty Centuries* (London: James Clarke).

Martin Wellings (2003), *Evangelicals Embattled* (Paternoster Press, Milton Keynes)

Westminster Divines (1646), *The Westminster Confession of Faith* [Online]. Available at https://books.google.co.uk/books?id=JFE1swEACAAJ.

J. L. Wile (2011), 'Modern Science Is a Product of Christianity', *Proslogion* [Online]. Available at https://blog.drwile.com/modern-science-is-a-product-of-christianity/ (Accessed 23 September 2019).

Sherwood E. Wirt (1969), *The Social Conscience of the Evangelical* (Harper & Row)

John Wolffe (ed.) (1995), *Evangelical Faith and Public Zeal* (S.P.C.K.)

Joseph Wood (1890), *The Bible—What it Is and What it is Not* (Midlands Education Co.)

B.G. Worrall (2004), *The Making of The Modern Church* (S.P.C.K.)

J.A. Wylie (1888–91), *History of Protestantism* (London: Cassell, Petter and Galpin)